THE ADVENT OF AMERICAN DEMOCRACY, 1815—18⋅

The ADVENT
of AMERICAN
DEMOCRACY
1815–1848

Leonard L. Richards
University of Massachusetts

Carl N. Degler, Editor
American History Series

Scott, Foresman and Company   Glenview, Illinois
Dallas, Texas   Oakland, N.J.   Palo Alto, Ca.   Tucker, Ga.   Abingdon, England

To my mother and father

Library of Congress Cataloging in Publication Data

Richards, Leonard L
The advent of American democracy, 1815-1848.

(Scott Foresman American history series)
Bibliography: p.
Includes index.
1. United States—History—1815-1861. I. Title.
II. Series.
E338.R48   973.5   76-28499
ISBN 0-673-07904-X

The publisher gratefully acknowledges the Carnegie
Institution of Washington for permission to reproduce
the maps "Density of Population, 1820" and "Density
of Population, 1840" from The Atlas of the Historical
Geography of the United States.

1 2 3 4 5 6 –CPC– 82 81 80 79 78 77 76

FOREWORD

This book is one in a series that encompasses the history of the United States from the early days of the Republic to the present. The individual volumes cover specific chronological periods and may be used either separately or in combination. Both this book and the series as a whole are intended to be different from the material covered in the usual survey text.

Customarily a textbook is largely filled with a chronological account of the "essential" facts of the past. Facts and chronology are, it is true, the building stones of historical knowledge, and familiarity with both is essential, but they do not provide the structure of the past by themselves. Rather it is the framework of an era that students must grasp if they are to retain and make sense out of the myriad facts that any book—text or other—throws in their path. By framework, however, we are not suggesting a skeleton or outline, but the unity or essential thrust of the period—in short, its meaning.

Emphasis falls throughout upon explanation of the past. Why did events turn out as they did? What significance did these developments have for subsequent American history? What importance do they have for the present? How does the American experience compare with that of other countries in similar circumstances? How and why did American attitudes and values alter during the period in question?

The organization and some of the less important facts that are to be found in more conventional textbooks are absent from these pages. It is the conviction of the author and the editor of the series that understanding the relationship among events is more important than just memorizing customarily agreed-upon facts. Therefore, some facts have been omitted simply because they do not contribute to an understanding of the structure of the period.

This book has been written for American college students; that is, readers who have some acquaintance with the history of the United States. While the usual effort has been made to clarify and define obscure or unfamiliar terms and persons, a certain basic familiarity with the subject has been taken for granted. No students who have passed successfully through an American high school need worry about their ability to comprehend what appears within these covers, but it is hoped that their understanding of the direction and the causes behind the movements of American history will be enhanced by reading this book.

Carl N. Degler

PREFACE

This book interprets the many changes that sifted through American society in the crucial years following the War of 1812. The period has always been known as one of striking changes. It was the time democracy came of age, Andrew Jackson set the tone of American politics, cotton became "king," merchants doubled and tripled their wealth, New York became "the" big city, factories sprang up in the Northeast, pioneers set out for the far West, and thousands of reformers stormed across the countryside demanding an end to privilege and favoritism, drunkenness and debauchery, war and slavery. It was the time, some say, when modern America was born, "when the old universe was thrown into the ash heap and a new one created."

This book is dedicated to the proposition that the historian's job is to explain major developments, rather than to recreate the past in as much detail as possible. What stimulated the new industrial economy? How did society's new wealth end up in the hands of the well-to-do? Why did democracy come of age? Who did democracy benefit? Who did it hurt? What effect did it have on American society as a whole? These are the kinds of questions that I try to answer. The book, then, is aimed at the intelligent student, young or old, who is not merely curious about the past, but wishes to know how and why the United States came to be what it is today.

In putting this book together, I followed several rules of thumb that perhaps the reader should know about. First of all, I made no attempt at what is known as "broad coverage." An accepted practice in history texts has always been to include as many heroes and memorable events as possible. At first historians provided a catalog of white heroes; then black heroes were added; then Indian heroes, and so on. That is not the approach taken here. There are plenty of great names who are not even mentioned in this book, mainly because their accomplishments add little to our understanding of the forces that shaped the lives of the unsung millions who kept house, picked cotton, ploughed fields, or sweated in the nation's new textile factories. Even my favorite author, Herman Melville, gets only a line or two.

By the same token, I have generally provided only a few examples to illustrate major points. Authors have a choice of including plenty of examples and thus hopefully mentioning everyone's favorite, or discussing a few in some detail. I have sacrificed numbers for in-depth coverage. Those who turn to the chapter on reformers, for example, will notice that the usual long list of reform movements is missing. Instead, a handful of reform movements are discussed at some length. And even these have been included, not so much for their intrinsic interest, but because they shed light on the larger forces that were shaping American society.

I had help in writing this book. I owe a very large debt to my colleagues at the University of Massachusetts, especially to Hugh Bell, Robert Jones, and Mario DePillis, who helped me more than once with my prose. I am also indebted to Carl Degler, who made numerous suggestions for improving the manuscript and saved me from several careless errors, and to Bonnie Smothers, my editor at Scott, Foresman and Company. I alone, of course, am responsible for any errors that remain.

Leonard L. Richards

CONTENTS

CHAPTER ONE

AMERICA IN 1815

W HAT WAS AMERICA like in 1815? The cultural underpinnings were much the same from the Maine coast to the Gulf of Mexico, even though customs and life-styles varied significantly from place to place. Travelers wrote extensively about gracious Southerners who spoke with a drawl, tight-fisted Yankees who talked with a nasal twang, and wild Westerners who were full of brag and told outlandish lies. But the same travelers were also quick to point out that a common culture pervaded most of the land, and that most Americans lived according to its dictates.

The foundation stones of this dominant culture were white supremacy and Protestantism, the pursuit of wealth and the belief in limited government. All were important. But in practice, if not in theory, everything else gave way to white supremacy. So let us begin there.

White Supremacy

Symptomatic of American culture in general, North and South, was Potter's Field in Cincinnati. Whites were buried east to west, and blacks north to south. Even among the destitute and the dead, white supremacy prevailed.

Patriots, it is true, always swore by the Declaration of Independence on the Fourth of July, and there is little doubt that they were well aware of the words "all men are created equal." But to most eminent men that hallowed phrase was merely an eighteenth-century shibboleth. It was often taken seriously, to be sure, when limited to "all white men." But it could never compete in the hearts of Northerners and Southerners with the concept of white supremacy. Only fools thought otherwise.

Blacks in 1815 made up nearly 19 percent of the total population. They outnumbered Indians, the other major victims of white supremacy, by about seventeen to one. Most of course were slaves whose labor was crucial to the nation's staple-exporting economy. And most were second, third, fourth, or fifth generation Americans. For nearly a century, natural increase had been more important than importation from Africa. Unlike the Caribbean, where slaves succumbed quickly to virulent tropical diseases, slaves in the American South had survived and multiplied. The prohibition of the Atlantic slave trade in 1808 thus only increased the importance of the birthrate. Planters knew that their well-being depended upon a healthy slave population and a high fertility rate. Thomas Jefferson put it bluntly: "I consider a woman who brings a child every two years as more profitable than the best man of the farm." Between 1810 and 1822 the young women on his plantation did their duty, providing him with one hundred new slaves.

In 1815 most slaves lived in the Chesapeake region, and the tidewater counties of the two Carolinas and Georgia. Since lands in these areas were declining, and the slave population was rapidly growing, the crucial question was where slaves

Washington, from the President's house. *Library of Congress* would be taken next. Although most proslavery men had their eyes on Alabama and Mississippi, some even considered land north of the Ohio River, where slavery was forbidden by Jefferson's Northwest Ordinance of 1787. Despite the ban, census takers reported 237 slaves in Indiana and Illinois in 1810 and 190 in 1820. But, in their fight to legalize slavery north of the Ohio, proslavery men were no match for antislavery and anti-Negro forces in the Ohio Valley.

The telling argument against slavery in the Ohio Valley—as elsewhere—was that it would produce a large black population and keep out free white labor. In keeping with this argument, states and territories north of the Ohio took a stand not only against slavery, but free blacks as well. In 1807 Ohio excluded free blacks from residence unless they posted a $500 bond guaranteeing their good behavior. Illinois in 1813 promised any black man who entered the territory thirty-nine lashes, repeated every fifteen days, until he left. Neither Ohio nor Illinois was capable of enforcing such laws, but both were eager to hang out "white only" signs.

The existence of so many slaves in "the land of liberty" was of course a constant source of embarrassment to the nation's leaders. Foreign critics never failed to point out that Jefferson and his fellow Virginians, who fancied themselves as the torchbearers of liberty in the western world, had hundreds of slaves back home. And the great planters were certainly aware of the discrepancy. For years Jefferson and other great planters had denounced slavery in the abstract. They hated slavery, so they said, and longed for the day "when the fires of liberty shall blaze throughout the South." But the "foul system" had been fastened upon them by their ancestors, and once established it was most difficult to eradicate. Simply turning slaves loose, in the eyes of Jefferson and others, was impossible even if slaveowners were compensated somehow for their losses; the two races could never live together peacefully as free men; racial distinctions would either have to be wiped out through intermarriage and interbreeding, or one race would eventually exterminate the other.

Such thinking, which prevailed throughout American society, had led to one half-baked program after another to ship emancipated blacks out of the country. Defenders of slavery, like William Loughton Smith of South Carolina, had always sneered at such "fanciful schemes." Shipping millions of blacks out of the country would cost half of the national income, and it hardly made sense for a nation that was short of both capital and labor to be spending millions getting rid of labor. Nevertheless, there were always plenty of wishful thinkers. And in 1817 gentlemen reformers concocted another hare-brained venture called the American Colonization Society.

Supported by such illustrious men as President James Monroe, Chief Justice John Marshall, and Henry Clay, the new society claimed that the answer lay in shipping free blacks "back to Africa." According to staunch supporters, African colonization would rid the country of the poor and despised free blacks, encourage planters to emancipate their slaves, and provide a nucleus of black missionaries to carry the Gospel to the Dark Continent. Zealots claimed divine inspiration! More aggressive than its predecessors, the Colonization Society sent out agents to whip up support among men of prominence. Soon churches, charitable groups, and even state governments began contributing money, and Congress appropriated $100,000 to aid the Society. Despite the contributions, the Colonization Society managed to send only 1400 blacks across the Atlantic by 1831. It thus had no effect at all in ending tyranny in America.

Hostility to Authority

What distinguished white culture in 1815 was not its bigotry—most cultures are bigoted—but its hostility to government. Americans believed that governments were a necessary evil, with special emphasis on the word "evil." Nearly everyone was certain that power corrupts, and that legislation was the parent of nine tenths of the trouble in the world. To keep trouble to a minimum, the vast majority endorsed the twin concepts of cheap government and small government. The public was horrified in 1816 when Congress voted itself a raise from $6 per diem to $1500 per year, and even though most of "the fifteen-hundred-characters" soon repented, the electorate was unwilling to spare the rod: more than two thirds of the miscreants were turned out of office at the next election.

It is hard now to imagine but it is a matter of record that the entire federal establishment, including army, navy, and marines, was no larger than the present Bureau of Indian Affairs. The Washington establishment, from the lowliest clerk to the President, amounted to no more than 500 men. Even then, according to Henry Clay, the most popular politicians campaigned on the theme that the government was getting too big and costing too much.

Weak government, in turn, meant that there was a noticeable lack of regimentation in white society. Laws were passed, and orders were given, but there was no way that a handful of government officials could force millions of Americans, scattered from Maine to Missouri, to obey the law. And few officials were foolish enough to try. This was a good thing according to many immigrants. In contrast to Europe, where taxes were high and conscription was common, American governments were rarely a burden to ordinary citizens. As one Swede happily wrote home (with only a bit of exaggeration): "It is a good country. There is no conscription here . . . no taxes . . . no poor relief . . . no police." America in 1815 was clearly a world we have lost.

But, like all good things, the absence of regimentation had its drawbacks. It was an unruly society. And its unruliness provided plenty of headaches for ordinary citizens as well as the governing elite.

The Problem of Lawlessness. By twentieth-century standards, America in 1815 was not a particularly violent society, but it was far from being law-abiding. The War of 1812 cost the country only 7000 lives, with less than 2000 dying in action. Yet, of 694,000 men enrolled in the militia, less than 5000 had responded to Madison's call to arms, and it was not until 1814 that the nation's effective fighting force reached 35,000 men. The governors of three New England states refused the President's order to supply troops. New York and New England contractors were guilty many times over of selling beef, flour, and other provisions to the enemy.

The war thus became a nightmare for Washington politicians who desperately needed help to withstand invading British troops. By 1814 they had to abandon the Capitol and flee to all points of the compass. Alone, President Madison wandered pathetically through the countryside while the British burned the Capitol. His wife, meanwhile, sought refuge at a country home—only to be cursed out of the house by a woman whose husband had just been called to arms to defend the Capitol.

Density of Population, 1820

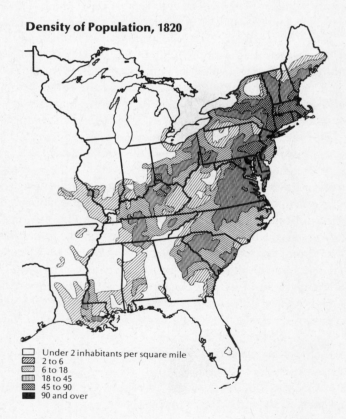

- ☐ Under 2 inhabitants per square mile
- 2 to 6
- 6 to 18
- 18 to 45
- 45 to 90
- 90 and over

The Breadth of Disorder. Men of power thus worried about unruliness. And one could argue that Americans were an unruly lot. Consider, for example, the West. When Lincoln was born, in 1809, the backwoods of Kentucky had a reputation for extreme lawlessness. According to travelers, fisticuffs, eye-gougings, knife and gun play were everyday events. One traveler recorded a typical western dispute—which was obviously as much tall tale as fact—between two boatmen who were fighting over a young Choctaw woman:

> One said, "I am a man; I am a horse; I am a team. I can whip any man *in all Kentucky,* by God." The other replied, "I am an alligator; half man, half horse; can whip any *on the Mississippi,* by God." The first one again, "I am a man; have the best horse, best dog, best gun, and the handsomest wife in all Kentucky, by God." The other, "I am a Mississippi snapping turtle: have bear's claws, alligator's teeth, and the devil's tail; can whip *any man,* by God." This was too much for the first, and at it they went like two bulls, and continued for half an hour, when the alligator was fairly vanquished by the horse.

Such "half-horse, half-alligator" stories had already become a part of the nation's culture. So when Louisianians wished "to describe the highest degree of barbarity," they called it "Kentuckian." And when the songwriter, Samuel Woodward, wanted to celebrate the Battle of New Orleans, he did not write about the riflemen of Tennessee who, according to Jackson, did most of the fighting. No, he entitled his song, "The Hunters of Kentucky!" Even Davy Crockett, another Tennessean, was later made into a Kentuckian. According to one almanac: "Gentlemen . . . I'm Davy Crockett, the darling branch o' old Kentuck, that can eat up a painter, hold a buffalo out to drink, and put a rifle ball through the moon."

Consider also the more "civilized" areas of Jeffersonian America. According to Thomas Jefferson, London, Paris, and the great cities of Europe were sordid dens of vice, corruption, crime, and murder. Yet most legal writers in America agreed that crimes of violence were much more frequent in the older, well-established communities of the East and of the South than in the sprawling urban centers of Europe. In 1793, for example, William Bradford showed that even though London had nearly twice the population of Pennsylvania, the Quaker state had far more executions for murder. Later, Edward Livingston wrote that between 1802 and 1818 New Orleans' homicide rate was nearly twenty-seven times greater, in proportion to numbers, than London's. Similarly, others produced figures indicating that in proportion to total population, the crime rate in Baltimore was 46 percent greater than in London, and the number of violent deaths in New York City was ten times greater.

While these commentators presented their data mainly in terms of convictions or executions, they all insisted that the number of unpunished and undetected murders in American cities was incredibly large. City officials often agreed. In 1828, for instance, the New York grand jury condemned Five Points, which was located on the site of the present Columbus Park, as "a rendezvous for thieves and prostitutes" and as one of the most lawless and ill-policed areas in the world. Particularly notorious was "Old Brewery," a dilapidated building that housed some one thousand Irish and blacks. It allegedly averaged one homicide a night for fifteen years.

Upper-Class Violence. Although men of power worried most about the misbehavior of the lower classes, it was very clear in 1815 that the upper classes also enjoyed a good brawl and the spilling of some blood. Today, men of property are expected to exercise self-control even under the most trying circumstances. In 1815, that was not entirely the case. The educational and social system taught that impulsiveness was a sign of spirit, that slights to one's honor could not be tolerated, and that loyalty to a friend included entering a quarrel on his behalf, regardless of the merits of the case. Thus men of property occasionally engaged in the most ferocious and childish brawls.

The best known involved Andrew Jackson, Thomas Hart Benton, and a half-dozen other men who were destined to lead the nation. After a summer of quarreling, in 1813, Jackson and Benton came face to face in a tavern at Nashville. "Now defend yourself, you damned rascal!" shouted Jackson. These words set off a donnybrook of shoving, kicking, eye-gouging, fist-fighting, knifing, and gunfire. Jackson, age forty-six, was shot in the left arm, and the thirty-two-year-old Benton received five knife wounds. The melee eventually came to a farcical conclusion when the massive Thomas Hart Benton, fighting off daggers and pistols, managed to fall backwards down a flight of stairs at the rear of the tavern. Needless to say, none of these men was ever brought to justice. And Jackson and Benton were not the only ones who later gained distinction in public service: several of the lesser figures in this brawl served in Congress; one later gained distinction in the courts and was offered a seat on the United States Supreme Court; and still another was nominated by his party for the vice-presidency.

But such behavior, one might object, was southern or western. Such incidents, so Easterners have frequently argued, never occurred among eastern gentlemen. This is largely myth. Between 1800 and 1816, according to historian David Hackett Fisher, eastern gentlemen "fought in the streets with pistols, muskets, knives, fists, canes, cudgels, and swords." Sometimes even New England town meetings "dissolved into a melee" between Federalists and Republicans. Joseph Story, later a Supreme Court Justice, got into a fist fight over politics in Salem, Massachusetts. In Boston, Federalist Thomas Selfridge got into a quarrel with Republican editor Benjamin Austin, and ended up killing Austin's son in a shoot-out on State Street.

Students at Harvard, according to one tutor, were so unruly that crimes "worthy of the penitentiary" were commonplace. Students fought in commons, drenched their tutors with buckets of ink and water, disrupted classes and chapel, dropped cannonballs from upper windows, and even blew up "public rooms in inhabited buildings." The faculty had so much trouble with the Class of 1823 that, just before commencement, they expelled John Quincy Adams' son and forty-two others out of a class of seventy. A few years later, the diarist Philip Hone watched

a famous Harvard commencement speaker, the illustrious poet William Cullen Bryant, horsewhip a rival editor on one of New York's most fashionable streets.

Even in the Halls of Congress, men in their thirties or forties or even fifties got into knock-down, drag-out brawls. Before the turn of the century, Republican Matthew Lyon, age fifty-one, and Federalist Roger Griswold, age thirty-five, went at it tooth and nail in the House chamber. Eight years later, two Republicans, Joseph Hopper Nicholson and Michael Leib, ages thirty-four and forty-four respectively, got into a real donnybrook in the House lobby. It lasted one hour and seventeen minutes! Both men, needless to say, were battered and covered with blood when the older man, Leib, finally gave in. Leib's age was apparently not much of a factor; what he needed most, according to one spectator, was a good left. None of these four men was from the wild West; they represented Connecticut and Vermont, Pennsylvania and Maryland.

Code Duello. Despite such roughhousing, the code duello was more typically upper class. If the Boston lawyer Thomas Selfridge had had his way, he would never have been involved in a State Street shoot-out. He would have met Benjamin Austin on the field of honor. The honor of a gentleman, said Selfridge, was "as sacred as the virtue of a woman. May we not then take life to preserve reputation, more valuable than life itself, and without which, life itself is neither desirable to its possessor, nor useful to the community?" The proper place to settle insults to one's honor—or to one's lady—was the duelling grounds.

Such sensitivity to a man's honor was a striking characteristic among gentlemen, in both the North and the South, in the first twenty-five years of the nineteenth century. Duelling, it seems, first became fashionable during the American Revolution among officers in Washington's army. After the Revolution, it subsided somewhat until the turn of the nineteenth century. Then it enjoyed an enormous revival from New England to Georgia, and among politicians on the mainland to officers in the Mediterranean fleet. About half of the forty-six duels reported in the *Dictionary of American Biography,* which includes the lives of most notable Americans, occurred in this period. Gradually, duelling seems to have drifted South, where it remained part of the southern way of life until shortly after the Civil War.

Many of the heroes of the early Republic were duellists. Besides such well-known men as Aaron Burr, Alexander Hamilton, Henry Clay, and Andrew Jackson, the list includes prominent New York newsmen such as James Watson Webb and William Leggett, naval heroes such as Stephen Decatur and Oliver Hazard Perry, the "father of the Erie Canal" DeWitt Clinton, Senator Thomas Hart Benton of Missouri, Congressman John Randolph of Virginia, and presidential hopeful William Crawford. In 1824, three of the four presidential contenders were duellists. And in 1832, both of the major candidates followed the code of honor.

Most of these duels were gentlemanly affairs, fought with pistols at ten paces, and often ending with a superficial wound and a reconciliation between the two parties. But some were utter madness. After the election of 1816, which led to more than a dozen duels, gossipy friends provoked General Armistead T. Mason, Senator of Virginia, to tangle with his brother-in-law, John M. McCarty. The two men agreed on shotguns at four paces! Mason's gun caught in his coat as he fired, and so he only blew off McCarty's arm. Mason himself was blown to bits.

The Dimensions of Authority. Obviously, the authorities were unable to contain duelling, even though laws in some states made duelling illegal. How did they fare against other forms of lawlessness and threats to social order? Traditionally, authorities in America relied on private citizens to maintain civil authority and civil order. The law, for example, gave parents and masters the right to use corporal punishment almost as they saw fit. Thus the flogging of sailors, children, and slaves was commonplace. And, with the exception of one's own children, public flogging was the norm. Indeed, the impression that flogging made on onlookers was considered far more important than actually punishing the offender. One of Jefferson's slaves, James Hubbard, ran away repeatedly, and by 1812 Jefferson was convinced that no amount of flogging would stop Hubbard from running away. Nevertheless, once Hubbard was captured, Jefferson reported: "I had him severely flogged in the presence of his old companions." And, as Jefferson predicted, Hubbard ran off again.

Northern philanthropists railed at the mistreatment of slaves only to be constantly reminded that northern sailors were "daily subject to the same treatment as slaves." Said one man who served between 1801 and 1815: "I have seen a man hauled up and made to receive eighteen lashes for a crime no more serious than spitting on the quarter deck. Such outrages on human nature ought not to be permitted by a government which boasts of liberty." James Garrison, brother of the famous abolitionist, revealed that once Matthew C. Perry had caught two men urinating on the deck, gave them thirteen lashes each, and ordered the master-at-arms to "fill their face and eyes with the excrement of man and to rub it well in." And in disgust, John Randolph wrote Jackson about a nightmare voyage he had with Perry. Even Randolph's slaves were "surprised and shocked" by the way Perry broke in a new crew. There was, claimed Randolph, more flogging in three weeks on board Perry's ship than in seven years on a large plantation.

Masters, then, were responsible for maintaining order. Even more important were parents. Since colonial times, ministers and statesmen had emphasized that the family was the key institution of social control. The family was to teach the child an honest calling and God-fearing behavior, and the church was to see that the family fulfilled its duties. Ultimately, so the argument went, the good order of the entire community rested upon family government. Loving parents had to use the rod and teach proper respect for authority. Sparing the rod ruined the child. Indulging or neglecting children were the worst things parents could do: untamed passions would grow furiously. "The mass of criminals," said a Pennsylvania report, "is composed of persons whose childhood and youth were spent in the uncontrolled exercise of vicious instincts." The confessions of most criminals, claimed the Boston Prison Discipline Society, revealed "that the course of vice, which brought them to prison, commenced in disobedience to their parents, or in their parents' neglect."

Dependence on Volunteers. Authorities also relied on private citizens to maintain order in both local and national crises. Indeed, for as long as anyone cared to remember, Fourth of July speakers sang the praises of voluntarism. Professional force was out of the question. Europeans might rely upon troops and professional police in a time of crisis, but Americans had been taught to despise both since colonial times. Every schoolboy knew that they were both "standing armies" and every patriot knew that standing armies destroyed liberty and brought oppression. Tyrants maintained social order through the use of professional soldiers and police; a free people had to rely mainly on the family and the church—and occasionally on citizen soldiers such as the heroes of Lexington and Concord.

In practice, too, the early Republic had a tradition of relying on amateurs. Even in major cities, daytime police protection consisted of nothing more than a handful of constables and marshals, who were either elected annually or served at the pleasure of the mayor. And nighttime protection was often a joke, depending on watchmen who were frequently ne'er-do-wells or drunks. In times of crisis, magistrates always had to rely on ordinary citizens. If the mayor had time, he could choose men for a posse comitatus. If not, the time-honored method was for the mayor and his men to walk through the streets, shaking a watchman's rattle and yelling "support the mayor," thus rallying law-abiding citizens to arms.

Even in war the Republic relied almost entirely on amateurs. In the War of 1812, for example, officers were almost invariably chosen for political reasons—and only incidentally for reasons of military prowess. There were, in fact, few professionals to turn to: Congress had established West Point in 1802, but Academy graduates were not yet numerous enough to be significant. Most of the political generals proved to be inept, but occasionally the country was lucky as in the case of Andrew Jackson. When war broke out, Jackson held the rank of Major-General in the Tennessee militia—but only because he had won an election, by a single vote, cast by a political friend. Once the war was over, the nation chose to forget the incompetence of its amateurs and focused on the Battle of New Orleans. Indeed, within a few years Americans forgot about Jackson's artillery, which had done much of the damage, and celebrated only the backwoodsmen for the slaughter of Lord Pakenham's seasoned army. It was Lexington and Concord all over again. Amateurs had routed professionals and proved once again that the nation could always count on the moral fibre and patriotism of ordinary citizens.

Thus men like President Madison, who had drawn different conclusions from the burning of Washington and other wartime debacles, were unable to strengthen the professional army. Madison recommended a standing army of twenty thousand men in 1815, but Congress fixed the peacetime army at ten thousand, stripped the armed vessels on the Great Lakes of their equipment, and put the navy's gunboat flotilla up for sale. John C. Calhoun, Secretary of War under President Monroe, recommended that there be no further cuts, but in 1820 Congress reduced the army to six thousand men. Soon, five state legislatures and several congressmen including Davy Crockett called for the abolition of West Point before it gained a stranglehold on the military establishment. They failed in their quest, but the basic hostility toward the professional soldier remained so that when a young West Point graduate, Ulysses S. Grant, wore his brand new uniform in public in 1843, even street urchins mocked him.

Clearly, amateur warriors such as the "embattled farmers" at Concord Bridge and the "hunters of Kentucky" at New Orleans were expected to defend the country. At the same time, however, the old ideas of an armed community and universal military training were rapidly breaking down. In theory, every man had to attend one or two muster days each year, or pay a fine. But state law and practice varied. After the war, Massachusetts and Vermont added to their exemption lists and excused most college students, salaried men, manufacturers, and professionals from militia duty; soon only artisans and farmers had the burden of attending muster, and they complained bitterly about the growing inequities in the system. New York had a militia fine of twelve dollars, which the wealthy could pay easily enough, but which the working man could not. Delaware abolished the mi-

Local and state militias may not have fought well in battle, but this lithograph suggest that they drilled worse. "The Militia Muster" by David Claypoole Johnston, c. 1829. *Courtesy, American Antiquarian Society*

litia fine in 1816, and most of the newer states never enforced it. Gradually, other states followed Delaware's lead, gave up the hallowed tradition of universal training, and turned more and more to volunteer regiments which strutted around in dazzling uniforms and had such ferocious names as Avengers, Snake Hunters, and Invincibles.

Could such feeble forces maintain the American polity? Could rag-tag militias and several thousand professional soldiers maintain a vast country which stretched from the Atlantic to the Great Plains? Clearly, the fate of the nation depended on the goodwill of England and other Atlantic powers, plus the goodwill of 900,000 farm families who were scattered along the Atlantic seaboard and deep into the backcountry. Many of these families were weeks away from Washington, days away from their state capitols, and living for all practical purposes under the jurisdiction of their own church, "land club," or "claim association." Many of these organizations not only lacked government sanction, but also ignored—and often openly resisted—government authority.

Could their presence be tolerated? The answer was invariably "yes." In a culture where all governments were regarded as a terrible nuisance, where few restraints on the individual were tolerated, it was impossible to make people conform to central authority. And one line of Jeffersonian theory even held that the people were sure to go right if left alone, that resistance to authority was a healthy sign because all authority was tyrannical, and that local authorities should be interfered with as little as possible by external powers. Said Jefferson: "It is error alone which needs the support of government; truth can stand by itself." Under this standard, the best governments were those that governed least. In 1815, American governments were incapable of governing too much.

The Unmanageable Money Market

Another constant source of headaches around 1815 was the money market. Cities and states, land speculators and farmers, industrialists and merchants—all desperately needed credit, and everyone needed money. There was never enough investment capital at home, and thus American entrepreneurs had to rely on foreign investors, especially the Dutch and the English. The English middle class had plenty of investment capital. Thanks to England's head start on industrialization and the sharp reduction in British taxes after the defeat of Napoleon, Englishmen had about forty to fifty million pounds annually for investment. How much would they invest in North American projects? That was a source of worry.

Fortunately, the Barings of London, who had been speculating in American land and merchandizing American cotton since 1795, had also developed an interest in placing American securities. After the War of 1812, they became the leading agents in London for American cities, states, businessmen, and bankers. They had close ties with the Bayards in New York, the Bank of Stephen Girard in Philadelphia, and other American banking houses. And, working with these associates, they distributed Erie Canal Stock and floated loans for New York, Pennsylvania, Louisiana, and Virginia during the 1820s. In the 1830s and 1840s, they acted as agents and underwriters for canal and railroad companies.

Politicians, especially those like Andrew Jackson who took delight in twisting the British lion's tail, never stopped harping on the danger of being in hock to foreigners. The British lion, they thundered, would soon devour innocent American lambs. But the common worry for most Americans was the domestic money market. Thomas Jefferson, John Adams, and many others agreed that it was utter madness at its worst, and bad even at its best. Historians, taking the long view, have often argued that they exaggerated the situation. But Jefferson and his contemporaries, of course, rarely took the long view when their own money was at stake. And to the modern reader the money market has always seemed to be rather strange and baffling.

The "Paper System." To begin with, legal tender and investment capital were always in short supply. Technically, the United States mint was supposed to supply the nation with metal currency for a sound monetary system. But that was largely a dream of the Founding Fathers. In reality, eagles and half-eagles, dollars, dimes, and half-dimes were as scarce as if no mint existed. Silver and gold coins simply could not be kept in the country. Indeed, so many went to London and Liverpool that the director of the mint, without any legal authority, stopped the coinage of many silver and gold pieces. No golden eagles were made after 1804, and not one silver dollar was struck from 1805 until 1836. Foreign coins were more plentiful, but they too were in short supply.

What, then, did people do for money? They created their own, or relied on paper currency created by others. Currency, in fact, came from scores of sources—from banks with state charters, from unlawful banks without charters, from towns, from cities, from importing companies and exporting companies, from canals and from factories, from the Treasury of the United States, and from private citizens. In a normal year, there were at least four hundred different kinds of currency in circulation. The system, moreover, changed from year to year and, while it worked well at certain times and places, it was on the whole wild and unruly.

Banking, everyone agreed, could be incredibly profitable. An "honest banker," many added, was a contradiction in terms. In theory, stockholders bought stock in banks by paying in gold and silver (usually called "specie"), and on the basis of this "specie" the banks made loans; the interest on the loans provided the banks with profits and the stockholders, in turn, with dividends. In practice, however, banks never lent specie. Instead, they gave borrowers bank notes, which were merely printed pieces of paper bearing a promise to pay a certain amount of gold and silver on demand. So long as people had faith in the bank's ability to redeem its notes in specie, they were seldom redeemed and circulated in the community as money. And that was what made banking so profitable. Bankers could safely lend and collect interest on many more notes than they had gold and silver to cover. So long as people had faith, they could lend five, ten, or even twenty times what they had in the vault.

Thus there were always plenty of would-be bankers in every community. But anyone who wanted to organize a bank, or any other corporation, was supposed to get a special charter from the state legislature. Since banks were most profitable, getting a bank charter was thought to be a political favor of the first magnitude. Potential bankers had to agree to certain regulations, and they often had to invest in state projects, support the "right" party, and sweeten the pocketbooks of key assemblymen. In 1811, when Congress refused to recharter Alexander Hamilton's national bank, hundreds of businessmen and politicians moved in quickly to take over some of the business of the big bank. They swarmed around state legislatures, bought votes, and often obtained unusually generous charters. Within five years the number of state banks tripled, and nearly everyone, including businessmen, associated corporations with favoritism and corruption.

But what happened to those entrepreneurs who lacked the influence, money, or standing to get a state charter? Often they simply ignored the legislature and established unlawful banks. This was particularly the case in areas where credit was desperately needed. In Virginia, for example, the legislature had chartered banks in 1803 and 1812 for the tidewater region, but it had failed to provide banks for the vast region west of Richmond. In that rapidly growing area, the demand for credit was enormous, and a host of uncharted banks sprang up. They had names such as the Bank of Winchester, Virginia Saline Bank, Bank of Martinburg, Farmers' and Mechanics' Bank of Harpers Ferry, and Bank of the South Branch of the Potomac. Without charters, they made loans, received deposits, discounted notes, and issued paper money. In addition, the great buyers and shippers of Virginia produce paid their debts with notes of their own issue. And these notes soon came to dominate the circulating medium.

The Virginia situation was hardly unusual. Indeed, it may have been less confusing than the situation in other states. In Pennsylvania, according to the state treasurer's report of 1817, there were forty-eight legal and chartered banks, twenty-two unlawful and unchartered banks, and thirty-nine private citizens issuing notes from five cents to two dollars in value. In Ohio, around Zanesville, there were more than thirty kinds of paper money in circulation. Which was worth more? That was the eternal question in towns like Zanesville. Should one accept a one-dollar bill of the Owl Creek Bank, or would it be better to take a one-dollar note of the Canton Bank? And what about the bills of the Virginia Saline, the Granville, the Perryopolis, the Mansfield, the New Philadelphia, and the Saddle-bag banks? Or the "shinplasters" issued by bridge and turnpike companies, city and borough authorities, merchants and tavern-keepers, barbers and shoeblacks? People had to be constantly on their guard in towns like Zanesville. Accepting the wrong kind of money, as everyone learned the hard way, could be costly. For how many merchants, in turn, would accept worthless currency?

Under such circumstances, of course, scoundrels had a field day. Counterfeiters plied their trade with so much success, complained newsman Hezekiah Niles in 1818, that false notes of at least a hundred banks were afloat in the country. One counterfeiter was caught with false notes of every important bank from Savannah to Albany. Four others, when caught in Pennsylvania, had $350,000 of counterfeit notes in their suitcases; and they were, so authorities said, just small fry in a large gang. The counterfeiters' enterprise differed little from that of the wildcatters, who simply created banks "out of thin air" and turned out hundreds of thousands of notes of these purely imaginary institutions. The owners of one, known as the City Exchange Bank of New York, did a thriving business throughout the South. Another, called the Ohio Exporting and Importing Company, victimized people from Philadelphia to Cincinnati. Newspapers all across the country were full of notices of false banks and notes of wildcatters.

All was not bad, of course. Thousands of honest farmers and manufacturers got their start with the help of bank credit and doubtful currency. Yet it is easy to understand the contempt and hatred that so many held toward the "paper system." Many got hurt time and again. And prominent men everywhere were certain that it was destroying simple, republican virtue and giving birth to a rotten, insubstantial world that paid off only the insider and the gambler. Snarled John Adams: "Every dollar of a bank bill that is issued beyond the quantity of gold and silver in the vault represents nothing and is therefore a cheat upon somebody." And Jefferson never tired of denouncing the system. "Shall we build an altar," he asked Adams facetiously in 1814, ". . . and burn on that all the bank charters present and future, and their notes with them? For these are to ruin both republic and individuals. This cannot be done. The mania is too strong. It has seized by its delusions and corruptions all the members of our government, general, special, and individual." The nation's currency was thus "trash" which would probably "blow all up in the course of the present year. . . . We must scud then before the gale, and try to hold fast, ourselves, by some plank of the wreck."

————The Second Bank of the United States. In the year that Jefferson predicted disaster, the nation's "trash" failed to "blow all up," but it led to a financial crisis during the war. Outside New England banks were forced to stop redeeming their notes in gold and silver; the notes quickly fell in value, and a paper dollar was soon worth 93 cents in New York and Charleston, 85 cents in Philadelphia, 75 cents in Washington, "with every possible variation in other places and states." Even though the resulting financial chaos fouled up the government's efforts to carry on the war, the government had difficulty in overcoming the power and influence of the bankers, and bringing them under control. "You might as well attack Gibraltar with a pistol," said John Randolph of Virginia, "as to attempt to punish them."

Suddenly, men who had vehemently opposed Hamilton's first national bank began to clamor for a second national bank. John Jacob Astor of New York, and Stephen Girard and David Parish of Philadelphia took the lead. They had been enemies of the first national bank, but they had subscribed heavily to government bonds to finance the war, and they were now concerned about their investments. They figured that their bonds would rise in value if they were made exchangeable for stock in a new national bank. Henry Clay of Kentucky, John C. Calhoun of South Carolina, and Jacob Barker of New York also reversed their positions. The war had proven, they said, that reform was necessary: a second national bank would restore the nation's credit and currency. Thus Republican stalwarts swallowed their pride and adopted a Hamiltonian measure, the very measure which they had previously condemned.

In 1816 they pushed through Congress a charter for the Second Bank of the United States. In many respects, the new bank was merely a larger version of Hamilton's old bank. It was granted a twenty-year charter. With headquarters in Philadelphia, it was to have a capital of $35 million as compared to the first bank's $10 million. It was to serve as depository for all federal funds, make loans to the federal government, and regulate state banks. Its power to regulate stemmed from its huge capital and its role as federal depository. Constantly receiving state bank notes, it could force state banks to curtail their issues by presenting the notes for redemption. It could also expand credit by increasing its own loans and bank notes. Like the state banks, it was essentially a private enterprise with the government putting up one fifth of the capital and appointing one fifth of the directors.

It too had problems with crooks and inefficient officers. The directors of the Baltimore Branch managed to buy $4.5 million in stock with only $3 million in securities, and one large shareholder, through chicanery, cast 1172 votes at meetings even though the law said no shareholder could have more than 30 votes. The bank's first president was a Philadelphia merchant, William Jones, who had recently gone through bankruptcy. An adroit politician, he simply let the bank's branches do what they pleased. And by the summer of 1818, the eighteen branches had issued more than ten times as many notes as they had specie to cover, which was twice what the law allowed. The Second Bank lost all control of the state banks, which also expanded their note issues. The overexpansion of bank notes, while it stimulated growth, also contributed to wild speculation and a postwar boom.

The boom burst in 1819. The web of credit collapsed; bank notes became worthless; state banks frequently shut their doors; and William Jones quit his job. The Second Bank's new president, Langdon Cheves of South Carolina, saved the bank by driving state banks and debtors to the wall. Times were hard: rents in Baltimore declined from forty to fifty percent; lands in Virginia were sold for less than a year's rent; and everywhere men cursed banks, bankers, and "the whole rotten paper system." The Panic of 1819 merely confirmed the prejudices of old bank haters. As Jefferson put it to John Adams: "The paper bubble is then burst. This is what you and I, and every reasoning man, seduced by no obliquity of mind and interest, have long foreseen." But hard times also created hordes of new bank haters.

Indeed, banks—and particularly the Second Bank—became convenient scapegoats for everything that went wrong. Cheves eventually restored the soundness of the Second Bank, and when Nicholas Biddle became its president in 1823 the bank was in good condition. For the next decade it would do much to stabilize the nation's currency. But it had left a host of enemies in its wake. "The bank was saved," said economist William Gouge, "and the people were ruined." In the 1830s, Andrew Jackson would capitalize on such sentiment.

The Preindustrial World

Probably the only reason such a loosely run society worked at all was that America in 1815 was still a preindustrial economy. There were only twelve cities in the entire nation with more than eight thousand people. Most Americans lived in small villages, or on isolated farms, where everyone knew everyone else's business, and where "strangers" were spotted instantly and sent on their way if they looked bad, where neighborliness was expected of everyone, and where tongues wagged everytime someone stepped out of line. Having a good name meant credit at the local store (usually the only store for miles around), a better chance to sell one's goods, and help when one needed it. Having a bad name was disastrous.

The sights and sounds of rural life were everywhere. Even in New York City herds of pigs roamed Broadway, and Harlem was farmland. Nationally, four out of five families were farmers. And if one believes William Cobbett, an Englishman who spent two years as a farmer on Long Island, the American farmer was one of the wonders of the Western world. He could accomplish much more in a day than his English counterpart. And he was a jack-of-all-trades. "Every man can

To protect themselves, many early Americans settled in compact communities surrounded by open fields rather than on isolated farms as this view of Windham, Connecticut, attests. *Courtesy of The New York Historical Society*

use an ax, a saw, and a hammer. Scarcely one who cannot do any job at rough carpentering and mend a plow or a wagon. Very few indeed who cannot kill and dress pigs and sheep, and many of them oxen and calves. . . . All are plowmen. In short, a good laborer here can do anything that is to be done upon a farm." In addition, farm families were responsible for most of the nation's manufacturing. Around Philadelphia country people turned out three or four times as much cloth as the city's textile factories. In New Hampshire, according to the Secretary of the Treasury's report, the average farm house had at least one spinning wheel, and every other house had a loom on which women turned out from a hundred to six hundred yards of saleable cloth each year.

However, farm families were not entirely self-sufficient. Even backwoodsmen needed the services of storekeepers, blacksmiths, tanners, and other artisans. And farmers in more settled areas depended not only on the services of the local village, but also, indirectly, on the urban working classes. The upper crust often lumped all these working people together and spoke of them as if they were part of a homogeneous class. In fact, this was hardly the case. From the top the social gap between a skilled artisan and a common laborer or factory worker may not have looked like much; but, from the bottom the gap was enormous. The skilled artisan had a vocation, rather than a mere job; he had a special calling, and a way of life that went with it; he had a skill, and stood far above the common laborer in the occupational hierarchy.

Traditionally, apprenticeship was the route to learning the "art and mysteries" of such trades as shoemaker, carpenter, tailor, blacksmith, printer, and silversmith. Some trades were partly identified with ethnic groups: barbers were often black, miners were Cornish, foundrymen were Welsh, and nearly all carpet weavers were Scots. Whatever the makeup, most craftsmen worked hard to keep "strangers" and "botches" out of their trades. And under apprenticeship rules in many towns, masters had the obligation of not only teaching a trade, but also seeing that their apprentices went to church, kept good company and regular hours, read practical books, and abstained from swearing and tavern-hopping. A trade, in short, was more than a job; it was a way of life.

While artisans were frequently members of the same clubs and churches as shopkeepers and farmers, they rarely had any significant contact with common laborers. Here was a group whose annual income was about half that of the artisan, and whose style of life was in marked contrast. The artisan usually stuck to one, or maybe two, trades; the common laborer was the epitomy of versatility, moving from seafaring to roadbuilding to woodcutting to hodcarrying, and often floating from town to town. Since the need for backbreaking labor was high in America, the unskilled American enjoyed an advantage over his English counterpart who faced ten competitors for every job. As a result, while the American artisan earned about ten to twenty percent more than his British counterpart, the unskilled American earned about 80 percent more than the English common laborer. Nevertheless, they were clearly at the bottom of the free labor market, and life was hard.

Factory workers were typically women and children, and rarely able-bodied men. And this was the nation's pride. Advocates of government aid to manufacturing always assured their readers that factories provided work for the "idle," made women and children "more useful," and did not take able-bodied men off the farm. In 1810, Secretary of the Treasury Albert Gallatin presented positive proof of this fact: the nation's 87 cotton mills needed a labor force of 3500 women and children, and only 500 men. And in 1820 the census revealed, to the delight of many, that 43 percent of all textile workers in Massachusetts were children; 47 percent in Connecticut; and 55 percent in Rhode Island. The typical advertisement was blunt: "Wanted. Four families with not less than four children each to work in the mill."

Two Distinct Economies. Ordinary citizens had plenty of problems to occupy their minds in 1815, but competition was not usually one of them. Less than half of the population produced goods for the staple-exporting economy and indirectly traded with the world-at-large through seaport merchants. The majority had little contact with the outside world and traded almost exclusively with their neighbors. Largely self-sufficient, they raised their own vegetables, grains, and livestock; made their own furniture, clothes, blankets, soap, rum, and cider; built their own barns, houses, and fences. Since the middle of the eighteenth century, when the population began moving into the forests beyond the Atlantic seaboard, this largely self-sufficient economy had grown at a faster rate than the commercial, or staple-exporting economy.

The chief difference between the two economies was transportation. Except for communities touched by navigable waters, production for sale was sharply limited by the cost of transportation. Bulky goods could be moved profitably no more than ten or fifteen miles by land. Emphasis was put on products such as whiskey, butter, and salted meats in which the value was high in relation to the weight. Even then the cost of moving goods overland was high. If a farmer lived twenty or thirty miles from water transportation, he might as well live on the other side of the Atlantic, for the cost of moving a ton of goods from Europe to America was the same as moving it thirty miles over wretched American roads. And the roads were wretched. The Vice-President's son, Elbridge Gerry, Jr., took the road to Pittsburgh in 1813. He lost his horse in a mudhole!

Even the old seaboard states had some of both economies. In New York, for example, the great landlords and farmers along the Hudson River were fully engaged in commercial farming. But Yankee farmers who had moved into western New York in great numbers since the Revolution were cut off from the Atlantic market. They could afford to send valuable goods like furs to market. But the cost of sending wheat from Buffalo to New York City was three times the market price; for corn it was six times; and for oats twelve times. Trading areas in western New York seldom extended beyond a five-mile radius. While such situations severely limited the commercial opportunities of farmers, storekeepers, shoemakers and other artisans, it also protected them from outside competition. Storekeepers and artisans, in particular, got all of the local run of trade.

Choosing Their "Betters." By 1815 most white adult males could vote. And sporadically a candidate or an issue would bring great numbers out of the woods, down the streams, and to the polls. In Delaware, the gubernatorial election of 1804 brought out 82 percent of the electorate, and 81 percent of New Hampshire's voters turned out to choose a governor in 1812. But these were whopping turnouts. Less extraordinary were record turnouts in other states:

Pennsylvania	72 percent
Massachusetts	67
Georgia	62
Rhode Island	49
New York	42
Louisiana	34
Virginia	26

Ordinary state elections attracted two thirds as many voters, and presidential elections brought out fewer still.

More often than not, ordinary farmers and workingmen concluded that government affairs—and particularly government affairs way off in Washington—had little effect on their lives. Even the federal postal service, which boasted some 3000 employees, was barely visible in most communities. And since the cost of mailing a letter, twenty-five cents for 400 miles, was prohibitively expensive, the average citizen used the postal service infrequently. So farmers and workingmen were generally willing to leave government to their "betters"—to men who had something to gain from political power such as land grants, bank charters, or simply government office.

SUGGESTED READINGS

There are several single-volume books that cover American society in 1815, but none does the job as well as an old one by John A. Krout and Dixon Ryan Fox, *Completion of Independence** (1944). Also invaluable is another old work, Volume IV of John Bach McMaster's *History of the People of the United States, from the Revolution to the Civil War* (7 vols., 1903).

The problem of white supremacy has spawned many books. The best one for learning how white supremacy developed in the colonial period is Winthrop D. Jordan, *White Over Black: American Attitudes Toward the Negro, 1550–1812** (1968), a long book which has been condensed by Jordan in *The White Man's Burden: Historical Origins of Racism in the United States** (1974). An excellent book which carries the same theme through the nineteenth century is George M. Fredrickson, *The Black Image in the White Mind: The Debate on Afro-American Character and Destiny, 1817–1914** (1971). A perceptive commentary on slavery and racism, North and South, is C. Vann Woodward, *American Counterpoint** (1971). For the attitude of Jefferson and his fellow Virginians, see William Cohen, "Thomas Jefferson and the Problem of Slavery," *Journal of American History,* Vol. 56 (1969); Robert McColley, *Slavery and Jeffersonian Virginia** (1964), and William W. Freehling, "The Founding Fathers and Slavery," *American Historical Review,* Vol. 77 (1972). For the hopes and dreams of the American Colonization Society, see P. J. Staudenraus, *The African Colonization Movement, 1816–1865* (1961). To understand American racism in a larger context, see Carl Degler, *Neither Black Nor White** (1971), a brilliant book which compares American and Brazilian race relations.

There is nothing outstanding on the unruliness of American society. But, through many books, one can get at it indirectly. On violence, for example, see David Brion Davis, *Homicide in American Fiction, 1798–1860** (1957); Arthur K. Moore, *The Frontier Mind** (1957); and John Hope Franklin, *The Militant South, 1800–1861** (1956). On citizen soldiers and the militia, see Marcus Cunliffe, *Soldiers and Civilians: The Martial Spirit in America, 1775–1865* (1968). On the weakness of federal authority and American attitudes toward authority, a good introduction is James Sterling Young, *The Washington Community, 1800–1828** (1965).

*Available in a paperback edition.

Much has been written on preindustrial America. For a delightful introduction to the subject, see Gerald Carson, *The Old Country Store** (1965) and Jared Van Wagenen, *The Golden Age of Homespun* (1927). Both books are written with zest and tell much about everyday life. For the preindustrial worker, see David Montgomery, "The Working Classes of the Pre-Industrial American City, 1780–1830," *Labor History,* Vol. 9 (1968). For the economy as a whole, see Curtis P. Nettels, *The Emergence of a National Economy, 1775–1815** (1962); Paul W. Gates, *The Farmer's Age: Agriculture, 1815–1860** (1960); and George R. Taylor, *The Transportation Revolution* (1951).

CHAPTER TWO

TWILIGHT OF JEFFERSONIAN DEMOCRACY

WHO RULED AMERICA in 1815? It was doubtful if anyone could actually rule such a loosely run society. But some clearly dominated it. Most Americans, in fact, divided their countrymen into classes and spoke of a governing aristocracy. Old revolutionaries such as John Adams and Thomas Jefferson never thought for a moment that it was necessary to have a royal court, or the trappings of nobility, to have an aristocracy. They knew that their own societies—Massachusetts and Virginia—were governed by the upper classes, even though the distribution of deference was less obvious than in a hierarchical society.

"The mass of our citizens," explained Jefferson in 1814, "may be divided into two classes—the laboring and the learned. The laboring will need the first grade of education to qualify them for their pursuits and duties: the learned will need it as a foundation for further acquirements." After elementary instruction, "the two classes separate—those destined for labor will engage in the business of agriculture, or enter into apprenticeships . . . their companions, destined to the pursuits of science, will proceed to college." That was Jefferson's plan for educating children in Virginia.

Who would govern? Under Jeffersonian theory, the "laboring" masses were good enough and wise enough to choose their own rulers, to separate "the wheat from the chaff," and in general they would elect "the really good and wise." But Jefferson never maintained that ordinary people should actually run the government or tell their chosen representatives what to do. Rather, once the election was over, they should leave government to their "betters" or, as he preferred to put it, to "natural aristocrats" of superior "virtue and talent." That was the essence of Jeffersonian democracy.

The Elite

Who actually had disproportionate power in American society? Who were the "aristocrats" in 1815? What groups dominated the "laboring" masses? These questions are hard to answer with precision. One reason is that historians have only recently begun the difficult task of measuring accurately the distribution of wealth and power. As a result, we have bits and pieces but not the entire picture. We know, for example, that in southeastern Pennsylvania, which had once been known as "the best poor man's country," the rich got richer as time went by, while the poor's portion of the economic pie got smaller; by 1802 the wealthiest 10 percent had ten times as much wealth as the poorest 30 percent. By comparison, in the village of Brooklyn in 1810, the upper tenth had much more wealth than the rest of the village combined. We need to know more, however, for American society differed markedly from town to country, from region to region, from old settlements to raucous frontier villages.

The Old House of Representatives by Samuel E. B. Morse, 1821. *In the collection of The Corcoran Gallery of Art*

Even with these reservations, it is obvious that at least three groups, and perhaps a fourth, dominated the nation in 1815.

Clergymen. The least secure was the clergy. In fact, some historians have argued that their time had passed. The old system of tax-supported churches, which still existed in three New England states, was on its last legs; and everywhere once powerful colonial churches had to fight off internal dissension, schisms, or challenging upstarts like the Methodists. In New Hampshire and elsewhere the old tradition of life tenure for Congregational ministers was giving way to short-term contracts; so towns could get rid of overbearing preachers.

Scores of New England clergymen, moreover, saw antireligious conspiracies all about them and insisted that the nation was rapidly descending into French revolutionary atheism. Students at Yale, so the lament went, had been corrupted by Tom Paine's *Age of Reason*; the "infidel" Jefferson had been elected President; Harvard had "fallen" to the Unitarians; and drunkards reeled through the streets with "entire impunity." Indeed, according to an 1816 report, the new areas of old cities were overrun with prostitutes, dives, and "ballrooms"—but were without churches. A Bible distributor had bravely set foot into the Seventh Ward of New York—only to be attacked by rogues, stripped naked, and left bleeding in the street.

But as always, when churchmen spoke of sin, they exaggerated. The most privileged colonial churches, the Episcopalians and the Congregationalists, may have been declining, and the Seventh Ward may have been overrun with whores, but 1815 was hardly Christianity's darkest hour. Clergymen still dominated education from Yale and Princeton down to the village schoolhouse. More than nine tenths of the college presidents from 1790 to 1830 were ordained ministers, who also served as college pastors and usually taught several courses. Moreover, clergymen had an enormous influence over women, who lacked the right to vote, but knew how to make themselves heard nevertheless. Evangelical Protestantism, which was rapidly expanding and soon would have missionaries "from Greenland's icy mountains to India's coral strand," provided the first organized religious work for thousands of women, who were encouraged to gather for prayer and study, and to spread the notion throughout their village of giving one cent a week to the missionary enterprise. Such "mite societies" spread rapidly throughout New England and New York and furnished churchmen with armies of steady workers for one religious cause after another—and later for one reform after another. The influence of clergymen thus may have been increasing in 1815.

Merchants. If there was some doubt about the power of the clergy, there was no question at all about the influence of seaport merchants. There were only twelve cities with more than 8000 people in 1815. All were inland or tidewater ports. They differed noticeably in size, wealth, and future prospects: Albany, Richmond, Providence, and Norfolk had about 10,000 people, while New York and Philadelphia had well over 100,000. Norfolk was losing population, while Baltimore was growing by leaps and bounds. Despite these differences, they had a common orientation toward the Atlantic trade. Their newspapers carried shipping schedules, news about foreign events and the state of foreign markets, and advertisements offering everything from Cantonese silk to anchor chains and ship bread.

The dominant figures of these ports were always the merchants. Operating out of small counting rooms, they engaged in virtually every aspect of the coastwide and foreign trade. They owned and sometimes built ships, bought and sold at both wholesale and retail, acted as bankers, shippers, agents, and insurance brokers. As a rule, they speculated heavily in real estate, but rarely in manufacturing. Most had solid local reputations and connections in every Atlantic port; a few, like John Jacob Astor of New York and Stephen Girard of Philadelphia, were known nationally as men of incredible wealth and power. Shipping ventures rewarded Girard so well that in 1812 he founded the "Bank of Stephen Girard" with a capital of $1,200,000. And Astor, despite the war's disruption of trade, owned nine ships and had $800,000 invested in trade in 1815. Together, Girard and Astor were the major subscribers of the $16,000,000 loan that the federal government had floated to finance the war.

Lawyers. Along with the merchants, lawyers also enjoyed power. Their position was somewhat peculiar in that most people regarded them with a great deal of suspicion. The old notion that lawyers lived off other folks' miseries was widely shared, and "pettifogger" was still a common epithet. But lawyers were a necessary evil: the "mystery" of the law had already become so complex that the layman could not plead his own case, and lawsuits had multiplied as commerce increased, land became valuable, and settlement spread. Thus, since the eve of the Revolution, leading lawyers were part of the upper crust from New England to the Carolinas.

Admission to the profession was never easy. Court regulations in most eastern states called for a clerkship of three to seven years with credit being given for college. Of Massachusetts attorneys practicing between 1800 and 1830, more than 90 percent went to college first and then began legal training in law offices. In some western states, the term of training was shorter. Whatever the term, the average lawyer learned his trade by reading Blackstone's *Commentaries on the Laws of England* and clerking for an established attorney. Once established himself, he began his search for clients. Except in seaboard cities, where maritime and commercial questions predominated, the most lucrative practices centered around the interests of land speculators and landed gentry. Many successful lawyers, in fact, used their practice as a gateway to business opportunities and became landed gentlemen and land speculators themselves.

Above all, lawyers held political office. And it mattered little what party, or what administration, was in power. Jeffersonian Republicans denounced John Marshall's Supreme Court and continually campaigned against Federalist "pettifoggers." Indeed, they often sounded like ordinary farmers and workingmen. But most of them, like their Federalist opponents, were lawyers. Of the one hundred men Thomas Jefferson appointed to high office, sixty-two were lawyers. And in 1815, more than half of the representatives, two thirds of the senators, and all the

Cabinet members except the secretary of the navy (a rich Salem merchant) were lawyers. The presence of so many lawyers, the French aristocrat Alexis de Tocqueville later observed, was "the most powerful, if not the only counterpoise" to democracy in America. Trained like English lawyers in the law of precedents, they had developed a "superstitious attachment to what is old" and were much less likely to innovate than French lawyers. So American lawyers, while they belonged "to the people by birth and interest," belonged also "to the aristocracy by habit and taste."

The Slaveholding Aristocracy. Of those who had disproportionate power in 1815, the slaveholding aristocracy was clearly at the top. Along with seaboard merchants and the owners of large northern manors, the planters dominated the staple-exporting economy, which had been the nation's primary money-making economy since colonial times. Owning more than half of the country's 1,600,000 slaves, as well as the best land, the great planters produced the lion's share of tobacco, cotton, rice, grain, and other staples for the overseas market.

The great planter-politicians, who were usually lawyers too, dominated much of national politics. During the first twenty-six years of the Republic, Virginia planters had held the presidency for twenty-two years. This fact, some said, could

Drawing by August Köllmer imparts the tranquil, leisurely life of the Virginia planter and his family. *The Bettmann Archive, Inc.*

be justified easily on the merits of the men involved: Washington was deserving as father of the country, Jefferson as father of democracy, and Madison as father of the Constitution. But why, in 1815, were the only acceptable candidates for the office natives of Virginia? Neither William Crawford, who had moved from Virginia to Georgia, nor James Monroe, who still resided in Virginia, was as illustrious as Washington, Jefferson, or Madison. Certainly there were other men just as deserving. So many concluded that their birthplace, along with their membership in the slaveholding aristocracy, gave them the edge. There was a Virginia Dynasty.

But why? Dissidents maintained that the system favored a dynasty of tidewater planters. In Virginia itself, farmers west of the Blue Ridge complained bitterly that the state constitution of 1776 grossly favored the tidewater aristocracy at the expense of the western part of the state. The system of representation, two delegates for each county, took no account of population. So Warwick in the Tidewater, with 620 free whites, had the same power as Shenandoah County with 17,000. In 1816 reformers from thirty-eight counties met at Staunton and demanded a constitutional convention. One speaker after another called attention to the hypocrisy of the state's leaders: Jeffersonians were the foremost spokesmen for republicanism nationally, but the basic republican tenet of majority rule was not to be found in Virginia.

Northern dissidents attributed Virginia's power to the Louisiana Purchase, which expanded slaveholding country, and to the constitutional compromise over slavery, which allowed the slaveholding states to count three fifths of their slaves for apportionment. Clearly, the three-fifths compromise gave the slaveholding states many more electoral votes and congressional seats than would have been the case if apportionment were based on free or voting population alone. North Carolina, with 78,000 free adult males, had the same number of electoral votes as Massachusetts with 166,000. Since Jeffersonian Republicans gained much of their support in the South, New England Federalists were quick to point out such inequities. In 1812, one pamphleteer calculated that in the crucial election of 1800, "the black representation from the SLAVE COUNTRY amounted to 15: so that *the negroes turned the majority, and actually put in the President!*"

Since 1800 the great planter-politicians had had little trouble controlling the political arena. Jeffersonian Republicans regularly won three fourths of all popular contests, and four fifths of all Senate races. So it was no surprise in 1816 when James Monroe, a tidewater planter who wore the knee-length pantaloons and white-topped boots of an earlier day, became the fourth Virginia President. It was American politics as usual. But trouble lay ahead for the plantation aristocracy. During the next sixteen years, they squabbled among themselves and were challenged first nationally—and then even at home.

Collapse of the First Party System

During the two terms of James Monroe (1817-1825), the nation's first political system fell apart. The nation began under Washington with a one-party system that gave way quickly to a two-party system under Adams and Jefferson. Two-party politics was never truly national or competitive in all states. The Jeffersonian Republicans gained a quick advantage in electoral votes and the nation always seemed to be on the verge of slipping back into one-party politics. And many Republicans dearly wanted to kill off the opposition and put an end to two-party politics. "Now is the time to exterminate the monster called party spirit," Andrew Jackson wrote Monroe in 1816. Monroe fully agreed.

Federalist vs. Republicans. The Federalists were dying without the aid of outsiders. Actually, they never established a party in the modern sense, for they failed to set up political operations throughout the nation. Federalist leaders often put principle above party, and only a few of them were capable of wheeling and dealing or making the necessary compromise to build a national coalition. They never even got a toehold in the new frontier states. They failed to maintain strength outside a few states like Massachusetts, Connecticut, and Delaware. And in the last year of the war, they sponsored the Hartford Convention, which toyed with secession and denounced the nation's leadership just at the moment that Jackson scored a smashing victory over British regulars at the Battle of New Orleans. Politically they seemed to do everything wrong.

In 1816 the Federalists nominated for President an able New Yorker, Rufus King, who was the leader of nine Federalists in the Senate. He won 34 electoral votes against 183 for Monroe. In 1820—in the midst of a depression—the Federalists did not even bother to put up a candidate, and Monroe won every vote in the electoral college but one. The Federalists thus left the Republicans in control of a one-party government. Since bad feelings were no longer channeled into a clearcut conflict between two national parties, they were easier to ignore. Hence, when Monroe began his first term with a goodwill tour of New England, and a great celebration at Boston brought together many men "whom party politics had long severed," a Federalist newsman dubbed the times "an era of good feelings." The name stuck, but bad feelings failed to go away.

The quest for unanimity was an impossible dream in a free and boisterous society. Neither the Virginia Dynasty nor the Republican party could hope to satisfy all the varied interests scattered across a vast Republic. Even when the Federalists provided the Republicans with some opposition, Republican Presidents had to worry constantly about the wolves in their own party, such as the Tertium Quids in Virginia, or the Smith clique in Maryland, or the Duane-Leib faction in Pennsylvania, or the Clintonians in New York. The only question was whether one party would give way to two, or perhaps to a dozen. And this question turned on whether political notables divided along regional or sectional or economic or ideological lines.

At first they went in half-a-dozen different directions. "There is no rallying point for any party," wrote Justice Joseph Story in 1818. "Indeed, everything is scattered. Republicans and Federalists are as much divided among themselves, as the parties formerly were from each other." Several years later, both Secretary of State Adams and Secretary of Treasury Crawford, who hated one another, insisted that Cabinet meetings were a disgrace: even trivial issues ended in deadlock. The administration, noted Adams, "is at war with itself, both in the Executive, and between the Executive and Legislature."

Battle for the Presidency. The immediate battle among Washington politicians was over who would be Monroe's successor when his second term expired in 1825. If things went according to custom, Republican congressmen, meeting in caucus, would choose the Republican nominee. They had always chosen Virginians who were usually secretaries of state. That pattern was clearly going to be broken since Adams, the present secretary of state, was neither a Virginian nor the likely nominee.

But could the caucus still make a binding nomination? That was the real question. Would the losers abide by the decision of the caucus as William Crawford did in 1816? In 1820 congressmen from Pennsylvania and North Carolina agreed unanimously to boycott the caucus, and only forty Republicans attended the meeting. Even though the caucus was being held to renominate a Virginia President, only two Virginia congressmen were willing to attend. There was good reason, then, to doubt the viability of King Caucus. Losers would probably not abide by the decision of a handful of congressmen.

That was exactly what happened. The dominant faction lined up behind William Crawford, the secretary of the treasury. But by the time they met to caucus, two things had gone wrong. First, their man was half-dead: the summer before, Crawford had suffered a paralytic stroke that left him dumb and blind, and doctors had bled him twenty-three times "to the verge of death." And second, there were already three candidates in the field when the caucus met. The names of John Quincy Adams, Henry Clay, and Andrew Jackson had already been placed in nomination by state legislatures or public meetings. The three men would have gladly accepted the blessing of King Caucus if they could have gotten it, but the caucus stood behind the battered hulk of William Crawford. It was a rump caucus, however, with only 66 congressmen out of 216 attending, and the three losers ignored the action.

Thus four men, all calling themselves Republican, ran for President in 1824. All but Adams were slaveholders. All but Jackson were experienced Washington politicians. Though Jackson won plurality of both the electoral and popular vote, no candidate had a majority, and the election went to the House of Representatives. There, an incredible amount of maneuvering, bargaining, and finagling took place. In the end, Clay threw his weight to Adams, and the President-elect promptly appointed Clay secretary of state. The appointment was doubly significant because the office traditionally had been the stepping stone to the presidency. Jackson men quickly concluded that a deal had been made. "So you see," snarled Jackson, "the *Judas* of the West had closed the contract and will receive the thirty pieces of silver."

Historians are fond of saying that the "people" were incensed, that they were angry to learn that the Hero of New Orleans had lost out to a gang of politicians, that "bargain and corruption" had turned the trick. Actually, it was impossible to discern the will of the majority. Jackson got nearly 98 percent of the vote in his home state of Tennessee, but not a single vote in Massachusetts, the home state of Adams. Indeed, there were real contests in so few states that only one fourth of the eligible voters bothered to go to the polls. And in New York, the most populous state in the Union, the voters did not even have a chance to vote. There, as in five other states, the choice was made by the state legislature. All we can say with some certainty is that Jackson had the support of 9 percent of the electorate, while Adams had the support of 6 percent, and no one had a clear mandate to govern.

The first two-party was dead. King Caucus had been dethroned. But what was to take their place? Would a new political system develop? Or would presidential politics remain a free-for-all? The election of 1824 only added to the murkiness of American politics.

The Loss of Political Control

Behind the struggle for the presidency was a more far-reaching crisis. What issues, what divisions, what lines of cleavage would dominate the nation's politics? What, in short, would politicians fight over? Under Jefferson and Madison the Republicans had managed to keep some particularly troublesome issues—like the future of slavery and the inordinate power of southern politicians—out of the political limelight. Under Monroe, however, party discipline was a shambles, and even the most explosive issues were fully debated. New lines of battle sprang up, and the political arena itself became something of a free-for-all.

Bad feelings emerged soon after the war. The nation had come within an ace of being split in two by an invading British army, and Washington had been burned. What was to be done to remedy the country's miserable wartime performance? Many older Republicans still adhered to the basic position that the best of all possible governments was the one that governed least. They wanted few changes and were generally content to blame wartime failings on "Hartford Convention Federalists" and other rascals. But Calhoun and Clay thought otherwise. Strong measures, they indicated, were a necessity to avert another disaster like the War of 1812. And, led by Calhoun and Clay, younger Republicans pushed through Congress in 1816 and 1817 a legislative program that created a new national bank, protective tariffs to encourage northern manufacturing and thus make the country less dependent on English factory goods, and a federal system of roads and canals "to bind the Republic together." So the party of Jefferson adopted the old program of Alexander Hamilton, and many commentators spoke knowingly of a new era of "Republican nationalism."

But Republican nationalism was largely wishful thinking. Only the Bank Bill passed Congress with votes to spare; the others squeaked through after an uphill struggle. Neither Clay nor Calhoun truly represented the views of their fellow planters. Only fourteen of fifty-one southern congressmen followed them in supporting protective tariffs; the remainder howled bitterly that raising the import duty on foreign manufactured goods would cost southern planters dearly in higher prices. And old Republicans in Virginia and North Carolina were furious that a program enhancing the power and prestige of the federal government had been adopted. Why adopt Hamiltonian measures? Why sell out the Republican heritage? Madison, who shared some of these doubts, vetoed the internal improvements bill on constitutional grounds just before leaving office.

Finally, the Panic of 1819 destroyed the illusion. Hard times proved to everyone that the remedies of Clay and Calhoun had failed to bind the nation together. Indeed, they had only become the source of endless friction. Hard-hit industrialists in New York, Pennsylvania, and Rhode Island demanded more protection to save them from British competition. Southerners blamed their troubles on high tariffs. And thousands everywhere pointed damning fingers at the Second Bank as it foreclosed on mortgages right and left and came to be known throughout the West as "the Monster."

John Marshall. Simultaneously, Republicans of the old school became incensed by the activities of Chief Justice Marshall. Since 1801 Jefferson and his colleagues had hoped to get rid of the great Federalist jurist. But they had failed to drive him off the high court, and they had failed to give the court a Republican cast. To their disgust, even their own appointees soon fell under the Chief Justice's dominance. And, in their eyes, Marshall was guilty many times over of abusing his great power in behalf of high Federalism, extreme nationalism, vested interests, and even his own pocketbook. In 1810, he had outraged many of his fellow Virginians by his decision in the famous Yazoo case *(Fletcher v. Peck).* He had ruled that a gigantic land grant, even though it was obtained by bribing the entire Georgia legislature, was a sacred contract and forever binding. So a subsequent legislative act repealing the grant was unconstitutional. What about states' rights? What about the people's rights? Could a crooked legislature simply barter away their rights, and leave them without a remedy? Marshall in effect said "yes": contracts must be strictly enforced or chaos would result.

Marshall carried such thinking even further in early 1819. In the Dartmouth College case, he pushed the sanctity of contracts to the point that the dead controlled the living. The case involved an attempt by the New Hampshire legislature to change Dartmouth from a private to a public institution. Dartmouth sued on the basis of a charter granted to the college by King George III in 1769. Despite the American Revolution against George III, Marshall held that the charter was still in force and neither party could alter it without the consent of the other; New Hampshire had acted unconstitutionally. News of the decision brought howls of protest. Everyone quickly saw that the decision cast a broad protective shield over scores of banks and corporations that enjoyed state charters, and that it took away from popularly elected representatives a large portion of their control over social and economic affairs.

Even more disconcerting was Marshall's decision a few weeks later in *McCulloch v. Maryland.* Responding to pressure from local banks, the Maryland legislature in 1818 had placed an annual tax of $15,000 on "foreign" banks. The Baltimore branch of the Bank of the United States refused to pay, and the state sued the cashier, John McCulloch. The Second Bank lost the case on the state level and appealed to the Supreme Court. It was a crucial lawsuit for the bank because five other states had levied taxes upon its branches, and other states would follow suit if the Maryland decision were upheld. It was also a crucial lawsuit for Republicans of the old school. Since 1791 they had argued that a national bank was unconstitutional. What clause in the Constitution gave Congress the power to establish a bank? The powers of Congress, they argued, were specifically enumerated, and the right to establish a bank was not one of them. And since 1816 they had wailed against their party's surrender to Hamiltonian principles in chartering the Second Bank.

In his decision, Marshall went out of his way to attack old Republican beliefs. In phrases taken from Hamilton's 1791 report to Washington, the Federalist judge held that the doctrine of "implied powers" gave Congress the power to charter a national bank. The powers of Congress were not limited to those spelled out in the Constitution. Not in the least! If the end was legitimate, if it was "within the scope of the Constitution," then "all means which are appropriate, which are plainly adapted to that end" are constitutional. Even more audacious, Marshall announced that Congress might withdraw *any* taxable subject from state taxation, and not merely those which the Constitution specifically mentioned. The power to tax was the power to destroy, he argued, and no state could be allowed to destroy an institution created by the federal government: the national government was supreme.

The decisions set off a storm of protest. Almost overnight, Marshall had succeeded in enraging strict-constructionists, states-righters, bank haters, debtors, and reformers. Public meetings and politicians screamed that the rights of the people and the rights of the states had been destroyed. "And for whom? The monster bank!" John Taylor of Virginia, the leading theoretician of the old Republicans, turned out a spate of books denouncing Marshall and the "insidious aristocracy of paper and patronage." Five state legislatures approved constitutional amendments giving states the power to exclude the national bank from their jurisdiction. Ohio met the challenge head on. When the Bank refused to pay $50,000 in state taxes, Ohio officials marched on the Chillicothe branch and seized bank notes and specie to meet the bill. Who said that the Supreme Court was the final expositor of the Constitution? Certainly not the people of Ohio! When the Bank then sued the state auditor, Ralph Osborn, the legislature declared the Bank an outlaw and banned it from the state. Again, the Bank took its case to court, and again Marshall used the Bank's case to strengthen federal authority. In 1824, when the Osborn controversy finally reached the Supreme Court, Marshall's court ruled that state officials were personally liable whenever they carried out an unconstitutional state statute. Federal law—and the high court—were supreme.

In the same year, Marshall also invalidated a monopoly that New York had granted over steamboat service between New York and New Jersey. In this case, *Gibbon* v. *Ogden*, the Court held that in giving Congress the power to regulate interstate commerce, the Constitution meant that *only* Congress should have that power; the New York monopoly, therefore, was an invasion of the federal government's exclusive right to regulate. Even more important, Marshall defined commerce so broadly that it included not only "traffic" but also "intercourse." No one had the foggiest notion what that meant, but it clearly laid the basis for future judges to expand federal power. "Is there no end to such heresies?" asked the Richmond *Enquirer*. The Federalist judge was clearly determined to make state governments weak, and the federal government strong.

The Missouri Crisis. From the standpoint of the Virginia Dynasty and the Republican leadership, banks, tariffs, roads and canals, and even Chief Justice Marshall were minor problems compared to the crisis that broke out in February 1819. Suddenly, the most divisive issues of the day—the future of slavery and the inordinate power of the South in national affairs—came to dominate Washington politics.

An obscure New York congressman lit the fuse. The House was in the process of enabling Missouri to apply for statehood, when Representative James Tallmadge of Poughkeepsie offered an amendment to the Enabling Act prohibiting "the further introduction of slavery" into Missouri and providing that all slaves born in Missouri after it became a state "shall be free, but may be held to service until the age of twenty-five years." Tallmadge's move came as a shock. Who was he? And what was he up to? First reports indicated that he was forty-one years old, a good Jeffersonian, and a freshman congressman who had already declined to run again. John Quincy Adams concluded hastily that the neophyte had just innocently opened a can of worms. But people who knew Tallmadge better claimed that he was a maverick who refused to play by the rules and who had an uncanny instinct for the jugular.

Tallmadge clearly went for the jugular. When he spoke, he seemed to be free of all pretense; he frankly admitted that the idea of extending the three-fifths rule to yet another state rankled him; the area west of the Mississippi had "no claim to such an unequal representation, unjust in its result upon the other States." And as Tallmadge explained it, "with the courtesy of a gentleman" and "the authority and dignity of a presiding officer," his proposal was in the best republican tradition. He did not wish to interfere with slavery in the older states, or even in the Alabama Territory, which was surrounded by slave states. That would be playing with fire: it might set off a slave insurrection.

But beyond the Mississippi, in new territory paid for by the entire nation, slavery was justly subject to national legislation. And his amendment merely applied to Missouri the same pattern of race relations that existed in neighboring states. It merely extended to Missouri the same program of gradual emancipation that the revolutionary generation had enacted in New York, New Jersey, and other northern states. Even the great Jefferson, in words that were frequently quoted, advocated that slavery be abolished gradually by "imperceptible degrees." Here, then, was the opportunity: the proportion of slaves in Missouri was no greater than it had once been in New York. Why let slavery, "with its baleful consequences," inherit the entire West? Why disgrace the republican heritage by letting the "original sin" engulf Missouri?

Tallmadge hit the chink in the South's armor. Defenders of slavery could simply dismiss Tallmadge's appeal as nonsense. But Jeffersonian liberals were being asked to live up to their word. For years they had denounced slavery in the abstract. Why then, asked one of Tallmadge's associates, did they want to fasten the same evil system on Missouri? They knew that slaves would be smuggled in from Africa to perform labor there; and they knew—better than anyone else—that future generations of Missourians would hate them for their decision. Was Jeffersonian liberalism real? Or was it just rhetoric? To meet the challenge, the eloquent Henry Clay of Kentucky and Philip Barbour of Virginia rose to speak for "the cause of humanity." They refused to defend slavery in the abstract: it was indeed an evil system. But they argued that the condition of slaves would improve immensely if they were spread over a large area. Indeed, everyone would benefit! The fertile West would provide slaves with cheaper and more abundant food, and they would be much happier than if they were cooped up in the Old South. At the same time, the scattering of the slave population would reduce the danger of insurrection.

Northern men responded with contempt: southern liberalism was a fraud. Look out the door, Tallmadge told his fellow congressmen, and see Clay's "diffusion" argument at work:

> A slave driver, a trafficker in human flesh, as if sent by Providence, has passed the door of your Capitol, on his way to the West, driving before him about fifteen of these wretched victims of his power. The males, who might raise the arm of vengeance, and retaliate for their wrongs, were handcuffed, and chained to each other, while the females and children were marched in their rear, under the guidance of the driver's whip! Yes, Sir, such has been the scene witnessed from the windows of Congress Hall, and viewed by members who compose the legislative councils of Republican America!

Tempers soon flared and men talked freely of disunion and civil war. Pointing at Tallmadge, Thomas Cobb of Georgia screamed: "You have kindled a fire which all the waters of the ocean cannot put out, which seas of blood can only extinguish."

Tallmadge had indeed lit a fire. Before he completed his one term in Congress, his amendment passed the House in a highly sectional vote, and then was killed in the Senate. When Congress met nine months later, Tallmadge was gone, but the battle quickly resumed. The admission of Alabama established an even balance of eleven free states and eleven slave states; so the admission of Missouri as the twelfth slave state would give planters control of the Senate, where they might strangle any legislation passed by the northern majority in the House. As a result, the struggle for "humanity" gave way to the struggle for power. Thanks to the three-fifths clause, noted Rufus King of New York, the South already had twenty "extra" seats in the House, and twenty additional electoral votes. Why give them more?

And so it went for nearly two years. But why? Why did the slavery question suddenly gain the upper hand? In the past, when slavery and southern influence came up for debate, the followers of Jefferson had always been able to side-track the issue, focus attention on Federalist "traitors" and other vermin, and generally control the political battlefield. Now, they failed miserably. Now, the moral leadership and political power of the southern elite was not only being questioned, but challenged directly day after day, week after week, year after year. It was due to the breakdown of party discipline, insisted Martin Van Buren, the master politician of the age. Without strict party discipline, wavering Republicans and schismatics got out of hand, and even long-time party members began playing with powder kegs.

The Missouri Compromise. In the end, it took all of Henry Clay's manipulative genius to get Missouri through the House of Representatives. First, by using his full power as speaker of the House, Clay tried to ram Missouri down northern throats by making "the admission of Missouri the condition of that of Maine," which was also applying for statehood. But that strategy failed to work. Finally, Senator Jesse Thomas of Illinois added a proviso to Clay's proposal that "forever prohibited" slavery in all parts of the Louisiana Purchase north of latitude 36° 30′

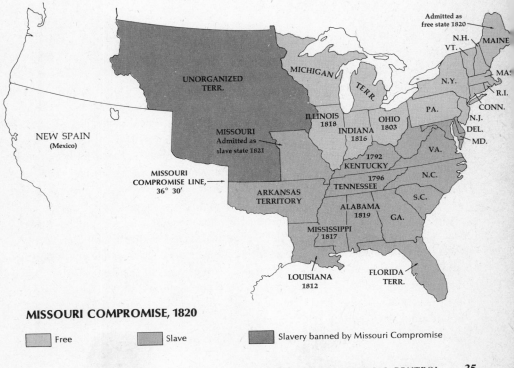

MISSOURI COMPROMISE, 1820

Free Slave Slavery banned by Missouri Compromise

with the single exception of Missouri. To get Missouri, then, the South would have to give up the lion's share of the Louisiana Purchase to the free states. And gradually it became clear that the Thomas Proviso was the best bargain that Clay and the South could get. So Missouri was admitted as a slave state, Maine as a free state, and the 36° 30′ line was firmly fixed on the nation's consciousness.

The donnybrook over Missouri, while it shook the entire nation, left its deepest impression on the leaders of the Old South. Everyone in power recognized the significance of what had happened. Historians quote them by the score as prophets but only fools missed the point: the nation would eventually divide free against slave. Here, noted John Quincy Adams, was "the basis for a new organization of parties terrible to the whole Union, but portentiously terrible to the South—threatening in its progress the emancipation of all their slaves, threatening in its immediate effect that southern domination which has swayed the Union for the last twenty years." The dispute, said Jefferson, "like a fire bell in the night, awakened me and filled me with terror."

Associates of Jefferson, who had helped create "southern domination," also saw the danger. Their moral leadership had been questioned; their "humanity" had been ridiculed; and their basis of power had been challenged. Almost immediately, they assumed that the battle over Missouri was part of a larger conspiracy to drive them from power. Who was behind James Tallmadge? That question rang through the South. Some mistakenly pointed their fingers at Rufus King, the kingpin of the dying Federalist party, while others erroneously blamed DeWitt Clinton, the arch-schemer in the Republican party, who once before had tried to drive the Virginia Dynasty from power. All agreed, however, that somebody was out to get them.

Northern Weaknesses. There were, in fact, only two matters in which the great planter-politicians could find any satisfaction at all. One was the final vote on the crucial bill to admit Missouri as a slave state; the South had held firm. Not one man failed to vote with his section. Eighteen northern congressmen, on the other hand, either voted with the South or were conveniently absent when the crucial vote was taken. John Randolph of Virginia declared that he had known all along that these men would give way. They were weak men, timid men, half-baked men. "They were scared at their own dough faces—yes, *they were scared at their own dough faces!* We had *them,* and if we had wanted *three* more, we could have had them, *whose conscience, and morality, and religion, extend to 'thirty-six degrees and thirty minutes north latitude.'* " Randolph's words stuck: "dough face" became a synonym for "northern men with southern principles," and it was applied indiscriminately to any northern man who voted with the South, regardless of his reasons. These eighteen men made sectional peace possible in 1820; they provided Clay with his 90 to 87 majority in the House on the crucial vote. Other "dough faces" would play the same crucial role, time and again, in the years to come.

The leaders of the Old South could also take some comfort in the predicament Northerners faced in what is sometimes called the "second Missouri crisis." After being accepted as a slave state, Missouri still had to present a constitution for congressional approval. The Missouri constitution included a clause *requiring* the state legislature to pass laws barring free Negroes and mulattoes from entering the state "under any pretext whatsoever." The clause clearly violated the federal constitution, which declared that "the citizens of each State shall be entitled to the privileges and immunities of the citizens of the several States." The free state majority thus had another opportunity to challenge the admission of Missouri.

This time, however, northern congressmen were vulnerable: free blacks were "citizens" in the North, but everywhere they were treated wretchedly. Charging northern congressmen with hypocrisy, Senator William Smith of South Carolina gleefully ran down a long list of northern sins: the constitutions of Connecticut and Ohio limited the franchise to white males, Vermont and New Hampshire barred blacks from their militias, and Indiana gave blacks the vote but forbade them from appearing as witnesses in any suits against white men. And in 1821 Tallmadge's New York raised the property qualification for black voters, while eliminating it for whites. In the end, Henry Clay won over the needed number of northern votes through a face-saving gesture: it gave President Monroe the right to proclaim Missouri a new state as soon as the Missouri legislature promised to obey the Constitution. Sarcastically, Missouri promised to be good, and Monroe formally admitted the new state in August 1821.

The Meaning of the Thomas Proviso. The architects of the Virginia Dynasty, however, took little comfort in counting the number of "dough faces" in Congress or watching Northerners squirm during the second Missouri crisis. The price of peace had been too costly. The rub was the 36° 30′ line. As soon as old Republicans in the South got word of the Thomas Proviso, they leapt to the attack. It was bad precedent, they thundered, to let the national government pass laws restricting slavery. Whatever the merits of the "peculiar institution," the presence of over 1.5 million slaves touched the heart of southern society: slavery was too important and too dangerous to be controlled by outsiders. "To compromise," said Nathaniel Macon of North Carolina, "is to acknowledge the right of Congress to interfere and to legislate on this subject; this would be acknowledging too much." "If we yield now, beware," wrote Thomas Ritchie in the Richmond *Enquirer.* "They will ride us forever." "We must in due time have Texas; we must have elbow room in the west." The jurist Spencer Roane of Virginia heartily agreed; as he explained it to Monroe, Southerners could never consent to be "damned up in a land of slaves."

The Thomas Proviso was thus a bitter pill. The great manipulator Clay avoided a showdown by splitting the Missouri Compromise into its component parts, and bringing each part through the House separately. Thus Virginians of the old school and southern hotspurs generally could hold out against the 36° 30′ line, while they joined the rest of the South in supporting the hotly contested bill to admit Missouri as a slave state. In the House, thirty-nine slave state congressmen followed Clay and voted for the Thomas Proviso; thirty-seven voted "nay." News of the vote and the final settlement was hardly welcome in Virginia. Thomas Ritchie reported: "We scarcely ever recollect to have tasted a bitterer cup." The followers of Clay, in Ritchie's judgment, had even failed to recognize the true interests of the South.

For the next decade, Ritchie and other Republicans of the old school would labor valiantly to teach their fellow Southerners that Republican nationalism was suicidal. If Congress had the power to charter the Second Bank, and now to ban slavery north of 36° 30′, then the federal government would soon claim other powers and would soon be meddling with slavery in the South. Marshall, Clay, and Calhoun—all had to be stopped. And the old Jeffersonian values of states-rights, strict construction of the Constitution, and a weak central government had to be restored. Above all, slavery had to be kept out of national politics.

Trouble at Home

During the next decade, these basic convictions were also reinforced by troubles that the great planter-politicians faced at home. Like all oppressed people, the black population in the South Atlantic states had generally endured the hard knocks of bondage and rarely rebelled against their oppressors. But, from time to time, enough had rebelled to create exaggerated fears among their masters. There was, moreover, the haunting fear that the ideology of the American Revolution, along with that of the French Revolution, had given birth to the great slave rebellion in San Domingo. That event, which lasted from 1791 to 1804, cost France the pearl of her empire and took the lives of hundreds of thousands. The bloody turmoil ended in a black victory ceremony, where triumphant revolutionaries established the Republic of Haiti and furiously ripped the white out of the French tricolor. From those days forward, even the sight of a slave listening to Fourth of July oratory troubled many Southerners. And tidewater planters, living in the midst of thousands of slaves, always trembled at the thought of a full-scale debate of the slavery question.

So the Missouri controversy racked much of the white South with fear. Would the South be devastated by a great slave revolt like the one in San Domingo? Northerners cruelly raised this question time and again, and played on southern fears. And Southerners were certain that the speeches of Rufus King and others would incite the slaves to rebel. Indeed, according to Senator William Smith of South Carolina, King's speeches were more provocative than anything ever heard in San Domingo. Such talk, predicted Andrew Jackson, "will excite those who is the subject of discussion to insurrection and masacre." And better grammarians agreed—especially after the decade that began with Denmark Vesey in 1822 and ended with Nat Turner in 1831.

Denmark Vesey. Denmark Vesey was a prosperous Charleston carpenter who had bought his freedom in 1800 with a lottery jackpot. He hated the racism under which free blacks constantly suffered, and he hated the system that kept his many wives and children in bondage. Brilliant and well-read, he found plenty in the Bible, the Declaration of Independence, and the Missouri debates that condemned slavery and justified insurrection. Armed with this ammunition, he moved freely through the slums of Charleston, and up and down the coast, winning black rebels to his cause. He bullied a few, and lied to others. He told one group that Congress had actually freed all slaves during the Missouri crisis; he told another that San Domingo had promised to send troops. Usually, however, he preached from a well-worn Bible, and likened his listeners to the Children of Israel. They, too, had been authorized by God to kill their masters.

In the late spring of 1822, Vesey and his followers made plans for a midnight massacre. Simultaneously, six battle units would seize the arsenals and main roads of Charleston, while small bands of slaves, armed with knives and axes, would wait in the shadows ready to kill their masters as they rushed to join the fray. At the last moment, however, the conspirators were betrayed by a "loyal" house servant, and the Governor ordered out five military companies to defend Charleston. Authorities then spent the next two months rounding up conspirators and trying to unravel the conspiracy. Eventually, Vesey and thirty-four blacks were hanged, thirty-seven others were banished from the state, and four white men were fined and imprisoned for encouraging the insurrection.

But Charleston aristocrats still slept in fear. For the investigations revealed that Vesey's followers were not poorly treated slaves. They were mainly skilled artisans who ran their own shops and hired out their own time, or trusted house servants. Indeed, the most trusted servants in South Carolina were part of the conspiracy. For years Governor Thomas Bennett had left his wife and children in the care of "his beloved slave" Rolla. It was shocking to learn that Rolla was a blood-thirsty conspirator! Even worse, Charleston aristocrats knew that most of the conspirators remained at large. How many Rollas remained in the nursery? How many "beloved" slaves wanted to see their masters dead? Such fears never subsided. In 1826, arsonists nearly gutted the city with fire after fire, and masters universally suspected their slaves. And in 1829, officials in Georgetown "accidentally" discovered another conspiracy just in time to avert bloodshed. How many lucky accidents could one reasonably expect?

Nat Turner. The good luck of the planters ran out—not in South Carolina—but in Southampton County, Virginia, in August 1831. There, a thirty-year-old, visionary slave preacher named Nat Turner touched off the greatest slave revolt in the nation's history. In 1828, according to Turner's own account, the "Spirit" appeared to him and told him to "slay my enemies with their own weapons." A heavenly sign would tell him when to begin. Thus, after an eclipse of the sun in early 1831, Turner and a small band began to make plans, and on August 21 they struck. Beginning with seven men, their forces soon expanded to fifteen, and then to fifty or sixty, as they carried terror and devastation along the road to Jerusalem. At each stop along the way, they seized money, horses, guns, and ammunition, and in less than three days they killed eleven men, fourteen women, and thirty children.

Within twelve hours of the uprising, wild rumors spread across the state. The rebels were said to have thousands of men, to be under the command of soldiers

Turner confessed that after, "the sign appearing in the heavens, the seal was removed from [his] lips, and [he] communicated the great work laid out for [him] to do, to four in whom [he] had the greatest confidence. . . ." *Culver Pictures*

from San Domingo, and to have been fired-up by wild-eyed antislavery men from the North. In response, the Governor sent company after company of state militia into Southampton County. By the time they arrived, however, local farmers and militiamen had crushed the rebellion. In doing so, they killed well over one hundred blacks, including many who were innocent and some who were probably on their own side. As for Turner, he outwitted thousands of pursuers for nearly two months, only to be finally captured, tried, and hanged from a tree.

Nat Turner sent a chill of terror through the white South. Quickly, leaders noted that a free black in Boston, David Walker, had published an *Appeal* in 1829 calling for slave uprisings throughout the South, and that a white printer in Boston, William Lloyd Garrison, had just recently launched a militant antislavery newspaper, *The Liberator,* which clamored for the immediate emancipation of all slaves. The southern leadership demanded the total suppression of such "incendiary" literature. Even more Southerners demanded that all-black churches be banned, and that laws be passed to ensure that no black man ever became a preacher. Still more demanded the elimination of the free Negro, the pariah of southern society, who traditionally bore the blame for making slaves uppity and rebellious. In response, state legislatures passed a flood of legislation to tighten controls.

The Virginia Debate. Such legislation, however, came far short of satisfying small farmers west of the Blue Ridge Mountains. They had lost a major battle in

1829 to gain equal representation in the Virginia legislature, and they were certain that the great planter-politicians of the Tidewater and Piedmont had abused them and misgoverned them for years. What was needed, they thundered, was total elimination of the danger. Blacks, whether they were free or slave, had to go! Virginia's enormous slave population, said western spokesmen, was not only inherently dangerous, but it was also a prime cause of Virginia's economic backwardness, and it ruined the white man's character. It bred bad habits, said George Summers, such as idleness, sensuality, and fondness for luxury—and even worse, it made children imperious and tyrannical. Slavery, echoed Charles J. Faulkner, always created "that unfortunate state of society in which freemen regard labor as disgraceful." And, if slavery continued to expand westward, it would drive out small farmers west of the Blue Ridge. The noble and virtuous "Virginia peasantry," said Faulkner, should not be forced to yield to "the slothful and degraded African." The African must go—not the white man!

Spokesmen for the white "peasantry" had but one chance to be heard—the winter of 1831-1832—when the spectre of Nat Turner still hung over Virginia. They had some support in the Tidewater and Piedmont, where blacks outnumbered whites. They had the aid of Governor John Floyd, who hoped to gradually abolish slavery at least on the west side of the Blue Ridge, as well as that of such powerful men as Thomas Ritchie of the Richmond *Enquirer* and Thomas Jefferson Randolph, grandson of the former President. And for three weeks Virginia's legislators debated the twin problems of abolishing slavery and ridding the state of blacks.

The leading voices favored either slavery or gradual, compensated emancipation. None of the emancipationists showed much concern for blacks who loved Virginia and regarded it as home: if freed, they had to be deported; that assumption ran through every plan. One proposal, for example, was that children born of female slaves after July 4, 1840, should become state property, and be hired out (which was common practice in Virginia) until they earned enough to pay for their own deportation. Such plans were hardly radical, given Jeffersonian rhetoric against slavery, but when a vote was taken spokesmen for small farmers lost, 73 to 58. Delegates from west of the Blue Ridge supported gradual emancipation, 49 to 6, but representatives from eastern counties opposed it by 67 to 9. Once again the great planters proved not only that they ran Virginia, but also that they had no intention of giving up their slaves.

Indeed, conservatives quickly launched a successful counter attack against slavery's critics. At the close of debate, one prominent slaveholder told Governor Floyd that he would rather have the state divided "than have the subject of abolition again debated." Within a few months, Thomas Roderick Dew, a thirty-year-old professor at William and Mary, published a *Review of the Debates*. Drawing from various speeches, he loaded his argument to prove that slavery was a "positive good," meriting the tenacious support of every good Southerner. The idea was hardly new, but more and more prominent Virginians gave it lip service. And soon politicians set out to convince themselves and everyone else that slavery was really a blessing for all concerned. At the same time, more and more southern legislatures curtailed freedom of speech and the press. Strident dissent dropped to a mere murmur. So triumphant was the plantation ideal that the large and important yeoman class, which Jefferson had once celebrated as the backbone of the South, dropped so far out of sight that it had to be rediscovered by twentieth-century historians.

Despite the great debate, there was always a common bond among small farmers and great planters regarding white supremacy. They might not agree on much else, but they always agreed that the black population was too large—and potentially too dangerous—to be tampered with by Bostonians, or New Yorkers, or other outsiders. And this common bond, in turn, strengthened the South's position in national affairs. For, while northern and western men had plenty of fears, they had no single, compelling fear that held them together. As a result, they never held to one position, year in and year out. Southern politicians, on the other hand, were unwavering in their insistence that slavery was a southern concern, never to be touched by outside hands. The "black strap" of slavery, observed Rufus King of New York, gave the white South a strong sense of unity that the North and West could never match. Thus, despite the passing of the Virginia Dynasty and Jeffersonian Democracy, the great planters were certain of controlling American politics for years to come.

SUGGESTED READINGS

An incisive book on the distribution of power in the early nineteenth century has yet to be written. For the most part, one has to rely on a variety of local, state, and regional histories, which invariably deal with the subject, although often indirectly. For the South, a good introduction is Clement Eaton, *The Growth of Southern Civilization, 1790–1860** (1961). More to the point is the analysis in Charles S. Sydnor, *The Development of Southern Sectionalism, 1819–1848** (1948); Fletcher M. Green, *Constitutional Development in the South Atlantic States, 1776–1860** (1930); Charles H. Ambler, *Sectionalism in Virginia* (1902); and the relevant chapters in J. R. Pole, *Political Representation in England & the Origins of the American Republic** (1966). For the North, there is much information in studies of various cities, as in Robert Albion, *The Rise of New York Port* (1939); Sam B. Warner, *The Private City: Philadelphia in Three Periods of Growth** (1968); Benjamin Labaree, *Patriots and Patricians: The Merchants of Newburyport, 1764–1815** (1962); and Edward Pessen, *Riches, Class, and Power Before the Civil War* (1973). On the professions, see Daniel H. Calhoun, *Professional Lives in America* (1965) and Gary B. Nash, "The Philadelphia Bench and Bar, 1800–1860," *Comparative Studies in Society and History,* Vol. 7 (1965). On those who held political office, see Sidney Aronson, *Status and Kinship in the Higher Civil Service* (1964).

George Dangerfield's *Era of Good Feelings** (1952) provides a general account of the

*Available in a paperback edition.

breakdown of the old political order, while James S. Young's *The Washington Community, 1801–1828** (1965) offers insightful analysis. For the political reaction to hard times, see Murray Rothbard, *The Panic of 1819: Reactions and Policies* (1962). For a good, short introduction to the role of John Marshall, see Edward S. Corwin, *John Marshall and the Constitution* (1919). In addition, Charles G. Haines' *The Role of the Supreme Court in American Government and Politics, 1789–1835* (1944) is thorough on the politican controversies associated with the Supreme Court, while Eugene T. Mudge's *The Social Philosophy of John Taylor of Caroline* (1939) is excellent on the leading critic of Marshall's nationalist doctrines. The standard work on the Missouri crisis is Glover Moore, *The Missouri Controversy, 1819–1821** (1953). For the reaction of the Old Republicans, see Norman K. Risjord, *The Old Republicans* (1965) and Richard H. Brown, "The Missouri Crisis, Slavery and the Politics of Jacksonianism," *South Atlantic Quarterly,* Vol. 45 (1966).

Studies of slavery are legion. For very different assessments, see Kenneth Stampp, *The Peculiar Institution** (1956); Stanley Elkins, *Slavery** (1968); John Blassingame, *The Slave Community: Plantation Life in the Antebellum South** (1972); Robert Fogel and Stanley Engerman, *Time on the Cross** (1974); and Eugene Genovese, *Roll, Jordan, Roll** (1974). For slave rebellions, and the fear masters had of their slaves, there are a number of first-rate books: Gerald W. Mullin, *Flight and Rebellion: Slave Resistance in Eighteenth-Century Virginia** (1972); William W. Freehling, *Prelude to Civil War** (1966); John Lofton, *Insurrection in South Carolina* (1964); Henry Tragle, ed., *The Southampton Slave Revolt of 1831* (1971); Stephen B. Oates, *The Fires of Jubilee: Nat Turner's Fierce Rebellion* (1975); Steven Channing, *Crisis of Fear* (1970). Among the better studies of white reaction to slave unrest are Clement Eaton, *Freedom-of-Thought Struggle in the Old South** (1964) and William S. Jenkins, *Pro-Slavery Thought in the Old South* (1935). The dissenters are ably covered in Carl Degler's, *The Other South: Southern Dissenters in the Nineteenth Century** (1974).

CHAPTER THREE

RISE
OF THE WEST

A T THE SAME TIME King Caucus was dethroned, and the hegemony of the old Virginia aristocracy fell into disarray, new forces arose that were destined to shape the nation. Of these, the one that first caught the eye of most contemporaries was the rise of the West. "The West," observed one European commentator, " . . . is ultimately destined to sway the country. The sea does not separate America from Europe; but behind the Alleghenies is springing up a new life and a people more nearly allied to the soil that nourished them than the more refined and polished population of the seaboard." Such thoughts were commonplace at the time, and later they came to dominate much of American historical writing. So let us look carefully at the rise of the West.

Haven for the Poor

The "West," in the common parlance of 1815, consisted of the vast territory stretching from the Alleghenies to the Great Plains. Somewhere beyond the Mississippi, so the mapmakers indicated, was the Great American Desert where white settlement would have to stop since "the land was fit for no one except Indians." In time settlers would come to know better, and as families pushed farther and farther west the vast region between the Appalachians and the Mississippi would come to be known as the Old West, the southern portion as the Old Southwest, the northern as the Old Northwest. It is the Old West that we shall mean by the term "the West."

Everyone sensed its destiny from the beginning. Indeed, the West's future was the talk of the nation, and the public appetite for facts and figures on the new "promised land" was often insatiable. Would the West, with its abundance of virgin land, provide economic salvation? How quickly? And with how much work? Those questions, and similar ones, were central for thousands of Easterners, for Yankees who lacked land for their children or were tired of fighting the stones of New England, for Virginians who had little left but worn-out tobacco land and a mountain of debts, for small farmers in the southern uplands who stood in the advancing path of plantation slavery and dreaded the shame of someday being treated like a "poor white," and for young farmers everywhere, as well as dissatisfied tradesmen, adventurers, ambitious lawyers, and a wide assortment of swindlers and rogues. And there were plenty of "answers." Foreign travelers and Yankee missionaries swarmed through the West and reported on what they saw, while land promoters and government statisticians turned out reams of data on the new "promised land."

Easterners were always of two minds about the West. On the one hand, many regarded pioneering as a drain upon the national economy. Instead of developing the East, where land was still abundant and the need for labor was great, young people were wasting the best years of their lives just subduing the wilderness. It took years to clear the land of huge sycamores and oaks, fourteen feet around and

Francis Asbury, pioneer Methodist preacher. *The Bettmann Archive, Inc.*

seventy feet to the nearest branch in southern Ohio, and turn the wilderness into first-class farm land. Back East these hearty young people could spend the same time fattening cows, or raising wheat, or working in mills—and generally adding their muscles more productively to the economy. "What a waste of labor!" exclaimed the Northampton, Massachusetts, *Gazette*.

On the other hand, most Easterners saw the West as a special haven for the poor and the desperate. Few spokesmen, to be sure, were anxious to see their own loved ones or their own employees take off for the wilderness. But everyone from labor radical George Henry Evans to crotchety old President Timothy Dwight of Yale advised the poor generally to head west. The West, said Dwight, had obviously been established by God to provide the poor with a "retreat"—and to rid older communities of restless idlers and potential troublemakers.

Even in Massachusetts, where industrialists worried about the shortage of labor, political spokesmen sang the praises of the West. The abundance of cheap western land, said conservative Edward Everett, "acts like a safety valve to the great social steam engine. There can be no very great pressure anywhere in a community where, by travelling a few hundred miles into the interior, a man can buy land at the rate of an acre for a day's work." Congressman Caleb Cushing repeated the same thoughts to a Fourth of July crowd in Boston: "Emigration to the West is the great safety valve of our population, and frees us from all the dangers of the poverty, and the discontent, and consequent disorders, which always spring up in the community when the number of its inhabitants has outrun its capacity to afford due recompense to honest industry and ambition."

"Safety-valve Thesis." The notion of the West as a "safety valve" gained wide scholarly attention after 1893, when Frederick Jackson Turner shook up the historical profession with his paper on "The Significance of the Frontier in American History." Turner argued that the "existence of an area of free land," among other things, worked as a "gate of escape" for Easterners in hard times. That was the reason labor radicalism failed to catch on in America. Since 1893, the safety-valve theory has undergone frequent revision. Research has demonstrated that most emigrants were farmers—not urban laborers; that the urban poor were prevented from going west by the cost of the trip and the cost of starting a farm; that free land was largely a myth, and that the available free land was so poor, or so far from transportation, that it was virtually worthless to a man seeking a fresh start. Yet it is abundantly clear that hundreds of thousands of struggling farmers went west. Since they might otherwise have flooded the urban labor market—as they did in England and other industrial countries—the frontier was obviously of real importance in draining off the surplus eastern farm population and thus keeping urban wages from becoming as depressed as they were in Europe.

Statistics on western migration bear this out. In 1810 the Old West had more than one million settlers. By 1820 this figure more than doubled, and even during the lean twenties when money was scarce and land sales were "down," every western state except Kentucky grew by leaps and bounds. Hard hit by the depression, Kentucky grew a mere 22 percent between 1820 and 1830, thus failing to keep up with the national average of 33 percent. But the "new country" as a whole registered a gain of 95 percent, as compared to the East's 23 percent. By 1830 nearly four million souls lived beyond the Appalachians, and by 1840 the Old West had a population of more than six million people—two million more than the Old South and twice the population of New England.

Such statistics, however, do not tell us who actually went west. Turner, armed with scores of eyewitness accounts, said that the typical pioneer was a poor eastern farmer. But his severest critics, in their zeal to cut the safety-valve theory to size, countered by showing that it took capital—indeed, "at least $1000" in some places—to transform eighty acres of wilderness into a "productive farm." Only middle-class farmers with capital, they implied, could afford to become pioneers. But in this instance Turner's critics were clearly guilty of overkill. Studies of eastern communities revealed that the economically successful seldom moved west, while the offspring of hard-pressed farm families left in droves. By 1850, for example, roughly one out of three persons born in Vermont had gone west. Vermont was notoriously poor. And a detailed investigation of migration from Vermont showed clearly that the migrants, who were generally under thirty years of age,

They erected their crude cabins on remote portions of the National domain where game was plentiful and settlement far behind. *The Squatters* by George Caleb Bingham, 1850. *Courtesy, Museum of Fine Arts, Boston. Bequest of Henry L. Shattuck in memory of the late Ralph W. Gray*

came largely from the poorest towns in the state.

Squatting. Statistics, of course, only tell a small part of the story. Records of government land sales tell us how much land was sold, and who bought it. But there were no records kept of the several hundred thousand settlers who lived on the land without paying for it. In fact, there is little reason to believe that settlement and sales went hand in hand. Some land was settled long before it went on the market, while much of the public land was sold to speculators who hoped to make a killing sometime in the future.

Those who settled on public land before it was up for sale—or without bothering to pay for it—were called squatters. Legally, squatting was trespassing, and in 1807 Congress had given the army the duty of driving trespassers off the public lands. But after 1815 squatting became almost universal, and there was no way the army could carry out this obligation. Legally, the land could be sold out from under the squatters. But buying such land was risky. Squatters associations treated the buyers as claim jumpers, tore down their cabins, and on occasion even sent them to an early grave.

Congress refused to recognize the change in circumstances for fifteen years. Then in 1830, Congress passed the first in a series of preemption laws, which led eventually to a permanent act in 1841. Preemption gave a man the right to settle on the public domain before the land was surveyed and put up for auction. When the land was offered for sale, the settler could buy a maximum of 160 acres at the minimum price. If he failed to buy the land, then it went up for auction. Westerners regarded preemption as long overdue, and thus gave Congress little praise for finally facing up to reality.

"Taming the Wilderness." Statistics also fail to tell us about success and failure, or the constant movement of people back and forth. Thousands went west only to be disappointed. Every road was filled with two-way traffic: struggling eastern farmers and dissatisfied tradesmen, young lawyers and confidence men went west only to meet hundreds of "go backers" who were returning East and who bore tales of woe, disease, and death. Life in the West was indeed harsh. Unfortunately, at this late date, it is hard for us to contemplate the human costs of what historians so lightly call "taming the wilderness." True, there were many success stories. Yet, for every success story of the rags-to-riches variety, there were undoubtedly dozens of families who lived out their lives in quiet desperation.

Even the most famous of pioneer families—the Lincolns—illustrates this point. Thomas Lincoln, the father of the President, was not "shiftless" as legend once claimed. He was a hard-working man who always paid his debts, had good credit, and stood well in his community. But success always eluded him. In December 1816 he gave up on Kentucky, according to his famous son, "partly on account of slavery, but chiefly on account of the difficulty in land titles." The Lincolns, with all their personal belongings, rode and walked to southern Indiana, where they threw together a pole shed or "half-faced camp" with a fire burning at the open end to protect them from winter. Within weeks, Thomas with the aid of neighbors built a log cabin, with no windows, a dirt floor, and a hole for a door.

Young Abraham slept on leaves in the loft. The next year, the Lincolns were joined by their good Kentucky neighbors, the Sparrows, who were to live in the pole shed until they located good land and settled.

Then misfortune struck. In 1818 came the dreaded "milk sick" which resulted, so it was thought, from cows eating white snakeroot or other poisonous vegetation. The Sparrows died in September, and Nancy Hanks Lincoln, Abraham's mother, died in October. She was thirty-four years old. Ten years later, Abraham's sister Sarah, age twenty-one, died in childbirth. Shortly thereafter, Thomas Lincoln decided to move his family to central Illinois. So in 1830, after fourteen years of sweat and sorrow, he sold his Indiana farm, with all its improvements, for $125. That was $35 less than the land alone had cost him!

Or consider another famous pioneer family. In 1816, the same year that Thomas Lincoln gave up on Kentucky, the parents of Joseph Smith, the Mormon prophet, gave up on Vermont. Joseph Smith, Senior, and his wife Lucy had spent nearly twenty years together in New England trying to eke out a living. Nothing went right. To satisfy creditors they lost their farm and Lucy's dowry. They moved constantly from one ill-begotten hill town to another. Then came the historic year of 1816, "eighteen-hundred-and-froze-to-death" in Vermont folklore. Snow fell in June and frost came in July. The senior Smith, along with hordes of Vermonters, went west, bound for Ohio, where the black loam was deep and summers were hot. He got as far as western New York, called for his family, and settled down. Western New York was booming, probably two or three stages beyond a raw frontier, and noted for instability. One revival after another swept through the region, dividing old churches and spawning new ones. Thousands left daily for cheaper land in Ohio, while thousands more came from the hills of New England to fill their places. The Smiths, unlucky as usual, settled just when land prices were at the peak of a speculative spiral—and just before their chosen settlement began to decline.

Then in 1830, the same year the Lincolns set off for Illinois, the prospects of the Smiths changed drastically. Young Joseph's Book of Mormon appeared. It was quite a story. The young man claimed that an Angel of the Lord had shown him the hiding place of sacred golden plates, along with a pair of magic "seeing stones" that enabled him to decipher the sacred writings. The golden plates, which allegedly had been compiled by Mormon long ago, covered American history from 600 B.C. to 421 A.D. and told the story of the family of Lehi, who had journeyed from Jerusalem to the New World. Two of Lehi's sons, Laman and Lemuel, had rebelled, and Laman's descendants had developed darker skins, which explained the origin of the American Indian. Lehi also had an obedient son, Nephi, who had white descendants. The Book of Mormon related the story of the good Nephites, their bloody battles with the Lamanites, as well as the teachings and rituals of Mormon.

Smith was ridiculed far and wide. "Just another crazy Yankee!" said a Rochester newsman. The book nevertheless proved to be most powerful—indeed, probably the most powerful of American religious books. Thousands quickly accepted it as scripture, and Smith was soon revered as "the Prophet." Success, notoriety, and persecution drove the prophet and his growing flock westward—first to Ohio, then to Missouri, and then to Illinois, where Smith reached the height of his power, presiding over the city of Nauvoo and about 15,000 saints. Then in 1844 Smith was shot by a mob. Two years later, his followers sought safety further west, and under Brigham Young began their famous trek to the Great Salt Lake.

It was mere coincidence, of course, that both Abraham Lincoln and Joseph Smith achieved success in Illinois, and that both were shot to death. In actuality, the Lincolns and the Smiths had little in common, except the long experience with disappointment and grinding poverty, experiences which they shared with millions of their countrymen. It was folly, Lincoln later told a campaign biographer, to make much out of his early life. It was the common experience of most Westerners. "It can all be condensed into a single sentence and that sentence you will find in Gray's *Elegy*—'The short and simple annals of the poor.' "

A Source of Disorder

The West, then, was supposed to be a good poor man's country—indeed, the best in all the world—and a safety valve for the rest of the country. That was the happy way of looking at western development. There was, however, a gloomier view. It held that the West would be the source of endless disorder.

The Problem of Governance. Was the Republic suited to indefinite expansion across space? Jefferson thought so, with some reservations, and so did Andrew Jackson and later President James K. Polk. The very nature of the Union, they insisted, made expansion possible. Thanks to the federal system of government with its decentralization of power, the Union could include areas that Washington did not control. Indeed, there was little need for much control, especially from Washington. After all, legislation was the "parent of nine tenths of all the evil . . . by which mankind has been inflicted." Simply let freemen go west, and they could be integrated into the Union at the time of statehood.

But there were many doubters. It was hard for some to forget the nadir of federal authority—the gloomy wartime days when much of Washington lay in ruins, the Treasury begged for loans from local bankers, and states were raising armies for their own defense. In addition, many recalled the haunting observation of the philosopher Montesquieu—that Republics were viable only when they were small in size. Would westward expansion increase the danger? Would it bring further disintegration? Many thought so. Alarmed at the rapid rate of migration across the Appalachians, John C. Calhoun called in 1817 for a national system of roads and canals to counteract disunion:

> Let it not be forgotten, let it be forever kept in mind, that the extent of the republic exposes us to the greatest of calamities—*disunion*. We are great, and rapidly—I was about to say fearfully—growing. This is our pride and danger, our weakness and strength. . . . Those who understand the human heart best know how pow-

erfully distance tends to break the sympathies of our nature. Nothing, not even dissimilarity of language, tends more to estrange man from man. . . . Let us, then, bind the republic together with a perfect system of roads and canals. Let us conquer space.

Madison's veto killed Calhoun's program in 1817. But over the next thirty years, a chorus of voices, led by the likes of Henry Clay and John Quincy Adams, called for national programs to foster unity and control western expansion. Some wanted to slow down the sale of government lands, while others put their faith mainly in transportation and technology—first, roads and canals—and later, telegraph lines and railroads. The railroad in particular, noted the philosopher Ralph Waldo Emerson in 1844, had great political promise. It would overcome the barriers of space, move officials and congressmen and judges over great distances, and provide the necessary connections to hold the country together. Otherwise, noted the philosopher, the days of the Republic were numbered.

The Distribution of Power. The growth of the West also upset the distribution of political power. So normal had the expectation of expansion become by 1815 that no one really expected each state to have the same number of congressmen, the same power, year in and year out. It had been mainly the Federalists, especially those who were discredited by the Hartford Convention, who wailed loudest about the country, in Josiah Quincy's words, falling into the hands of "wild men on the Missouri" and "Anglo-Hispano-Gallo Americans who bask in the sands in the mouth of the Mississippi." The dominant Jeffersonian Republicans had welcomed an agrarian empire stretching half way across the continent.

But few Jeffersonians had expected a rapid shift in political power. Virginia Republicans, in particular, had got used to the idea of providing the country with one President after another. So the rapid development of the West after 1815 was rather unsettling. Five new states quickly entered the Union: Indiana in 1816, Mississippi in 1817, Illinois in 1818, Alabama in 1819, and Missouri in 1821. And, to the dismay of Easterners, the census of 1820 revealed that Ohio and Kentucky were the fifth and sixth largest states in the nation, and that Ohio was entitled to more representatives in Congress than the old commonwealth of Massachusetts.

By 1820 Easterners could only watch and grumble as the West grew in power. Unlike the situation in Virginia, where backcountry farmers first had to change the state constitution before they could gain equal representation in the Virginia legislature, the new western states only had to abide by the existing rules to gain in power. The basic procedures for admitting new states had been laid down by the Northwest Ordinance of 1787, and the rules for apportionment had been established by the Constitution. Technically, the old seaboard states could change the rules if they could muster enough votes, but tampering with the rules of apportionment was certain to reopen the thorny question of the three-fifths rule, and the slaveholding states wanted none of that. More basic, the old seaboard states were hopelessly divided. Unlike the situation in Virginia, where in 1829 the slaveholding aristocracy united vigorously against granting equal representation to farmers living west of the Blue Ridge, the eastern states were simply incapable of presenting a united front. The admission of each new western state, in fact, was always seen as a gain for either the free states or the slave states.

So the old seaboard states were unable to keep power from slipping out of their hands. And their losses were startling. In a House of 181 men, Virginia alone had the same number of congressmen—23—as the entire West in 1810. After the census of 1820, the West's total increased to 47 seats. By 1840 all had changed: Virginia now had 15 seats, Ohio 21, and the West as a whole 92 in a House of 223. Even more noteworthy was the change in the Senate: the West had 6 seats compared to the East's 28 in 1810; by 1840 the ratio was 22 to 30. Up to 1828, the first forty years of the Republic, Virginia and Massachusetts provided the nation with all its Presidents; during the next forty years, six Presidents came from the West: Jackson, Polk, and Andrew Johnson from Tennessee; Harrison from Indiana; Taylor from Louisiana; and Lincoln from Illinois. None came from Massachusetts. And Virginia, once the nursery of Presidents, could boast only of John Tyler, the first Vice-President to succeed an incumbent who died in office, and the first President who was never elected to the office.

Controlling the West

Even before the West became a political power, there were plenty of Easterners who wanted to impose some kind of order on the West. Invariably churches led the way. Indeed, nowhere was the fear of disorder more pronounced than in the churches.

Churchmen looked west—and saw disorder. Westerners, so eastern ministers were told, had lapsed into a state of ungodliness or nonconformity. Revivals were ungodly orgies where men and women barked, jerked, howled, screamed, and generally behaved like wild beasts. Schisms were frequent: the Methodists split four ways between 1814 and 1830, and the Baptists split into Reformed Baptists, Free-Will Baptists, Seventh-Day Baptists, Primitive Baptists, Two-Seed-in-the-Spirit Baptists, Footwashers, and other sects. Nonconformists were plentiful: the followers of Jemima Wilkinson, who thought herself to be Christ, held forth in western New York, while Isaac Bullard and his "Pilgrims" moved through the West to Missouri, preaching free love and communism, and denouncing bathing as a sin. The West was not totally lost, explained one religious journal after another, but there was a definite need for a well-trained ministry, sound schools and colleges "to dispel ignorance, check vice, and create a pure public opinion, favorable to sound morals and true religion."

The more evangelical of the Protestant churches were more than willing to meet the challenge. The best prepared were the Methodists. Having been founded by John Wesley during a period of social disorganization in England, the Methodists had already perfected methods to cope with a scattered population. The key was the circuit rider, who like the modern traveling salesman covered a wide area and made regular rounds from settlement to settlement. A legendary figure in the

West, he rode his circuit through sleet and snow, preached daily, organized small "classes" and then churches, and more often than not burned himself out by the time he was thirty or thirty-five.

The Baptist farmer-preacher was his closest rival in the West, but the circuit rider was clearly the man to beat. One Presbyterian minister explained it this way: "I at length became ambitious to find a family whose cabin had not been entered by a Methodist. In several days I travelled from settlement to settlement on my errand of good, but into every hovel I entered, I learned that the Methodist missionary had been there before me." Educated clergymen from the East, especially Yankees who knew Latin and Greek, never tired of ridiculing the half-educated circuit rider. At the same time, however, they paid him the supreme compliment by adopting some of his methods. For his diligence paid off: the Methodists easily outdistanced their rivals in taming the West.

Other churchmen were hardly lacking in zeal. They formed dozens of missionary societies, Bible societies, tract societies to carry the Gospel to the West. Founded in 1826, the American Home Missionary Society soon had well over seven hundred missionaries in the Ohio Valley, while the American Education Society raised funds to send poor boys through colleges such as Amherst and Williams for work in the missionary field. Even the notable Lyman Beecher, one of the most eminent divines in New England, set off for the West in 1832. "The moral destiny of our nation," said Beecher, "and all our institutions and hopes, and the world's hopes turn on the character of the West. . . . If we gain the West, all is safe; if we lose it, all is lost."

The Importance of the Ohio Valley. In the battle for the West, attention focused mainly on the Ohio Valley. The reason for this was basically simple: the Southwest was settled almost entirely by Southerners, while the Old Northwest attracted an assortment of cultural groups. The economic life of the southern frontier was caught up in the expansion of cotton, and with the expansion of cotton came the planters, who quickly took charge and set their stamp upon the region. The Old Northwest, on the other hand, was settled by swarms from several hives: the upland South, New England, Pennsylvania and New Jersey, Germany and Ireland.

These stocks differed sharply in outlook, attitudes, and habits—and on occasion they stung one another:

How do you make a Kentuckian out of a Yankee?
    It's easy, Sir; Knock his brains out.
How, then, do you make a Yankee out of a Kentuckian?
    Can't do it, Sir; ain't stock enough.

The people from New England generally looked upon the others as little better than heathen, while the others regarded them as hypocrites or pious-talking thieves. "A Kentuckian," noted one traveler, "suspects nobody, but a Yankee, whom he considers as a sort of Jesuit." Indeed, a popular character in one of

James Fenimore Cooper's novels referred to Yankees as "the locusts of the West."

Yankee Dominance. Whose ways would govern the Old Northwest? That was a crucial question, and it explains in part why Lyman Beecher and scores of others went West. They hoped to tip the balance in favor of the "right" way. Yankees, in fact, were accused time and again of cultural imperialism. They had a reputation for invading an area, digging in, and soon dominating everybody with their books and schools and teachers and newspapers. They had already come to dominate much of New York. Indeed, in the New York Constitutional Convention of 1821, a majority of the 127 delegates were either born in Connecticut or sons of Connecticut men. Would they have the same impact on the Ohio Valley?

It seems that they did. They had to share influence, of course, with other insistent and vigorous stock. But they had one enormous advantage over their rivals: they were a literate people; they already knew how to read and write and how to pass on these skills to their children. Thus, almost automatically, they came to dominate schools, libraries, and newspapers; and in time children throughout the Old Northwest came to be more familiar with the story of Plymouth Rock, of Roger Williams, the Salem witches, and Paul Revere than they were with the tales of their own forebears.

Contemporaries, moreover, were also quick to note Yankee influence in politics. In 1830, observed French commentator Alexis de Tocqueville, "the little state of Connecticut" was entitled to only five representatives in Congress. Yet thirty-one western congressmen also hailed from Connecticut. As a result, even though Connecticut's population constituted only one forty-third of the nation's, Connecticut Yankees held one eighth of the seats in Congress. According to John C. Calhoun's calculations, at one time the number of congressmen who were either born or educated in Connecticut were just five short of being the majority! And one had to be impressed with the unbelievable record of Litchfield, Connecticut: by the time of the Civil War it could list among its distinguished sons eleven governors and lieutenant governors, thirteen United States senators, fifteen state supreme court judges, eighteen college professors and nine college presidents, and scores of congressmen—twenty-two from New York alone.

The Tame and the Wild West

What about the actual development of the West itself? Easterners, as we have noticed, often emphasized the unruliness of the West. Frederick Jackson Turner and his followers, on the other hand, pointed mainly to the creativeness of the West. The frontier, Turner argued, remade the Europeans and Easterners who entered it. First, it mastered the pioneers. The environment was "at first too strong for the man." It stripped him of "the garments of civilization," and put him in the log cabin, the hunting shirt, and the moccasin. Then, after the initial seasoning, the pioneers gradually conquered the wilderness, and created a new civilization that was strikingly different from the one they left behind. The new society, according to Turner, was truly American—not European. It was uniquely individualistic, opportunistic, nationalistic, and democratic.

The Resilience of Old Ways. Oddly enough, both Turner and the eastern doomsayers erred in the same way: they both underestimated the durability and toughness of cultural patterns. As one of Lincoln's kinfolk noted, "we lived the same as the Indians, 'ceptin' we took an interest in politics and religion." That word " 'ceptin' " turns out to be an important one when considering the history of the West. Pioneers, research has shown, hung on desperately to their cultural heritage. Thus, they were rarely as innovative as Turner claimed—or as dirty and nasty as Easterners often insisted.

Consider, for example, state constitutions—a matter that interested Turner. The new state constitutions were neither radical nor boldly innovative. The drafters of western constitutions, in fact, showed no zeal at all in devising fundamental documents filled with original and revolutionary ideas of democracy. They were basically rewrite men. Armed with scissors and paste, and copies of the Ohio and Kentucky constitutions, plus an assortment of other documents, they pieced together and edited their basic plans of government. The founding fathers of Indiana put together a constitution in nine days in 1816. It was essentially the Kentucky constitution, minus slavery, plus the Ohio bill of rights. The Mississippi constitution, written a year later, followed the Kentucky slavery provision to the letter—including even the same punctuation marks—with the addition of one minor phrase. Similarly, the founding fathers of Illinois and Alabama, who drafted their constitutions in 1818 and 1819 respectively, borrowed much from older states.

These scissors-and-paste creations, of course, were not exact replicas of their parent documents. Like all offspring, they differed here and there. Older documents, for example, required governors to be at least thirty-five years old, senators to be thirty, and representatives to be twenty-four. The framers of the Indiana and Mississippi constitutions lowered the age limits to thirty, twenty-four, and twenty-one respectively. Some of the older constitutions, moreover, had not explicitly excluded free blacks from voting. From 1819 until the end of the Civil War, every new state limited the suffrage to whites only. At the same time, it should be pointed out, many of the old states revised their constitutions and stripped from free blacks their right to vote.

The Question of Orderliness. Given a choice among older examples, the framers of new constitutions usually chose the more orderly way. This was particularly the case when it came to voting. Since the days of colonial Virginia, voice voting and three-day elections had been the norm in much of the country. It was both disorderly and great fun. Three days of stump-speaking, free liquor, and an occasional fist fight provided many a thirsty patriot with recreation and excitement. Voice voting enabled both candidates and voters to keep tabs on the progress of an election. With the aid of barrels of whiskey and apple toddy—and on occasion a few ham-fisted thugs—candidates and their supporters went to great lengths to win over the wavering and to intimidate the weak in a close election. Everyone watched eagerly as freeholders stepped forth and announced their choice.

"I vote for you, Sir," said the freeholder, nodding in the direction of his favorite. And a cheer or a moan would follow each vote.

Kentucky and Virginia would continue to enjoy and deplore such practices for years. Writing in 1838, Benjamin Drake described an election in Macon County, Kentucky. It was a bit extreme, admitted Drake, but it showed what could, and did, happen. In the eleventh hour of a close contest, the losing candidate rolled out two barrels of "stout" liquor, mounted one and told the crowd that his father was a poor "canebrake" pioneer, that he himself was a native son who had been raised on "possum fat and hominy," while his opponent was a "New Englander by birth, a college-learnt dandy schoolmaster, who carried his sheepskin in a tea cannister." The native son then made his pitch: while he himself was a captain of the militia, who had waded in muck and mire fighting for his country, his opponent was a "damned blue-belly" Federalist who had aided the British during the late war. Inviting "all true sons of Ol' Kentuck to come to the trough and liquor," the patriot jumped to the ground and began ladling out the "spirit of democracy." Soon drunken shouts of "Huzza for old Kentucky" and "Down with the Yankees" filled the air. The opposition responded with "stones, clubs, and brickbats." And, in the end, "so hot waxed the patriotism of the belligerents, that many of them were trampled under foot, some were gouged, others horribly snake-poled and not a few knocked clear into a cocked hat."

The framers of the new constitutions, however, rejected this tradition. Instead,

Election Day at the State House, Philadelphia, 1816 by John Lewis Krimmel captures the aggressive, noisy behavior of Americans engaged in political activity. *The Historical Society of Pennsylvania*

they provided for one-day elections and the secret ballot. The results were readily apparent: their elections, while never models of decorum, were strikingly different. Noted the traveler James Flint: "A few days ago I witnessed an election of a member of Congress from the state of Indiana—members of the state assembly and county officers, and the voters for the township of Jeffersonville were taken by ballot in one day. No quarrels or disorder occurred. At Louisville in Kentucky the poll was kept open three days. The votes were given viva voce. I saw three fights in the course of one hour." In at least one respect, then, the new West was tamer than the old one. And, in time, the secret ballot and one-day election became the norm everywhere.

The Myth of Western Unity. Besides the tendency to exaggerate western democracy, western creativity, and western unruliness, there has also been a tendency to exaggerate western unity. After the War of 1812, scores of politicians rose in Congress and said majestically: "I rise to speak in behalf of the West." And Easterners often spoke of western men as if they were all alike.

But were they? Was there really a "western" point of view? Turner had no doubts in his earlier writings: he insisted that the West was a distinct section with a distinct point of view. Later, Turner modified many of his earlier statements, hedged on others, and generally indicated that even in pioneer days the Northwest differed radically from the Southwest. But it was his earlier statements that captured the limelight and left their mark on the teaching of American history. So the notion that the West was a political unit runs through scores of textbooks. The rise of the West, so the story goes, led to the demise of the Indian, the rise of the "common man," and the triumph of Andrew Jackson. Then, as time passed, the Northwest became socially like the Northeast, while the Southwest became an extension of the Old South, and the West was no longer a distinct political unit.

While there is some truth in each of these notions, the idea that the West was once a political unit is largely make-believe. In truth, the vast region west of the Alleghenies was the scene of many voices, some shouting in unison, others in contention. Henry Clay of Kentucky and Thomas Hart Benton sat in Congress together for close to thirty years; both claimed to "speak in behalf of the West"; more often than not, they were at loggerheads. And, in the nation's mythology, there have never been two men more "western" than Andrew Jackson and Davy Crockett of Tennessee. They too were political enemies.

Rather than regard the West as a political unit, it is more realistic to picture it as a series of rural settlements oriented around small trading centers or burgeoning cities. Places like Pigeon Creek, where the Lincolns settled in Indiana, had no idea what was going on in the West as a whole, and it is a bit far-fetched to insist that they developed deep inner feelings of comraderie for isolated settlements way off in Mississippi, or Alabama, or Arkansas. Pigeon Creek had close ties with the neighboring trading center of Gentryville, which in turn dealt with Troy, a larger trading center sixteen miles away on the Ohio River. Thanks to the river trade, the people of Troy had some idea what was happening up and down the river. But families of Pigeon Creek and other inland settlements had little contact with the outside world. They were always at the mercy of wretched roads and poor communications.

Under these circumstances, rural settlements were at a disadvantage politically, and small cities and trading centers dominated public opinion and western politics generally. If these towns and cities promoted any ideology at all, it was an ideology of local self-interest. What's in it for Pittsburgh? For Lexington? For Cincinnati? Given the mild boosterism of modern chambers of commerce, it is difficult for us to fully appreciate the amount of zeal and energy that nineteenth-century boosters spent in fighting over the location of state capitals, canal lines, railroad lines, and the like. Thousands of budding cities plunged recklessly in debt to build canals and railroads, and to gain an advantage over nearby rivals. According to one writer, intercity rivalries, such as the long and bitter battle between Pittsburgh and Wheeling over trade routes, evoked passions that "were akin to those found in a revolution or a religious war." He may be exaggerating, but Cleveland and Ohio City nearly went to war in 1836 over the construction of a bridge; as it was, ten men were killed and twenty-three were wounded.

Panic of 1819. Probably no event sheds more light on the question of western unity than the Panic of 1819. That catastrophe, which pricked the postwar inflationary boom, brought incredible hardship to the West. No part of the country suffered more. Trade stood still and crops rotted in the fields. Thousands of farmers and land speculators were over their heads in debt. During the boom years, they had bought public land on credit under the Land Act of 1800, which called for one-fourth down, and the rest to be paid in four annual installments. The amount owed the federal government for public land had risen from $3 million in 1815 to $22 million in 1819.

With hard times, thousands faced the danger of losing their land—and perhaps even spending time in debtors' prison. Naturally, they howled for relief. In response, Congress extended payment periods, dropped interest charges, and permitted delinquents to forfeit a portion of their land equal to the debt and to keep the remainder. At the same time, in the Land Act of 1820, Congress cut the minimum price on public lands from $2 to $1.25 an acre, thus making it possible to buy an eighty acre tract for $100 cash. But how many settlers had $100 cash? Very few. And against their wishes Congress ended the credit system. There was considerable doubt, in fact, whether the nation's leaders paid heed to the plight of the West. In his annual message of 1820, Monroe dismissed the prostration of the western farmer as merely a "mild and instructive admonition." Indeed, he hoped that it would teach all concerned "lessons in economy."

Most dramatic was the depression in the urban West. The manufacturing center of Lexington collapsed; thirty percent of the population moved out of Pittsburgh; and everything from hotels to stables went under in Cincinnati, often ending up in the hands of the Second Bank. As Senator Thomas Hart Benton of Missouri put it: "All the flourishing cities of the West are mortgaged to this money power. They may be devoured by it at any moment. They are in the jaws of a monster! A lump of butter in the mouth of a dog! One gulp, one swallow, and all is gone!"

What was to be done? Men could neither pay their own debts nor collect on loans to others. Foreclosures and bankruptcies swept entire communities in Kentucky and Tennessee. Land speculators were left holding vast tracts of land with no buyers in sight. Prominent men suddenly faced financial ruin and even imprisonment for debt. What was needed, they hollered, was time and money: time to get back on their feet, and money to hold their creditors at bay. In response, one legislature after another established "banks" or "loan offices" to turn out millions in paper money for loan to hard-pressed debtors.

Such measures invariably proved divisive. Kentucky, for example, created a Bank of the Commonwealth with no capital, no specie, no stockholders; the bank's only asset was a $7000 appropriation to cover the cost of printing $3 million in bank notes. Such money was not worth much in gold and silver. What if the creditor refused to accept such dubious currency? What if he demanded to be paid in "good" money? To remedy this situation, Kentucky passed a relief measure in 1820 that was designed to give the debtor two years to get back on his feet. Under this law, it was unlawful to sell property by court order for less than three fourths of its value (as assessed by the debtor's neighbors) unless the creditor agreed to take state paper. If the creditor refused to take state money, which by 1822 was worth about fifty cents on the dollar, then the debtor could get a stay of two years before he had to meet his debt. It left the creditor with the option of taking about half of what he had lent, or waiting two years for payment in gold and silver.

Creditors raised a storm. Howling that the new law was a flagrant violation of contract law, they took it to court, and in 1823 the Kentucky Court of Appeals declared the relief law unconstitutional. In retaliation, the relief party in the state legislature cut the judges' salaries to twenty-five cents a year, tried to remove them, and finally pushed through a bill creating a new Court of Appeals, which it packed with sympathetic judges. For two years there were two supreme courts in Kentucky, and citizens lived in a state of judicial anarchy until voters restored the old court to preeminence. Out of this struggle two parties sprang up—an Old Court party and a New Court party. They fought furiously in the streets and through newspaper invective. Yet, for national purposes, both called themselves Republican.

The West and the Nation

It was in the midst of these grim years that western congressmen first became a sizable force in Congress. Following the census of 1820, reapportionment nearly doubled the size of the western delegation in the House, and twenty-one new districts sent representatives for the first time in 1823. "It represents a new era in our politics," declared Representative George Holcombe of New Jersey. Thoroughly shaken by hard times back home, westerners all agreed that such a debacle must never occur again. But could they agree on a remedy?

Henry Clay's American System. As usual, the chief remedy came from the lips of Henry Clay, the pride of Kentucky. By the time the newcomers arrived in 1823, Clay was a seasoned veteran in Washington politics, yet a long career still lay before him. Snuffbox in hand, cracking jokes and swearing freely, Clay dominated his colleagues everywhere, in Congress and at all-night card parties, in formal gatherings and at the races. With charm and wit and fire, he could speak for hours and turn the grubby measures of everyday politics into broad and exciting visions.

The West's problem, argued Clay, was the nation's problem. Rural poverty everywhere stemmed largely from the collapse of European markets. English Corn Laws kept hungry workers in industrial Manchester, Liverpool, and London from buying American foodstuffs, while the hungry European continent of earlier days had recovered from the Napoleonic wars and was now feeding itself. The future, moreover, looked gloomy: agricultural production in America was clearly outstripping European power to consume.

What was to be done? The answer was obvious, said Clay. "We must speedily adopt a genuine American policy. Still cherishing the foreign market, let us create a home market, to give further scope to the consumption of produce of American industry." Home markets for farm goods must be created by stimulating the industrialization of the Northeast; by building a nationwide network of roads and canals at federal expense; and by supporting the Second Bank in its efforts to stabilize the nation's currency and to provide sound credit. With a genuine "American system" of protective tariffs to encourage industry, roads and canals to stimulate interstate commerce, and a strong national bank, argued Clay, rural poverty would disappear and home markets would be provided for everyone. Industrial cities would buy up everything farmers could raise, and prospering farmers in turn would buy up factory goods. Everyone would profit, and all America would develop by leaps and bounds.

Not everyone agreed. The "American System," argued Republicans of the old school, was a sham. It was merely Hamilton's old program, with a few new wrinkles, and shorn of elitism. It was little more than a grab bag of gifts to special interests. Western entrepreneurs would get roads and canals at federal expense. Industrialists would get high tariffs to keep out English goods. And hemp growers in Clay's Kentucky would get tariff protection against Russian competition. But what would the South get? "Nothing!" thundered John Randolph of Virginia. "On whom bears the duty on coarse woolens and linens, and blankets, upon salt and all the necessaries of life? On poor men and slaveholders." And, added William Brent of Louisiana: "Who wants to buy Kentucky hemp? We much prefer paying forty cents per yard for the foreign article to making use of the bagging of Kentucky at twenty-five cents."

The Western Response. How did westerners respond to Clay's program? They never got a chance to vote on the Bank in the 1820s, since it still had many years to run on its charter. Perhaps that was fortunate for Clay, for the Bank was hardly riding a crest of popularity in the grim years following the Panic of 1819. Indeed, men everywhere bitterly referred to it as "The Monster." But the other two parts of Clay's program came up time and again, and western congressmen were originally united behind one, and sharply divided over the other.

On the one hand, support for roads and canals at federal expense was nearly universal. In 1817, when Madison vetoed a bill designed to foster internal improvements nationwide, the West was outraged. Madison's objection that the constitution did not specifically give such powers to the federal government was absolutely absurd, said Clay. "Just look at what has been done for the seaboard states!" Sea walls have been constructed; coast surveys have been made; public buildings and lighthouses have been erected—"and all at federal expense." Surely if Congress had the power to improve coastal navigation for the seaboard states, it must have the power to construct roads and canals for "the great interior of the country." Western congressmen agreed with Clay fully in the early years, supporting one measure in 1824 by a whopping margin of forty-three to nothing.

On the other hand, the West never united behind the tariff. The Southwest had no need for "home markets," since cotton producers had a growing market in in-

The Cumberland wagon road was passable as far as Wheeling in 1817. Federally financed extension of this and other roads was a valuable phase of Clay's "American System." *The Bettmann Archive, Inc.*

dustrial England. High tariffs meant only higher prices for southern consumers. Why support tariffs? The Northwest saw things differently. Small manufacturers in the Ohio Valley demanded protection, and so did farmers who saw eastern workers as potential consumers of their surplus wheat, corn, and hogs. So, when the tariff came up for a vote in 1824, the West divided along North-South lines. The "home market" appeal carried Kentucky and the Northwest by twenty-nine to nothing; the Southwest rejected it by fourteen to two.

Western unity, then, depended almost entirely on the matter at hand. On some issues, when the self-interests of the new states coincided, the West voted as a bloc. On others, the West was sharply divided, and the basic alignments were North against South, Northwest against Southwest, city against city, or party against party. In this respect, western politics differed little from that practiced in the East.

SUGGESTED READINGS

The literature on the West is immense. Very readable are four volumes by Dale Van Every, which trace the frontier from 1754 to 1848: *Forth to the Wilderness,* * A Company of Heroes,* * Ark of Empire,* * and *The Final Challenge* * (1961–64). So too are John A. Caruso's *The Appalachian Frontier, The Mississippi Valley Frontier, The Southern Frontier,* and *The Great Lakes Frontier* (1959–66). The history of the West is told in great detail in Francis S. Philbrick, *The Rise of the West, 1754–1830* * (1965) and Ray Allen Billington, *The Far Western Frontier, 1830–1860* * (1956). For details on the Southwest, see Thomas P. Abernethy, *The South in the New Nation, 1789–1819* * (1961). Also especially good is Richard A. Bartlett, *The New Country* * (1974), which seeks to recapture what the entire frontier experience was like from 1776 to 1890.

For years historians have been arguing about the merits of Frederick Jackson Turner's seminal ideas. Some idea of the immensity of this argument can be found in Gene M. Gressley, "The Turner Thesis—A Problem in Historiography," *Agricultural History,* Vol. 32 (1958). Turner's most significant essays, plus criticisms of them, can be found in: Ray Allen Billington, ed., *The Frontier Thesis: Valid Interpretation of American History?* * (1966); George Rogers Taylor, ed., *The Turner Thesis* * (1956); and Stephen Salsbury, ed., *Essays on the History of the American West* * (1975). Besides his controversial essays, Turner wrote two superb books on the West: *Rise of the New West: 1819–1829* * (1906) and *The United States: 1830–1850* (1935). The latter book was completed after his death thanks to the efforts of his dedicated students.

The best overall study of land policy is Roy M. Robbins, *Our Landed Heritage* * (1942). Other general studies are Benjamin H. Hibbard, *A History of Public Land Policies* (1924); Everett Dick, *The Lure of the Land* (1970); Malcolm Rohrbaugh, *The Land Office Business* * (1968).

On Yankee influence in the West, see Lois Kimball Mathews, *The Expansion of New*

*Available in a paperback edition.

England: The Spread of New England Settlement and Institutions to the Mississippi River 1620–1865 (1909); Stewart Holbrook, *Yankee Exodus* (1950); Dixon Ryan Fox, *Yankees and Yorkers* (1940); and Richard Lyle Power, *Planting Corn Belt Culture* (1953).

On the Mormons, there is an abundance of material, but much of it is biased. The best studies include Thomas F. O'Dea, *The Mormons** (1967); Nels Anderson, *Desert Saints* (1942); Norman Furniss, *The Mormon Conflict* (1960); and Fawn Brodie, *No Man Knows My History: The Life of Joseph Smith* (2d ed., 1971).

On western cities, the best introduction is Richard C. Wade, *The Urban Frontier** (1959). Also excellent are Stefan Lorant, *Pittsburgh* (1949); Gerald Capers, *Biography of a River Town* (1939); and Kenneth Wheeler, *To Wear a City's Crown* (1968).

On western politics, see Curtis Nettels, "The Mississippi Valley and the Constitution, 1815–1829," *Mississippi Valley Historical Review,* Vol. II (1924); Louis Hartz, *Economic Policy and Democratic Thought: Pennsylvania 1776–1860** (1948); Harry N. Schieber, *Ohio Canal Era* (1969), in addition to the general histories of the West listed above. For further information on Henry Clay and the American System, see Glyndon G. Van Deusen, *The Life of Henry Clay* (1937) and Clement Eaton, *Henry Clay and the Art of American Politics* (1957).

CHAPTER FOUR

TRIUMPH OF THE ATLANTIC ECONOMY

I N EXPLAINING what happened after the War of 1812, Americans invariably looked at themselves. It was their axes, plows, and energy that tamed the wilderness. It was their ambition and enterprise that created factories and plantations. And it was clearly internal affairs, not foreign affairs, that troubled the nation after 1815. And so the story came to be told, time and again, for over one hundred years.

Yet, while there is much merit to this traditional view, it has serious limitations. Nineteenth-century Americans were ambitious and hardworking, but they had a short-sighted view of the world. Had they been able to look candidly upon themselves in relation to the Atlantic world, they would have realized that their country was in no position to will its own destiny. The War of 1812 proved conclusively that the nation was incapable of defending itself. One invading army nearly cut the country in two along the Hudson Valley, and another easily captured the nation's Capitol. Thanks only to the British preoccupation with Napoleon, the war came short of being a total disaster. America, in short, was clearly a second-rate power, and its future depended partly on the policies of the mighty. President Madison and the nation's leadership were certainly well-aware of this fact in 1815; subsequent generations conveniently forgot it.

The United States was also an underdeveloped country. It had plenty of land and natural resources, but lacked the capital, techniques, and manpower to develop them. To conquer the wilderness, the country needed more muscle, more investment capital, more machinery and hardware, and better breeds of sheep and cattle than Americans could provide. These resources had to come, in part, from the more developed countries of western Europe. Like today's struggling new nations, then, the United States in 1815 was dependent upon the giants.

The mightiest giant in 1815 was clearly Great Britain. America's old enemy had been a great nation, of course, long before Napoleon's defeat at Waterloo, but the period after 1815 was truly Britain's heyday. France had finally been beaten. Germany was not a state, but a politically divided area in which a common language was spoken. The British navy controlled the seas, and British industrialism dominated the world. England already produced 40 percent of the world's pig iron in 1815, and British industrialism had just entered its golden years. The period of most rapid industrial advance lay ahead—between 1815 and 1847.

The special pride and symbol of British supremacy was the cotton industry concentrated around Manchester in Lancashire. The growth of industrial Manchester dominated the Atlantic economy. Textile manufacturers had pioneered the Industrial Revolution in England, and textile mills and "factories" were virtually synonyms. The output of cloth increased by fifty times from 1785 to 1850. Fortunes were made overnight: Robert Owen, a former draper's assistant, started in 1789 with a £100 loan; twenty years later he bought out his partners for £84,000 cash; and his success story was modest by Lancashire standards. Rich men accu-

New York from Brooklyn Heights. *I. N. Phelps Stokes Collection, Prints Division, The New York Public Library, Astor, Lenox, and Tilden Foundations*

mulated money so fast that they soon had a vast amount of capital for foreign investment. Fortunately for the United States, many were willing to risk their money on American banks, canals, and railroads.

The cotton trade also assured the preeminence of the port of Liverpool. The importation of raw cotton rose more than fifty-fold between 1785 and 1850. In early days, the main markets for finished products had been at home and on the European continent. During the Napoleonic wars, when the European markets were often cut off by blockades and warfare, Manchester and Liverpool built up a large Latin American market, which grew prodigiously after the war. By 1814 England exported four yards of cloth for every three sold at home, and during the next thirty years textiles made up 60 percent of all British exports. Increasingly, raw materials flowed in and manufactured goods flowed out. The island kingdom was truly "the workshop of the world."

It is against this background that American energy, ambition, and enterprise must be understood. The new lines of trade, the new wealth, and the new industrial metropolis—all shaped the young nation's growth. Ironically, the country prospered not by breaking away from Europe as myth would have it, but by remaining an important cog in an interdependent Atlantic economy dominated by the Republic's old enemy, Great Britain.

The British Man of War

Between 1815 and 1914, the United States had the marvelous opportunity to develop free of serious external threat. The "Century of Security," as it is sometimes called, was guaranteed primarily by British domination of the seas.

In 1815, however, few would have predicted a long peace. The London *Times* anticipated "the recurrence of a new and more formidable American war." John Quincy Adams, one of the peace negotiators, wrote that the treaty was merely "a truce rather than a peace. Neither party gave up anything; all the points of collision which had subsisted between them before the war were left open." John C. Calhoun called for aid to industry through a protective tariff so that the nation would be better prepared "once war broke out again" with England. And many saw new dangers on the horizon: an epidemic of revolutions had broken out in South America, and rumor had it that Great Britain would soon join hands with the crowned despots of Europe to crush the revolutionaries and uphold the principles of monarchy. If the monarchs triumphed, the American republic would be virtually surrounded by powerful and hostile forces.

But the anticipated troubles never came. Englishmen were tired of war, and Liverpool merchants and Manchester industrialists had little concern for the principles of monarchy. Indeed, they looked forward to a booming trade with independent republics in the New World. And, in the end, the interests of trade prevailed: English exports to Latin America easily surpassed exports to the United States; London bankers floated loans of the revolutionary governments; and by 1820, at the latest, Latin America became a captive British market. Hence British ministries sat back and watched as the Spanish Empire crumbled in the New World. And gradually even English Tories accepted the permanence of the United States and other New World republics.

The happy change in British-American relations became clear two or three years after the war, when the outstanding questions between the two nations were cordially settled. In the Rush-Bagot Agreement of 1817, the two nations agreed to severely limit naval armament on the Great Lakes. And in the Convention of 1818, they specified American fishing rights in Canadian waters, established the boundary between the United States and British North America at the forty-ninth parallel from the head of the Mississippi to the Rocky Mountains, and provided for joint occupation of the vast Oregon country for ten years. Together, these agreements put to rest southern and western fears that England still had devilish plans to detach Louisiana Purchase territory from the United States, or to keep the Indians constantly on the warpath.

The Invasion of Florida. The real test in British-American relations came in 1818 when Andrew Jackson marched into Spanish Florida to pacify the Indians along the southern frontier. Jackson captured the Spanish fort at St. Marks, lowered the Spanish flag and raised the Stars and Stripes. Then, in the pursuit of Indians, Jackson discovered and arrested two British subjects, Robert Ambrister and Alexander Arbuthnot, whom he court-martialed on charges of inciting the Indians and supplying them with weapons. The court sentenced one man to death by hanging, and ordered fifty lashes for the other. Jackson reversed the court and had both men executed. Marching on, Jackson captured the Spanish post at Pensacola, told the Spanish governor that he was assuming command of Florida, and sent the governor and his garrison packing to Havana. The Hero then returned home expressing regret that he did not hang the Spanish governor.

News that Jackson had "murdered" two Englishmen on Spanish soil led to a series of diplomatic crises. The Spanish minister, Luis de Onis, demanded indemnity for Spanish losses and punishment for Jackson. The London press clamored for apologies, disavowals, and reparation. War might have broken out, said Lord Castlereagh, if the British ministry "had but held up a finger." But, in the end, the British ministry neither demanded redress nor supported the protests of Spain.

Their failure to do anything, in turn, strengthened the hand of the American Secretary of State, John Quincy Adams, who alone in Monroe's Cabinet had fought off efforts by other Cabinet members to punish Jackson. Adams held out for a defiant course in dealing with Spain. Far from apologizing, Adams charged the Spanish with encouraging Indian atrocities. He even demanded an indemnity for the expenses that Jackson had incurred in pursuing Indians and in policing Florida. Spain had the choice, said Adams, of either placing sufficient force in Florida to maintain order, or ceding the province to the United States. If Spain did neither, Adams threatened to seize Florida.

Spain, although she protested vigorously, saw clearly that without British help Florida was beyond her practical control. So the Spanish minister, Onis, traded away Florida in 1819 for a clearly defined boundary between Spanish Texas and the United States. Onis was prepared to give up much more western territory than he gave, but he was a tough bargainer, and the Adams-Onis Treaty established a line which began at the mouth of the Sabine River, zigzagged north and west to the forty-second parallel, and then due west to the Pacific. Adams regarded the treaty as only a temporary settlement. The absorption of all North America, said Adams, was "as much a law of nature . . . as that the Mississippi should flow to the sea."

The Monroe Doctrine. The unseen hand of the British navy also supported the legendary Monroe Doctrine. For years, both London and Washington had been disturbed by the Russians, who had founded a colony, Fort Ross, north of San Francisco in 1816, and subsequently claimed all of the Pacific coast from Alaska to Fort Ross. Adams, in fact, had sternly rebuked the Russian expansionists. Then in 1822 both countries learned, to their dismay, that the powers of continental Europe, led by France, were considering intervention against the revolutionaries in Latin America. The British foreign minister, George Canning, proposed the following year that the United States join England in warning France to keep her hands off South America. Both Jefferson and Madison, President Monroe's unofficial advisers, favored acceptance. But Adams was opposed. There must be, argued Adams, a declaration against European intervention, but the United States should not "come in as a cockboat in the wake of the British man-of-war." It must be an independent assertion by the United States alone.

Following Adams' advice, Monroe told Congress and the world in December 1823 that the New World was now closed to further European colonization and that any intervention by European powers in the affairs of the Americas would be regarded as an unfriendly act towards the United States. Neither European nor Latin American leaders were impressed. The United States, with its tiny navy, was obviously in no position to guarantee Latin American independence. But everyone was impressed with the size and power of the British navy, and European powers had no enthusiasm for reconquering Latin America against British opposition. So, until the United States had sufficient power to back up some of Monroe's words, American principles prevailed only because of the British man-of-war. By the same token, without the opposition of the British navy, European nations violated the Monroe Doctrine with impunity. In 1838 France blockaded Mexico and invaded and blockaded Argentina, while Britain itself seized the Falkland Islands off Argentina in 1833 and one of the Bay Islands off Honduras in 1838. Washington either made token protests or simply ignored the episodes.

Atlantic Capitalism

The years following the Peace of Ghent also marked a transitional period for the American economy. Before the War of 1812, when Europeans were constantly at war, American shipowners and merchants faced little competition on the high seas and could make enormous profits carrying goods for belligerents. After the war, the carrying trade was never again so important. Instead, the United States was caught up in a rapidly expanding Atlantic economy. English manufacturers, cut off from lucrative American markets during the war, tried to make up for lost time and dumped a vast quantity of goods on the market; American manufacturers quickly felt the pinch and called for help. At the same time, the European demand for raw materials was much greater than the supply. American commercial agriculture thus enjoyed an unprecedented four-year boom. Profits were high, credit was easy, and thousands of farm families ventured for the first time into the larger capitalist economy, raising cash crops such as wheat and cotton on a commercial scale.

King Cotton. Cotton led the way. The English demand for cotton was insatiable. Cotton prices thus began to rise in 1812, reached twenty cents a pound in 1815; twenty-nine cents in 1816; and remained high until 1818. Hoping to get rich quick, planters turned more and more land to cotton production, and soon were hooked on the miracle crop. Many were soon sorry, for the boom was followed by an equally spectacular bust in 1819, then a depression in the 1820s, and another boom-bust cycle in the 1830s. But, in good times or bad, cotton remained king. Production skyrocketed from 146,000 bales in 1814 to 349,000 bales in 1819 to 732,000 bales in 1830. Cotton was the country's chief export, making up about 40 percent of export values between 1816 and 1820, and reaching a high of 63 percent in the 1830s.

At one time cotton production in the South had been limited by the difficulty of separating the seeds of upland cotton from the fibres. But with the rapid development of Eli Whitney's cotton gin, which almost any blacksmith could reproduce, it became profitable to raise upland cotton as well as sea island cotton. Before the war plantations had sprung up in the Carolina and Georgia uplands. After the war the desire for rich cotton land—and rich lands generally—led to an amazing surge of population into the Southwest.

Much of this land had been previously closed to white settlement due to the strength of the southern and western tribes. But during the war, while William Henry Harrison suffered heavy losses in putting down Tecumseh in the Northwest, Jackson crushed the Creeks and Cherokees in the Southwest. "We shot them like dogs," Tennessee's Davy Crockett later boasted. Indeed, so overwhelming was the all-day bloodbath at Horseshoe Bend, where the Creek dead added up to over eight hundred men, women, and children, that Jackson was able to drive harsh terms at the peace table. He took from the tribes, friendly and hostile alike, half their ancestral lands—23 million acres—which included one fifth of the state of Georgia and three fifths of Alabama.

Following the war England and Spain abandoned their former Indian allies. Thus the broken tribes in the southern states, along with those in the Northwest, were almost completely at the mercy of white settlers who poured over the Appalachians to take up rich lands which could be bought from land speculators or from the federal government, on credit terms, for as little as $2 an acre. Nevertheless, the powerful tribes of the South, such as the Chickasaws, the Choctaws, the Cherokees, and the Creeks—along with Chief Blackhawk and his tribesmen in the Northwest—managed to hold on for nearly twenty years before they were finally forced to move west of the Mississippi.

Yet, long before the great tribes were finally dispossessed, the West generally, and the Southwest in particular, became crucial to the nation's economy. During the postwar boom years, migration and land speculation soared to new heights. Federal land sales, which had gone over 500,000 acres in 1813, shot up to 1,300,000 acres in 1815, and then to 3,500,000 acres in 1818. Sales tapered off during the lean twenties, boomed during the mid-thirties, and reached a peak of 38,000,000 acres between 1835 and 1837. Speculators bought up the lion's share of public land—as much as 75 percent during the mid-thirties—mapped out towns and plantations, lobbied for roads and canals, gave would-be cities stirring names such as Cairo or Paris or Rising Sun, and waited for settlers to turn their dreams into reality. And while reality seldom matched their dreams, settlers did come in droves.

Almost overnight the Southwest became the center of the cotton kingdom. Before the war the old states of South Carolina, Georgia, Virginia, and North Carolina had completely dominated the cotton market. They produced thirty-nine times as much cotton as the Southwest in 1801, and fifteen times as much in 1811. South Carolina led the way, producing about half of the South's cotton. But South Carolina's lands were worn, and soon Carolina planters and their slaves joined the march west, cleared the land, and within three or four years brought the former wilderness into production. Once these new lands came into production, planters who had remained in the East found that their yields could never match those of a good farm in Alabama or Mississippi. Before their competitive positions completely deteriorated, many of them also picked up stakes and took their slaves to the new promised land. Again and again the pattern was repeated. Thus by 1839 Mississippi produced more than three times as much cotton as South Carolina, and the new Southwest outproduced the Old South by a margin of nearly two to one.

The rise of the cotton kingdom dramatically changed the United States' position in the world's economy. In 1801, only 9 percent of the world's cotton came from the American South, while 60 percent came from Asia. India led the way with an output of 160 million pounds per year, and the rest of the Asian countries together produced an equal amount. By 1821 the South had pulled even with India, and by 1850 it was producing about five times as much cotton as India, and three times as much as all Asia. By 1850 Asia's share of the world market had declined from 60 percent to 22 percent, while the South's had risen from 9 percent to 68 percent. Southern productivity was the key to world productivity, and thanks mainly to the South worldwide production in the first half of the nineteenth century increased from 531 million pounds per year to 1482 million pounds. The South thus provided industrial Manchester with about 80 percent of its raw material. It kept, as Southerners liked to put it, industrialism going.

The Cotton Myths. The spectacular rise of King Cotton and its dominance of the Southwest has led to several misconceptions. One is the tendency to treat the other western states as poor cousins and to minimize the importance of other commercial crops. Even in the South, other staples were important money crops. Tobacco, while it had taken its toll on the worn-out tidewater lands of Virginia and Maryland, expanded rapidly along the Virginia-North Carolina border and in Kentucky, Tennessee, and Missouri. Rice remained the specialty of the South Carolina and Georgia swamplands, and sugar became the specialty of Louisiana planters from Baton Rouge to below New Orleans. Both rice and sugar were rich man's crops, providing enormous returns but also requiring expensive machinery and a huge labor force; some of the most highly skilled men in the South—more often than not slaves—worked with rice and sugar. Hemp, used for rope and baling cotton, came to dominate central Kentucky and parts of Missouri.

More important than these staples, however, were the old standbys—corn, hogs, cattle, wheat, and hay—which provided the principal source of income for most farmers, whether they were small operators or ran highly developed farms in the Genesee Valley of New York, southeastern Pennsylvania, the Nashville Basin of Tennessee, or the Bluegrass Region of Kentucky. Wheat, in particular, was an important cash crop. Wheat and flour made up 16 percent of the nation's exports between 1816 and 1820. Great landlords like the Rensselaers and Wadsworths of New York insisted that rent be paid in wheat. And settlers in the great wheat-producing regions—Virginia, Pennsylvania, New York, and later the Ohio Valley—raised wheat in order to make payments on their land. Like wheat, corn was also grown in every state, but the top producers were concentrated in Kentucky, Tennessee, and Virginia, followed by the states north of the Ohio River. They sent corn-fed animals and other products down the Mississippi to New Orleans, then to overseas destinations or markets in the Deep South.

When cotton and sugar boomed, planters of the lower South relied heavily upon food producers in the Nashville Basin, the Bluegrass Region, and the Ohio Valley. But when times were bad, sugar kings and cotton barons tried to make themselves self-sufficient. The great planters in particular sought diversification. They worried constantly about even being partly dependent on outsiders for foodstuffs, and they complained bitterly about the amount of money that went north to Cincinnati and other "porkopolises." "Corn and hogs are the true kings," advised a Mississippi farm journal, and many planters agreed. The typical slave thus spent much of his time tending livestock, milking cows, or raising corn.

A second misconception is that slavery was dying until cotton came along and gave it new life. For years, scholars maintained that the Founding Fathers had slavery at bay, and the institution would have died out had it not been for Eli Whitney's cotton gin and the rise of King Cotton. This old tale, once widely believed, rested on remarkably few facts: patriots like George Washington freed their slaves; revolutionary leaders like Thomas Jefferson denounced the institution; and the Virginia tobacco economy was declining.

But how many planters actually freed their slaves? Alas, Washington was the exception—not the rule! The average planter might free his own children, a remarkable number of freedmen were half-white, but he showed little inclination to free anyone else's. Jeffersonian Virginians took for granted Negro inferiority and

Slave Population, 1800–1860

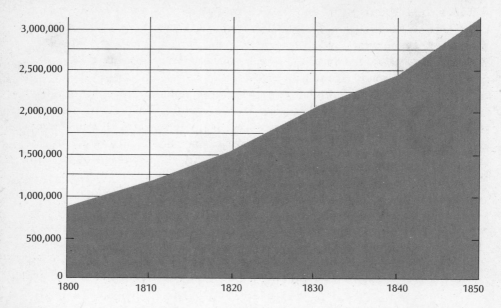

Negro slavery. The planter's wealth, status, and political position rested largely on the number of acres and slaves he owned. Jefferson, for example, owned ten thousand acres and over two hundred slaves; giving this all up would have been most difficult; Jefferson never did. Instead, he took a philosophical position that never could endanger the system. Wrote Jefferson in 1821: "Nothing is more certainly written in the book of fate than that these people are to be free. Nor is it less certain that the two races, equally free, cannot live in the same government." So the blacks had to be deported and that, Jefferson reckoned, was too costly to ever work. Thus in the end there was no real alternative to slavery in Jefferson's thinking.

It is possible, of course, that planters would have to mend their ways in the face of an economic disaster. But a general disaster never came. True, some planters did poorly after the Revolution. Yet others did very well. Indeed, Americans imported more slaves from Africa between 1780 and 1810, the period when slavery was supposedly declining, than in any other thirty-year period in the nation's history. Far from declining, then, slavery was actually increasing before cotton became king. After 1815 planters merely redirected their labor force to the new miracle crop, so that by 1850 seventy-three percent of all slaves in the staple-producing economy lived on cotton farms.

Triumph of the Big Cities

The triumph of King Cotton and the growth of the Atlantic trade also affected the port cities. Only Philadelphia and Providence developed much industry after

1815. The others continued to be geared almost entirely towards the Atlantic trade as they were before the War of 1812. The focal points of most urban economies were still the dock, the wharf, the warehouse, and the counting house. And the city's leading capitalists continued to be the great merchants who no longer dabbled as much in every aspect of trade, but specialized more and more. Thus as the Atlantic trade grew, so did the port cities.

But they did not grow evenly. Indeed, this became the striking feature of the nation's urban development: everywhere growth was selective; some ports stagnated, while others flourished. In New England, for example, Boston soared ahead of its smaller rivals, as the following figures on population growth between 1810 and 1840 reveal:

Boston	181 percent growth in population
Providence	132
Salem	19
Newport	5

Similarly, in the Chesapeake Region, Baltimore boomed at the expense of its smaller rivals:

Baltimore	187 percent growth in population
Richmond	107
Norfolk	9

Ships and warehouses dominated the scene on South Street along New York's East River. South Street's fifty piers spanned three miles—a stretch known as Packet Row. *I. N. Phelps Stokes Collection, Prints Division, The New York Public Library, Astor, Lenox, and Tilden Foundations*

Even among major ports there were striking contrasts. Charleston, the fifth ranking port in 1810, grew a mere 18 percent over the next thirty years, while sixth-ranked New Orleans grew a whopping 494 percent.

Gradually, five giants—New York, Baltimore, Boston, Philadelphia, and New Orleans—completely dwarfed every other port between Maine and Louisiana. At the expense of their smaller competitors, they gobbled up more and more of the nation's trade. Of the nation's twelve port cities, the big five handled about 56 percent of total exports in 1815; by 1840 they handled 68 percent. The most striking gain was made by New Orleans. Thanks to the produce of the Mississippi Valley, it increased its portion from less than 10 percent to more than 25 percent.

New York. The most spectacular success story, however, was New York City's. It came to completely dominate the import trade. Though Manhattan took first place in volume of exports and imports as early as 1797, its lead was slim for many years. In the year before the War of 1812, custom receipts indicated that New York, Boston, and Philadelphia were about equal in the value of foreign imports each handled. After 1815 New York took a commanding lead which it never lost. By 1821 it handled one third of the nation's imports; by 1825 over one half; and by 1836 nearly two thirds. Perhaps one fact sums up New York's dominance: when Andrew Jackson was elected President in 1828, the New York Custom House collected enough money to pay all the current expenses of the federal government!

The port's spectacular growth occurred before the opening of the Erie Canal. It was partly due to London and Liverpool merchants who in 1815 decided to dump their surplus goods on the Manhattan market, causing a rush of buyers to New York City. New York merchants then took two bold measures to further their port's prosperity. Auctions, which enabled ship captains to dispose of their goods quickly for cash, were common in all ports. In most ports, if the bids were too low, the goods could be withdrawn. New York auctioneers got a tax measure enacted in 1817 that made withdrawals costly and guaranteed that goods would be sold for "whatever they would bring." Again, buyers swarmed to Manhattan to get a bargain; and when the buyers came, more sellers came also. The second innovation was the establishment of the Black Ball Line in 1818. The Black Ball Line inaugurated regular service to Liverpool: four packets, each making three round trips a year, would sail on a regular schedule, "fair weather or foul," "full or not full." Elsewhere, both exporters and importers were at the mercy of ships which came and went whenever the captains saw fit.

New York's lead thereafter fed upon itself, but Manhattan merchants lent a helping hand. In order to settle their accounts for overseas manufactures and luxuries, they sent their ships to Charleston and Mobile and New Orleans, and hauled cotton to Liverpool and the continent. Southerners soon complained that forty cents of every cotton dollar actually went north, and most of it went to New York for freight bills, commissions, insurance, and interest. In the year Jackson was elected President, it was estimated that the rest of the nation constantly owed Manhattan entrepreneurs $50 million.

In the 1820s, New York shipping interests also discovered the value of attracting the immigrant trade. Their ships, which carried bulky goods such as cotton, wheat, beef and pork to European ports and then loaded up with less bulky items such as pots and pans, salt, and textiles, often had extra room on the westward crossing. Filling the "'tween decks" with human cargo meant extra profits. Little trouble was taken to accommodate passengers, and even less was done to care for them on the high seas. Very few ships specialized in passenger traffic until the 1850s.

But thousands of Europeans were desperate enough to make the voyage. Between 1815 and 1845 about 850,000 Irish found it necessary to cross the Atlantic. Then came the potato famine, a disaster so complete that in only eight years nearly 1,250,000 Irish rushed to the United States. The Irish were joined by thousands more who came out of poor and overpopulated valleys in Norway, from the Black Forest district of Wurttemberg, from Bavaria and Baden and Prussia, and from England—and which altogether outnumbered Irish immigrants by about three to two. The immigrant trade thus became a big business, and by the 1850s New York completely dominated the trade. In 1854, a peak year, Manhattan counted 328,000 arrivals from Europe, as compared to New Orleans' 51,000, Boston's 27,000, and Philadelphia's 15,000. Many immigrants, particularly the Irish, tended to remain where they landed. By 1850 nearly half of New York's population was foreign born, and more than half of the foreign born were Irish.

The Transportation Revolution. The cities' most spectacular achievements were in transportation. In earlier days seaport merchants had shown little interest in innovations like John Fitch's steamboat, which made a trial run on the Delaware in the 1790s. But with the rapid growth of the West, the idea of being cut off

European Immigration, 1820-1848

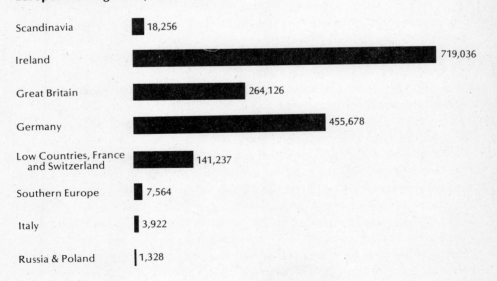

Scandinavia	18,256
Ireland	719,036
Great Britain	264,126
Germany	455,678
Low Countries, France and Switzerland	141,237
Southern Europe	7,564
Italy	3,922
Russia & Poland	1,328

from the interior became intolerable to seaport capitalists, and they began looking for ways to overcome nature's obstacles.

The obstacles were most obvious on the Mississippi River and its tributaries. Flatboating down the river to New Orleans, which had been commonplace since the American Revolution, was hazardous and slow. The return journey upstream was so slow and backbreaking that boatmen usually broke up their boats and sold them for lumber at New Orleans, and then walked home. Keelboats were a great improvement over flatboats; twelve strong men, like the legendary Mike Fink and the "half-horse, half-alligator" men of Kentucky, could row and pole them back up river. But the trip from New Orleans to Pittsburgh took at least four months, and freight charges were prohibitive except for luxury goods. Upstream traffic was never more than one tenth of downstream traffic.

Thus, after Robert Fulton's steamboat, the *Clermont*, steamed up the Hudson in 1807, western entrepreneurs eagerly sought his patent. And under a Fulton patent, Nicholas Roosevelt built the *New Orleans* at Pittsburgh in 1811. Soon forerunners of the classic Mississippi sternwheelers appeared on western waters. Fulton and his partner, Robert Livingston, tried to monopolize steamboat traffic on the Mississippi, just as they did in New York. But by 1817 their monopoly grants were broken, and the flamboyant era of the steamboat with its colorful pilots, gamblers, races, and explosions began. In 1817 there were 17 steamboats on western waters; by 1845 there were 557; in no other part of the world were so many steamboats built and operated. Downriver rates soon dropped to one quarter of what flatboat rates had been, and upriver rates plummeted to one twentieth of keelboat rates. Thus steamboats made it possible for New Orleans' merchants to tap trade far up the Mississippi and its tributaries, while simultaneously enabling farmers in remote areas to raise wheat, cotton, and other bulky commodities for the commercial market.

New York City's most spectacular success—and its most important contribution to transportation—was the Erie Canal. It was the result of the strenuous rivalry between northeastern cities to capture trade. Baltimore, it was thought, had a definite advantage when the federal government under Jefferson began building a "National Highway" from Cumberland, Maryland, to the interior; by 1818 it reached Wheeling on the Ohio River and was supplemented by hundreds of turnpikes that fed into it. Manhattan merchants also dreamed of federal aid to tap the backcountry but lost hope when Presidents Madison and Monroe indicated that such programs violated their constitutional scruples. Meanwhile, New York City's powerful mayor, DeWitt Clinton, tried to interest the state of New York in building a 364-mile canal running from the Hudson River to Lake Erie. What he had in mind, said his numerous enemies, was preposterous: a canal, ten times longer than any in the world, across a sparsely settled wilderness, costing at least $5 or $6 million, without the aid of a single experienced engineer. Nevertheless, when Clinton became governor, he prodded the state legislature in 1817 into accepting his proposal. And the value of the project was obvious even before it was completed in 1825. By 1822, when the middle section was

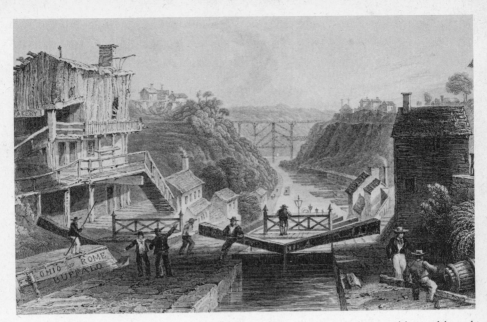

The Erie Canal quickened industrialization in the North as it stimulated competition and brought great wealth to New York. The Canal carried such a volume of traffic that it repaid its initial construction cost within twelve years. *Library of Congress*

open for one hundred miles, Manhattan surpassed Philadelphia as a flour market; and by 1827 it overtook first-place Baltimore. Two figures explain the Erie's success: it cut freight rates from Buffalo to New York City from $100 to $9 a ton, and travel time from twenty days to eight.

The Erie's success agitated entrepreneurs everywhere. Philadelphia merchants in particular were desperate to catch up with their Manhattan rivals. In thirty years they had declined from first place to fourth in volume of trade. They faced enormous geographical handicaps: New York in the Mohawk River had a low pass through the mountains; Philadelphia had to scale the Alleghenies, heights as great as two thousand feet, to reach Pittsburgh. But Philadelphia also had more options. Since the New York decision, railroads had been rapidly developing in England and the Stockington and Darlington railroad, which had opened in 1825, was a smashing success. It proved that one of George Stephenson's locomotives could pull an eighty ton train uphill at fifteen to twenty miles per hour. The problem, argued conservative Philadelphians, was that the railroad had not been tested in the United States, where mountains were higher, snows deeper, and spring floods more violent. Instead of the railroad, they lobbied through the Pennsylvania legislature a mind-boggling plan that included horse-drawn railroads, canals, incline planes, cable cars, and canal boats that split into sections. Completed in 1834, this colossal work had so many bottlenecks that it never threatened the Erie's preeminence.

Baltimore merchants, who took credit for the city's rapid growth, were probably more rational in their choice of options. They began to build the Baltimore and Ohio Railway in 1828. Unfortunately, they ran into a thicket of legal snares: a rival canal, which Maryland supported, took them to court time and again; Virginia declared Baltimore a "foreign port" and delayed progress over the mountain; and Pennsylvania took them to the Supreme Court. As a result, when the B & O finally reached the Ohio River, more than twenty years had passed. It was 1852, and Baltimore had lost too much time to catch New York. By then, New York had its own railroads.

Other states, and other entrepreneurs, also tried to emulate New York's success. The states of the Old Northwest completed a series of canals linking the Great Lakes with the Ohio and the Mississippi. By 1834 the nation as a whole built over 2200 miles of canals, and by 1860 still another 2000 miles. The total cost was $188 million. States and local governments bore over 70 percent of the costs, and most of the government money was borrowed—a handsome slice coming from British investors. The greatest beneficiary in the end was New York City. By way of the new canal system, farmers in the Northwest began to send their goods to Manhattan, rather than down the Mississippi to New Orleans. By 1835 the Erie had one third as much business from the Northwest as the Mississippi; by 1844 it had pulled even; and by 1853 the Erie enjoyed a commanding lead of nearly two to one. Thus New York became the Empire State.

Industrialization

The most significant northern developments after 1815 were in industry. Yet the great merchants, as a rule, showed little interest in infant industries. There were a few exceptions, notably in Boston, but not many. Astor made most of his fortune in Manhattan real estate. Girard owned millions in Pennsylvania real estate, plus many slaves and 280,000 acres of rich plantation land in the Southwest. By comparison, their investments in industry amounted to a pittance.

The postwar years, moreover, were rough ones for most manufacturers. British merchants dumped vast quantities of cheap English goods on the American market immediately following the war. Manchester and Liverpool even cut prices below cost "to stifle in the cradle those rising manufactures in the United States." Congress tried to retaliate with the tariff of 1816, the first protective tariff in American history. In a wave of patriotism or hatred for the British even some southern congressmen—sixteen out of fifty-one who voted—supported the measure although the South clearly benefited from the flood of cheap English goods. Nevertheless, most of the infant industries, which had cut their first teeth during the war years, quickly succumbed to British competition, or struggled valiantly only to be wiped out by the Panic of 1819. Within just four years, wailed protectionists, the number of workers in cotton goods plummeted drastically: from 2300 to 150 employees in Philadelphia; from over 15,000 to under 4000 in Rhode Island.

The Survivors. Yet, despite the wailing, industry survived the lean years and then flourished in the 1820s. Why? One reason is that British dumping devastated some concerns, but not others. Tariff protection eased the pressure on producers of sheeting, but English calicoes were so cheap that manufacturers of ginghams, a Rhode Island specialty, either went bankrupt or switched to another product. And some manufacturers—either through good judgment or good luck—modernized their plants just in the nick of time, installed the Gilmore power loom and other cost-saving devices, and just barely survived the holocaust.

The most striking success in these lean years was the Boston Manufacturing Company. Founded in 1813 by rich Yankee merchants led by Francis Cabot Lowell, this company had from the beginning much more operating capital than the typical Rhode Island mill. The merchants, moreover, believed that huge profits could be made from the economies of large-scale operation, complete mechanization, and integrated production. At Waltham, Massachusetts, they built the first textile mill in the world where all operations were under one roof, installed the latest in power-driven machinery, and established their own selling agencies to eliminate costly middlemen. Their machinery made it inexpedient to rely heavily on child labor. So, rather than hire whole families like the small Rhode Island mills, they hit upon the idea of employing unmarried Yankee farm girls. To overcome the general fear that factory life would corrupt the daughters of respectable farmers, they devised a boardinghouse system with watchful house mothers, a ten o'clock curfew, various educational activities, and required religious worship. Instead of making fine cloth like the British, the Boston industrialists specialized in a cheaper, coarser cloth that had many uses in a pioneer society with many slaves.

Beginning operations in the worst of the postwar years, the Waltham mill was an instantaneous success. Within six years, Lowell and his associates had earned back their initial investment. These earnings they used to develop costly but more productive water-power sites on the Merrimack and Saco rivers, to establish insurance companies and banks, and, most of all, to build bigger factories. Within a generation, the Boston Associates established factory towns on the edge of rapid rivers in southern Maine and New Hampshire and northern Massachusetts.

Their showpiece was Lowell. Begun in 1823 and named after the company's founder, the town was purposely laid out by Kirk Boott to take full advantage of the peaceful, rural setting as well as the water power of the Merrimack River. Hence, even though the town grew from nothing to 28,000 in two decades, European travelers never got over the fact that one could pick violets or wild geraniums, or relax under peaceful old maples, in a city of factories, "the Manchester of New England." The town, in fact, became a tourist attraction, and everybody of importance—from Charles Dickens to Andrew Jackson to the legendary Davy Crockett—was given the red-carpet treatment. And most tourists, in turn, praised the owners for establishing an industrial utopia, and even attributed the "healthy

The title page of the *Lowell Offering. The Bettmann Archive, Inc.*

and wholesome look" of the girls, not to the farm families from which they came, but to the owners of the mills!

The Ebbing of British Competition. A second reason for the success of American industry—and one that is often ignored—is that British mill owners became less concerned with the American market. By the 1820s, they fully realized that their best markets were in Latin America where both economic conditions and warmer climates insured that there would be a heavy demand for cotton goods every month of the year. After 1820, Liverpool and Manchester concentrated on expanding first their Latin American trade, and then their East India trade. Eric Hobsbawm, an eminent English historian, regards this shift in British interests as world-shaking. We may lift our eyebrows in skepticism, but the figures he presents on British cotton exports to various parts of the world are staggering. Look at the magnitude of change between 1820 and 1840:

	1820	1840
To the United States	24 million yards	32 million yards
To Africa	10	75
To East Indies	11	145
To Europe	128	200
To Latin America	56	279

The British did not drop out of the American market; they remained fearsome competitors; but, as their Rhode Island competitors noted, they hustled less. What if things had turned out different? What if British mill owners had increased the pressure on their upstart American competitors? There is no telling how many small firms, with less capital and less know-how than the Boston Associates, would have survived another onslaught of British dumping. It depends partly on how high Congress would have pushed protective tariffs. But a textile war would hardly have encouraged upstarts to expand operations. Obviously, then, the British preference for Latin American markets was a boon for infant industries in the United States. Working in conjunction with protective tariffs, it gave American producers a larger share of the growing domestic market.

The Importance of Commercial Agriculture. A third reason for the expansion of American industry is the triumph of commercial agriculture. Many industries expanded largely because the rural economy became more commercial and expanded westward. Every farmer wanted better axes to clear new land, better plows to open the plains, scythes to cut wheat, and hoes to chop cotton. And the bulk of the nation's iron production went into producing axes, scythes, pitchforks, plows, hoes, and other farm tools. While such everyday items never look impressive on paper, in real life they meant industry—and lots of it. Even in New England there were more factories turning out simple tools than making impressive machinery for the giant mills. A typical small factory in Litchfield, Connecticut, had an output of $178,000 in 1831; more than half of the total came from scythes, axes, and pitchforks.

Bigger operations also owed their existence to the nation's farms. Consider, for example, meat packing which became a moderate-sized industry by 1845. In the Ohio Valley as elsewhere, it was easy for farmers to raise great herds of swine. Abundance of land made it possible to let hogs run loose in the woods, reproduce like rabbits and literally raise themselves on acorns and beechnuts until five or six weeks before killing time; then they were turned loose in a cornfield to fatten. This led to overproduction, and on the spot hogs had little value; no consumers lived nearby.

To take advantage of this situation, Cincinnati developed slaughterhouses as early as 1818. In the words of a contemporary, the city "originated and perfected the system which packs fifteen bushels of corn into a pig and packs that pig into a barrel, and sends him over the mountains and the ocean to feed mankind." In the early days of pork packing, "there was so little demand for any portion of the hog, other than hams, shoulders, sides and lard, that the heads, spareribs, neckpieces, backbones, etc. were regularly thrown into the Ohio River to get rid of them." As time passed, however, the throwaways fostered other industries, and the city was soon making soap and glue and even brushes out of hog bristles. By 1828 Cincinnati packed 40,000 hogs a year; by 1833, 85,000; by 1848, nearly 500,000. The town grew from a small trading center of 2500 people in 1810 to an industrial city of 46,000 in 1840. It had become, as one New Orleans journalist put it, "the most *hoggish* place in all the world."

Still larger industries processed wheat and corn, turning out cornmeal, flour, and whiskey. Soon after the American Revolution, Oliver Evans had established an automated gristmill on Redclay Creek in Delaware. Evans used waterpower not only to turn millstones, but also to run his conveyor system, which included a belt conveyor, a screw conveyor, and a bucket conveyor—the three basic types still used today. The grain passed through the various milling processes without the help of human hand. At first, millers labelled "the whole contrivance" as "a set of rattle traps," and Jefferson pointed out, correctly, that the various details like the bucket and screw conveyors had been used by the ancient Persians and Greeks.

More important, even when the advantages of Evans' system became obvious, millers were reluctant to take it up because of installation costs. Only wheat centers like Baltimore with both waterpower and access to large markets could afford to fully mechanize. The others had to wait. Thus, when the wheat empire expanded after 1815 and transportation was revolutionized, millers in strategic locations took advantage of mechanization and transformed grist-milling into large-scale commercial industries. Baltimore was the king of flour in 1815; by 1850 it had to share its domain with Richmond, Rochester, Oswego, and St. Louis. And in terms of the value of the product—$136 million—milling was the nation's most important industry in 1850.

Entrepreneurship. A final reason for industrial expansion is innovation and entrepreneurship. If we accept the accounts of foreign travelers, every American was a risk-taker, and therefore some were bound to succeed. The promoters of canals, for example, were not investing their money or the state's money on sure things; they were betting on the future, and in many cases they were clearly betting on long shots. New York's "act of faith" turned out to be immensely successful, and the Father of the Erie Canal, DeWitt Clinton, has been celebrated in history books as a man of vision. Most of the other canals turned out to be flops. We remember the Pennsylvania system, in the words of a recent scholar, only as "a cumbrous mongrel . . . that technological monstrosity, a canal over mountains."

For all that, it is clear that Americans were more likely to take some risks than others. They were obsessed, according to travelers, with labor-saving devices. Wrote Friedrich List in the 1820s: "Everything new is quickly introduced here, and all the latest inventions. There is no clinging to old ways, the moment an American hears the word 'invention' he pricks up his ears." Richard Cobden noted in 1835 that the machine shops of Lowell had more "machines and contrivances for abridging labour" than even the major firm of "Sharp and Roberts" in England. And in the 1850s, two groups of English experts reported that Americans excelled the English in standardization and mechanization in dozens of fields. "Every workman seems to be continually devising some new thing to assist him in his work." In New England there was a much stronger desire among both masters and workmen "to be 'posted up' on every new improvement . . . than is the case in England."

Why were Americans this way? The universal answer was "labor." First, industrial wages were higher in America than England: "twenty-five percent higher," wrote Nassau Senior in 1829; "particularly the wages of females," reported James Montgomery in 1840. Second, it was much more difficult for an American manufacturer to expand his labor force. In England, there were always more hands than work, and industrialists could always draw even more workers out of densely populated agricultural slums. In America, even though the hill towns of New England and the worn-out farm lands of New York and Pennsylvania quickly turned into rural slums, farmers still had the option of going West. Thus, as two economic historians once put it, "the abundance of western land drew away many thousands of *potential* wage earners. . . . who might otherwise have crowded into the factories." Finally, the American labor force turned over much faster than the English. Unlike Great Britain, reported Montgomery, where there was always an abundance of experienced hands, the factory girls in America were "constantly changing, old hands going away, and new ones learning." For this reason, American cotton manufacturers had to have "some contrivance connected with the machinery" to prevent the work from being injured by inexperienced hands, and American manufacturers had to constantly look for ways to simplify the work process.

Division of Labor. Hence Americans took the lead in many aspects of mechanization, standardization, and mass production. On the one hand, they introduced machinery—like Evans' mill—to replace hand labor. On the other hand, they broke down handcrafts into their component parts. This led to a minute division of labor, even in industries which did not become mechanized.

Consider again the slaughterhouses and packinghouses of Cincinnati. They never had much in the way of machinery, and in the early days all the operations were *not* carried on under one roof as in the cotton factories of the Boston Associates: the slaughterhouses were outside the city, and the meat had to be carried through the city to the packing houses, which were located near the wharves for water transportation. Yet, every traveler marveled at the organization of the slaughtering process. The work had to be done quickly since the entire pig crop came in the fall. The answer was one of industry's most effective tools—the assembly line.

The idea of the assembly line, or disassembly line if one wants to be technical, apparently developed slowly. At first, butchering was divided into several steps, and work was done by teams. By 1837, a team of twenty men could kill and clean, without machinery, 620 hogs in eight hours. By 1840, five men could cut up, weigh, and trim hogs at the rate of more than one a minute. By mid-century, "it was found economical to give each workman a special duty . . . one cleaned out the ears; one put off the bristles and hairs, while others scraped the animal more carefully. . . . To show the speed attained at Cincinnati in 1851 the workmen were able to clean three hogs per minute." By this time, slaughterhouse and packinghouse had been united under one roof. Pigs were driven up an inclined plane to the top of a four-story building, slaughtered on the top floor, transported downwards from floor to floor by the force of gravity, and then out the front door ready for market.

The designer of Central Park in New York, Frederick Law Olmsted, left a vivid impression:

> We entered an immense low-ceiled room and followed a vista of dead swine upon their backs, their paws stretching towards heaven. Walking down to the vanishing point we found there a sort of human chopping machine where the hogs were converted into commerical pork. A plank table, two men to lift and turn, two to wield the cleavers, were its component parts. *No iron cog wheels could work with more regular motion.* Plump falls the hog upon the table, chop, chop; chop, chop; chop, chop, fall the cleavers. All is over. But before you can say so, plump, chop, chop; chop, chop; chop, chop, sound again. There is no pause for admiration. By a skilled sleight-of-hand, hams, shoulders, clear, mess, and prime fly off, each squarely cut to its own place, where attendants, aided by trucks and dumbwaiters, dispatch each to its separate destiny—the ham to Mexico, its loin for Bordeaux. Amazed beyond all expectation at the celerity, we took out our watches and counted thirty-five seconds, from the moment when one hog touched the table until the next occupied its place. The number of blows required I regret we did not count.

Thus, even with the absence of cogwheels, men had been trained to function like machines.

And, by the same token, the celebrated factory girls of Lowell were little more than cogs in the system. True, the factory owners provided them with boardinghouses, housemothers, and churches, and European travelers found them to be healthier and better-groomed than their European counterparts. But the Lowell arrangement, for its time, was the ultimate in impersonality. Unlike the Rhode Island magnates, who frequently lived across the street from their mills and their workers, the officers and directors of Lowell never rubbed shoulders with their employees. They lived in Boston, many miles away, and dealt with the girls only through overseers. The girls, moreover, came and went with such rapidity that they were usually just names on the payroll. They were merely interchangeable parts—just necessary to keep the machinery going. One mill manager even apologized to Andrew Jackson in 1833 that the girls' uniforms were not exactly alike. Another put it bluntly in the mid-1840s: "I regard my work people just as I regard my machinery. So long as they do my work for what I choose to pay them, I keep them, getting out of them all I can."

Results. For these reasons, then, American industry survived postwar dumping and expanded in the 1820s along with the transportation network and the growing domestic market. Each year, more and more Americans came to depend on factory-made goods. Household manufacturing, which had been the dominant industry in 1815, declined rapidly over the next forty years, first in the older regions and then in newer settlements. In New York state, for example, the output of homemade fabrics and clothes reached a high point around 1825 and then declined as follows:

1825	8.95 yards per person
1835	4.03 yards per person
1845	2.74 yards per person
1855	.27 yards per person

And, just as homemade clothing gave way to factory goods, imported from England or made in the United States, rural farmland also gave way to factory towns. Today, we normally think of cities when we think of industry; but in the early nineteenth century, when waterpower dictated the location of factories, most industries were located in rural areas. This was particularly true of southern New England, where by the 1840s every stream boasted a mill or two. The Blackstone River, a creek flowing from Worcester to Providence, supplied power in 1840 for ninety-four cotton mills, twenty-two woolen mills, and thirty-four machine shops and iron works. In just two decades, cow pastures were turned into mill towns, and mill towns grew quickly into industrial cities.

George Tucker, a professor of moral philosophy at the University of Virginia, summed it all up in 1843: industrial employment increased at a greater rate between 1820 and 1840 than any other field of employment; it had more than doubled in New York, Pennsylvania, and the other "Middle States"; nearly tripled in Massachusetts; and more than tripled in Rhode Island. "In the Southwestern States, alone, the proportion of the agricultural class had increased; in all others it had diminished." Industrialism had yet to come of age, but the basic framework was established.

Consequences

What were the results of all these changes? Generally speaking, Americans everywhere became more productive. As agriculture expanded westward, declined in some areas and grew stronger in others, farm labor generally became more effective. Both free labor and slave labor, according to a recent study, accomplished much more in 1850 than at the turn of the century. What it once took one hundred men to produce, sixty could do in cotton production, fifty-five in wheat, and seventy in corn.

Yet, despite the striking gains in productivity, the basic structure of the agrarian South changed little. The South remained a society with few industries of its own and a small urban population. In 1800 at least four out of five Southerners made their living off the land; in 1850 the ratio was exactly the same. Men and women, whites and blacks, great planters and struggling farmers moved to more productive land; but few took up a new way of life. Even the white illiteracy rate, always a source of embarrassment to southern leaders, remained the same from one generation to the next. In 1817 about 24 percent of the men who applied for marriage licenses in Virginia could not sign their own names. Twenty years later, to the dismay of Governor David Campbell, the figure was almost exactly the same.

In contrast, the North—and particularly the Northeast—underwent something of a metamorphosis. Looking back, it often seems that many Northerners had little choice: the New England soil was so poor that it could never support the growing population; thus Yankees only had the option of either stagnating on their declining farms, moving West, or trying something new. Yet Yankees were not the only ones to take up a new way of life; they merely did so in larger numbers. In the North as a whole, the percentage of the labor force in farming declined from 70 percent to 40 percent. The portion living in towns of 2500 or more doubled. And in southern New England the percentage living in larger towns of 10,000 or more increased from about 7 percent to 25 percent.

The North also became more productive. For one thing, the proportion of able-bodied workers in the total population increased. Around the turn of the century, one out of three Northerners was under ten years of age. Then, for reasons which are not entirely clear, the birthrate in many rural areas, as well as urban-industrial areas, dropped precipitously. Indeed, by 1850 Yankee women had only about half as many children as Mississippi women. At the same time, far more immigrants settled in the Northeast than in the South or in the West. Over 60 percent were men, and the vast majority were in their twenties or thirties. So foreign muscles, along with fewer dependent children, gave the Northeast a definite advantage in terms of overall productivity. In addition, the implementation of laborsaving methods increased production so that the average worker in the pig iron industry turned out twice as much iron as had been the norm in 1800, while the average textile worker produced close to four times as much cloth.

The result was that the Northeast not only became more productive than either the Cotton Kingdom or the farm states of the Old Northwest, but also much wealthier. The following figures, which were compiled by a modern economist, show the differences in per capita income for 1840 and 1860:

	1840	1860
Northeast	$129 per capita	$181
South	74	103
Northwest	65	89

Southerners, even though they lacked these figures, were keenly aware of the uneven distribution of income. And, although planters generally saw themselves as

Density of Population, 1840

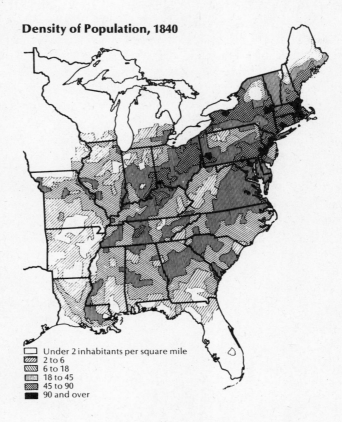

- ☐ Under 2 inhabitants per square mile
- ▨ 2 to 6
- ▧ 6 to 18
- ▥ 18 to 45
- ▦ 45 to 90
- ■ 90 and over

prospering, they complained bitterly. While cotton was king, wailed one southern congressman after another, forty cents of every cotton dollar ended up in northern pockets. Why? Some blamed southern ways, but others pointed their fingers at greedy capitalists and unfair legislation. The bill of indictment included everything from high tariffs to profits made by New York middlemen and moneylenders, to southern travelers who squandered their money in northern resorts, to Yankee schoolteachers in the South who sent money home. From an economic point of view, complained southern congressmen, the South was never liberated from its colonial status: first, the South was a colony of Britain; now, the North.

Many modern historians have agreed. But is the conclusion warranted? We must remember that southern compaints rang through the Halls of Congress largely because the planters had political clout; they still had the benefit of the three-fifths compromise; and they had spokesmen like John C. Calhoun, Henry Clay, and John Slidell who rarely let an opportunity pass to point out the needs of cotton, hemp, and sugar growers. But who spoke as loudly for the farmers of the Northeast? Certainly not Daniel Webster! Not even a calamitous potato blight that ruined the farmers in his native state stirred him to action.

In fact, northern farmers faced the same problems as southern planters. They, too, had to share profits with middlemen and moneylenders. Indeed, all the villains of southern propaganda—factors, brokers, and commission agents—were to be found in great numbers in Buffalo and Rochester, Cincinnati and Chicago, as well as in Mobile and New Orleans. The woes of southern agriculture, then, were primarily the expenses of farming—and not expenses peculiar to the South.

Moreover, by the world's standards, the South was hardly poor in the early nineteenth century. It was certainly richer than Germany and Italy, and at least on a par with France. Indeed, according to one estimate, it was the fourth richest area in the world by the time of the Civil War. And, in per capita income, it was doing far better than the farm states of the Ohio Valley. But it was falling behind the Northeast, which was well on its way to becoming one of the bastions of industrial capitalism. And that was hard to take. And in the long run a sign that they would never catch up.

SUGGESTED READINGS

In *The Age of Revolution, 1789–1848** (1962), E. J. Hobsbawm provides a brilliant analysis of the dominant forces in the Atlantic world. Among the better accounts of American efforts to deal with the great powers is Samuel Flagg Bemis, *John Quincy Adams and the Foundations of American Foreign Policy** (1949). Useful specialized studies include Dexter Perkins, *The Monroe Doctrine* (1927), and Arthur P. Whitaker, *The United States and the Independence of Latin America, 1800–1830* (1941).

Two excellent brief studies of American economic growth after 1815 are Douglas C. North, *The Economic Growth of the United States, 1790–1860** (1961) and Stuart Bruchey, *The Roots of American Economic Growth* (1965). Paul W. Gates, *The Farmers' Age* (1960) and George R. Taylor, *The Transportation Revolution, 1815–1860* (1951) discuss the economy sector by sector. Allan Pred, *The Spatial Dynamics of U. S. Urban-Industrial Growth, 1800–1914* (1966) analyzes the growth rate of various kinds of cities. Especially valuable are two studies by Stanley Lebergott: *Manpower in Economic Growth: The American Record Since 1800* (1964) and "Wage Trends, 1800–1900," in *Trends in the American Economy in the Nineteenth Century* (1960).

*Available in a paperback edition.

Useful specialized studies include J. Van Fenstermaker, *The Development of Commercial Banking, 1782–1837* (1965); Samuel E. Morison, *The Maritime History of Massachusetts, 1783–1860** (1921) Robert Albion, *The Rise of New York Port* (1939); Blanche Hazard, *The Organization of the Boot and Shoe Industry* (1921); Caroline Ware, *The Early New England Cotton Manufacture* (1931); Albert Fishlow, *American Railroads and the Transformation of the Ante-Bellum Economy* (1965); Louis Hunter, *Steamboats on the Western Rivers* (1949); and Stuart Bruchey, ed., *Cotton and the Growth of the American Economy* (1967).

Basic works on technology include J. W. Oliver, *History of American Technology* (1956) and Roger Burlingame, *The March of the Iron Men** (1938). A more sophisticated analysis is presented in H. J. Habakkuk, *American and British Technology in the Nineteenth Century** (1962). But for fascinating reading, nothing matches Siegfried Giedion, *Mechanization Takes Command** (1948).

The best work on immigration is Phillip Taylor, *The Distant Magnet** (1971). Exceptional also are Oscar Handlin, *Boston's Immigrants** (1941), and Marcus Lee Hansen, *The Atlantic Migration, 1607–1860** (1940).

CHAPTER FIVE

THE TURBULENT NORTH

T HE SOUTH ENJOYED one advantage over the North. Since it underwent less change, there were fewer tears in its social fabric, and its ways were always steadier and far more predictable than the North's. In the North, little was certain from one generation to the next. The growth of the division of labor and the spread of the factory system shattered many traditional crafts. Newcomers from Ireland and Germany, as well as other parts of northwestern Europe, fought with native-born whites and blacks for jobs. The centralization of commerce squeezed out many middle-class entrepreneurs. New reforms—and even new religions—suddenly appeared. Utopians, spiritualists, eccentrics, faddists, crackpots, charlatans—all suddenly emerged and tromped across the northern countryside in great numbers. "What a fertility of projects for the salvation of the world!" exclaimed Ralph Waldo Emerson.

The World of Emerson

In trying to find their way through this confusion of voices, poets, writers, and historians once looked to the philosopher Emerson for guidance. He was generally optimistic, a booster as well as a critic of northern society, and his observations, coupled with others, added an upbeat note to the telling of the story. In his eyes, the tumult and shouting were like springtime storms, awful at the moment, but signs of brighter days to come. The angry voices were chiefly forward-looking protests against the passivity and pessimism of the Old World. The new immigrants were not the "indiscriminate masses of Europe," but "the blue eyes of Europe," "the liberal, adventurous, *America-loving* part of each city, clan, family." The future, in sum, looked bright.

Today it is hard to imagine how much weight Emerson's observations once carried. His star has waned in recent years, and many of the lesser lights of his own generation, such as Herman Melville and Henry David Thoreau, have surpassed him in literary prominence. Only a generation ago, however, Emerson was hailed as "the voice of America to America," "the high priest of democracy," "the poet who pierces the crusts that envelop the secrets of life," "the superb critic who reduces a whole chapter of human experience to a single sentence." Two eminent historians even went so far as to claim that his essay *Nature,* which appeared in 1836, marked a turning point in American thought comparable to the Declaration of Independence in American politics. And thus, over the years, he was quoted and paraphrased so often that his thoughts left their mark on the teaching of American history.

Did he know what he was talking about? Not so much, surely, as his followers once assumed. His world was a limited one. He knew genteel poverty and sickliness as a youth, but as an adult his world was largely one of comfort, books, refined culture, and handsome dividend checks. He was generally oblivious to the lot

The first painting, *The Savage State,* in *The Course of Empire* by Thomas Cole, 1833–1836. *Courtesy of The New York Historical Society*

of ordinary workingmen and dirt farmers, not to mention half-starved immigrants. Yet he knew much about the intellectual ferment that swept the northern countryside. He was a central figure in part of it. And he himself, in thrusting aside the faith of his fathers, experienced an agony of soul-searching and fumbling.

Descended from six generations of New England clergymen, Emerson served as minister to the venerable Second Church of Boston until 1832. Then, at the age of twenty-nine, he resigned the ministry, having grown miserable and disgusted with "the corpse-cold Unitarianism of Brattle Street and Harvard College." Several years later, in the quiet Boston suburb of Concord, Emerson, Henry David Thoreau, and others fashioned a new social philosophy. It came to be known as Transcendentalism.

The heavy hand of society and tradition, Emerson now insisted, had perverted the human spirit. But liberation from the past was easy—and a totally invigorating experience. Emerson thus urged his many readers to break free of society, go into solitude, commune with nature, and in this way recapture the original natures they had lost as children. "In the woods I feel nothing can befall me in life . . . which nature cannot repair." "In the woods . . . a man casts off his years . . . and, at what period soever of life, is always a child." Indeed, by establishing an "original relation" with nature, man can "transcend" his environment, stretch far beyond his known capacities, and realize his unlimited potential. Such thoughts, while they seem hackneyed today, represented a sharp break with the teachings of Emerson's Puritan ancestors, who not only feared solitude but also focused less on the innocence of children than on their inheritance of Adam's sin. This literary critics have often maintained that Emerson's exhortations marked the beginning of a fresh new "American voice."

Emerson's philosophy may have been new and fresh, but it was never much of a threat to the status quo. Transcendentalism inspired Henry David Thoreau to take to the woods on Emerson's property, where he lived alone in a hut for two years. Recounting his experiences vividly in *Walden,* his finest book, he exceeded Emerson in censuring established institutions and called for a more total immersion in nature. And he spent a night in jail rather than pay taxes to support the Mexican War. Other Transcendentalists tried their hands at communal living, and quickly set up two communes, Brook Farm and Fruitlands, famous in literary circles. Emerson, however, kept his distance from such ventures, not to mention the more radical mass movements of his day, and in time his eloquent preaching of self-realization and self-reliance captivated thousands of middle-class Americans, who flocked to his lectures, named their children after him, and made pilgrimages to his Concord home. Emerson was all too well attuned to the yearnings of his day to be a "superb critic" of his society.

Romanticism. Underlying the Transcendentalist spirit was a new configuration of ideas and attitudes in the Western world known as Romanticism. A vast and complicated movement, Romanticism took so many different forms, led in so many different directions, that it served many intellectual creeds besides Tran-

One of the finest genre paintings of George Caleb Bingham is *Fur Traders Descending the Missouri,* c. 1845. *The Metropolitan Museum of Art, Morris K. Jessup Fund, 1933*

scendentalism. It provided intellectual underpinnings for reactionary thought as well as progressive, for suicidal pessimism as well as Emersonian optimism. Basically, Romanticism represented a sharp reaction against the thinking of the eighteenth-century Enlightenment. Enlightenment thinkers believed that a benevolent Creator had laid down certain "natural laws" regulating both the physical and moral universes for the benefit of mankind, and that rational men through careful observation and reasoning could understand these "natural laws" and thus achieve happiness. Romanticism rejected this mechanical view of the world and its emphasis on scientific observation and reasoning. The world, said Romantics, was not predictable like a clock, but wild and unruly, dynamic, constantly changing, growing and decaying. Distrusting intellect, Romanticism celebrated man's emotional and intuitive qualities, insisting that the highest truths came instantaneously when man was in deep, spiritual communion with nature.

Romantic assumptions pervaded Emerson's America. Landscape painters of the Hudson River School tried to capture on their canvases the wild and the marvelous, the emotion of the "sublime," the "very spirit of Nature herself." As landscape artist Thomas Cole put it:

> Ye mountains, woods and rocks, impetuous streams,
> Ye wide-spread heavens, speak out, O speak for me!
> Have I not held communion deep with you,
> And like to one who is enamoured, gazed
> Intensely on your ever-varying charms?

Similarly, in his more popular novels, James Fenimore Cooper celebrated the superior wisdom and virtue of such "natural" men as the untutored woodsman Leatherstocking and the noble redskin Chingachgook. And, in laying out New York's Central Park, Frederick Law Olmsted tried to duplicate the wild and irregular patterns of nature, rather than the formal patterns of classical landscape architecture.

Romantic assumptions also found their way into politics. Among Andrew Jackson's other virtues, according to the distinguished historian and Jacksonian politician George Bancroft, was that he had been lucky enough to escape the long schooling and formal training that impaired the vigour and intuitive judgment of his arch-rival John Quincy Adams. Indeed, to the disgust of most of his fellow New Englanders, Bancroft rhapsodized over Jackson's "natural" mind:

> Behold, then, the unlettered man of the West,
> the nursling of the wilds, the farmer of the
> Hermitage, little versed in books, unconnected
> by science with the tradition of the past . . . .
> What policy will he pursue? What wisdom will
> he bring with him from the forest?

Against this unlettered hero, whose wisdom came out of the woods, anti-Jackson men countered by quickly discovering the superior "wisdom" of rustics like Davy Crockett, who to Bancroft's chagrin roasted Jackson for betraying the common people of western Tennessee. Suddenly, Crockett sayings and Crockett autobiographies appeared in eastern bookstalls, and overnight Crockett became a major folk hero, a Romantic primitive and rip-roaring comic who could "wade the Mississippi, carry a steam-boat on his back, and whip his weight in wild cats." No one knows for sure what effect all this had on the ordinary voter. But by 1840, political strategists of all stripes were willing to go along with what one newspaper called "The Davy Crockett Line" and portray their candidates as simple backwoodsmen who were raised on possum fat and hominy.

The Problem of Meaning. Until recently historians, in evaluating American Romanticism, pictured it as primarily a chorus of hope, singing triumphantly about progress and the perfectibility of man. Such an interpretation seemed justified since optimistic writers like Emerson abounded. There were some dissonant voices of major concern, to be sure, who were conveyers of gloom, doom, and horror, and who dwelt often upon the vulgarities of northern life. But such "naysayers" as Edgar Allan Poe, Nathaniel Hawthorne, and Herman Melville were either explained away, treated as exceptions to the general rule, or even quoted in support of the basic argument. Indeed, Hawthorne had even complained about "the difficulty of writing a romance about a country where there is no shadow, no antiquity, no mystery, no picturesque and gloomy wrong, nor anything but a commonplace prosperity, in broad and simple daylight, as is happily the case with my dear native land." What more was needed to cinch the argument!

Hawthorne's evaluation, moreover, squared nicely with the era's reputation as being the Age of the Common Man, the period when Tom, Dick, and Harry came into their own. The words "commonplace prosperity" coincided perfectly, in fact, with the most influential single book ever written on the period, Alexis de Tocqueville's *Democracy in America*. Tocqueville, along with another young French aristocrat, visited the United States for nine months in 1831 and 1832, having been sent by the French government to study the American prison system. But, besides studying prisons, Tocqueville studied American society, and the result was a book that was so dazzling and original in its insights that American scholars have held Tocqueville in awe. And Tocqueville emphasized particularly the "equality of conditions" that he found in the United States. Nothing, in fact, struck him "more forcefully." Not only a political equality, but also a rough economic equality existed among white Americans.

In recent years, however, scholars have laid bare a situation of dramatic inequalities, not only between blacks and whites, but also among whites. Judged by the standards of a French nobleman, American equality was no doubt astounding in 1831 and 1832. But in terms of dollars and cents, comfort and hardship, it has been greatly exaggerated. And many of the Americans whom Tocqueville interviewed told him as much. John Quincy Adams, no flaming radical, told Tocqueville that while in the North there was "a great equality before the law . . . it ceases absolutely in the habits of life. There are upper classes and working classes." And an eminent Philadelphia attorney told him that "there is more social equality with you at home than with us. Here . . . wealth gives a decided pre-eminence."

Along with Emersonian optimism, moreover, scholars have uncovered convincing evidence of widespread uneasiness about America's future. Indeed, a common theme of the period's poems, novels, paintings, and historical works was that of peaceful progress ending in catastrophe. For example, in a series of paintings called the *Course of Empire,* Thomas Cole depicted society moving from a simple pastoral state, to magnificent commercial metropolises, followed by social chaos and war, destruction, and finally desolation. Other popular paintings depicting annihilation included Ashur Durand's *God's Judgment upon Gog,* Benjamin West's *Death on a Pale Horse,* and Joshua Shaw's *The Deluge.* So the gloomy pessimism of Melville and Hawthorne and the melancholy horror of Poe were not bizarre exceptions in the otherwise optimistic world of Emerson and his admirers. They were very much a part of Emerson's America.

The Growing Ranks of the Poor

One reason for northern uneasiness was that not everyone shared in the North's growing prosperity. Tocqueville was right in emphasizing the size and importance of the American middle class. It was large by European standards and politicians clearly aimed their pitch at middle-class voters. But Tocqueville was wrong—indeed, dead wrong—in claiming that glaring inequalities in the distribution of wealth were rapidly disappearing.

In fact, the uneven distribution of wealth in the rapidly developing Northeast was clearly going from bad to worse. While the economic pie as a whole was getting bigger and bigger, so that most Northerners had a few more dollars in their pockets, the middle and lower classes were getting a smaller and smaller share of the total pie. In prosperous Massachusetts, for example, the "bottom" 90 percent at the time of the American Revolution had held more of the state's total wealth than the richest 10 percent. But by the time of Tocqueville's visit, their share of the total wealth was about one half that of the richest 10 percent, and by the Civil War about one quarter.

Many middle-class citizens, of course, prospered some as the wealthy prospered a great deal. But others did not. In Boston, the proportion of *propertyless* taxpayers rose from 29 percent at the time of the Revolution to 44 percent in 1830 to 57 percent in 1850. In New York, the Society for the Prevention of Pauperism estimated that one out of fifteen New Yorkers was utterly destitute in 1819; in 1844, estimates were one in seven. In the long run, perhaps the vast majority benefited from cheaper goods and a more efficient economic system. But in the short run, hundreds of thousands lost out as the division of labor destroyed old crafts, and local and regional markets came under the control of larger establishments.

The Plight of the Artisan. At one time, for example, teenage apprentices could expect to rise in their trade, become journeymen in a small shop, and then with a little luck open small shops of their own when they became middle-age masters. They could also expect to do much of their own work to the order of individual customers. But the new set of economic conditions undermined the old order so that trade was no longer a local affair, and shopkeepers either succeeded in the race to capture a larger and larger slice of the citywide or regional market, or lost out to merchant-capitalists and became journeymen once again working under someone else. In the end, losers outnumbered winners by a wide margin. In cities such as Philadelphia, the population doubled, tripled, and even quadrupled, yet the number of shops remained the same, and the proportion of master craftsmen in the total work force dropped by more than one half. Several rungs in the urban social ladder were virtually cut out; no longer could young apprentices expect to own their own shop.

At the same time, to meet the competition ambitious shopkeepers and merchant-capitalists pressed their journeymen harder and cut labor costs whenever they could. Traditional skills were broken down, and labor was divided so that the shoemaker, for example, no longer made the whole shoe. He did a single operation all day long. And, wherever possible, masters replaced skilled craftsmen with convict, female, child, and other unskilled labor to cut labor costs. In self-protection, shoe workers, printers, blacksmiths, chairmakers, bakers, tailors, weavers, jewelers, and dozens of other tradesmen organized journeymen's societies. In 1827, sixteen journeymen's societies banned together in Philadelphia to increase their effectiveness. The idea soon caught on in other cities, and "unions of the trades" became common in both large and small cities. By the mid-1830s some 300,000 skilled workers marched under the banner of one organization or another.

Skilled craftsmen, like the nation's small farmers, had always regarded themselves as the "bone and sinew" of American society. So they never thought of limiting their scope to just shop conditions. They often complained as much about pauper schools and the failure to keep the streets clean as they did about working conditions. Out of the Philadelphia "union of the trades," therefore, came the Philadelphia Working Men's Party in 1828. And, once again, the idea caught on and workingmen's parties sprang up in small towns and big cities throughout the North.

Typically, these organizations soared to great heights in one or two years, did well at the polls, and then collapsed. They invariably had their own newspapers which cried out in favor of a wide range of reforms, including a less expensive legal system, land reform, revision of the militia system, and the end of imprisonment for debt. But, above all, they clamored against "free" schools, which were only open to families who were willing to make a public confession of poverty, and which were run on a shoestring budget. In place of such wretched schools, they demanded tax-supported schools which were not tainted with the concept of being for "the poor only." They were a proud people, fighting as much for respect and a way of life as for dollars and cents.

Skilled craftsmen, of course, never ignored bread-and-butter issues. The traditional working day, from sunup to sundown, was long enough even when the job involved a variety of tasks and the pace was leisurely. Once the work was reduced to doing the same task over and over again at a faster pace, the same twelve or thirteen hours became torture. Similarly the traditional pay of most journeymen, between $1 and $2 a day, was hard enough to live on in ordinary times. In the mid-1830s runaway inflation took over, and it became impossible for skilled workers to maintain a decent standard of living.

Journeymen thus waged hundreds of strikes in 1835 and 1836, many for the ten-hour day, and many more for higher wages. Outside New England, the ten-hour movement was largely successful. The gains made during the strikes, however, turned out to be short-lived. The inflationary boom was followed by an equally spectacular bust. And during the grim depression following the Panic of 1837, jobs disappeared, pay was cut, and the workingmen's movement collapsed. Once again skilled craftsmen had to scramble on their own to find a niche in the new economy.

Native-born workingmen soon faced a new threat in the 1840s, with the arrival of thousands of able-bodied, eager workers from Ireland and Germany. Generally, new immigrants would work for less. But the Germans differed from the Irish in that many came with skills and expected skilled wages. Invariably the Irish were half-starved peasants, desperate and unskilled. So the impact of immigration on a city's tradesmen depended on how many immigrants entered the city, how many were Irish, and how many broke into the trade. In New York City, where immigration was by far the heaviest, native-born shoemakers lost out to the Irish, while tailors lost out mainly to Germans. Other trades were less affected. By 1855, almost all of the city's shoemakers, tailors, and stonecutters were foreign born, as compared to over half of its carpenters and dressmakers, and only a small portion of its printers. In Boston, where most immigrants were Irish, the Irish soon made up two thirds of the tailors, but less than one tenth of the carpenters and printers.

In tandem, the division of labor and the influx of cheap labor destroyed many ancient crafts. And by the mid-1840s, the standard of living of many craftsmen had noticeably declined. The New York *Tribune* noted in particular the sad state of the city's once-proud shoemakers:

> There is no class of mechanics in New York who average so great an amount of work for so little money as the journeymen shoemakers. . . . We have been in more than fifty cellars in different parts of the city, each inhabited by a shoemaker and his family. The floor is made of rough plank laid loosely down, the ceiling is not quite so high as a tall man. The walls are dark and damp, and a wide, desolate fireplace yawns in the center to the right of the entrance. There is no outlet back and of course no yard privileges of any kind. The miserable room is lighted only by a shallow sash, partly projecting above the surface of the ground and by the little light that struggles down the steep and rotting stairs. In this . . . often live the man with his workbench, his wife and five or six children of all ages, and perhaps a palsied grandfather or grandmother or often both. In one corner is a squalid bed and the room elsewhere is occupied by the workbench, a cradle made from a dry-goods box, two or three broken, seatless chairs, a stew-pan and a kettle.

The ancient craft of shoemaking, then, had become a poor man's calling. Oldtime craftsmen either got out, became bosses, or joined the ranks of the poor.

The Plight of the Very Poor. The poor immigrants who took their place, of course, had it no better, and they had even less opportunity to find better jobs. The advantage still lay with native-born whites. The Irish especially were likely to start at the bottom and remain there all their lives. They were not only unskilled, but also Catholic—and native Americans hated them for it. Irishmen could be found fighting with blacks in New Orleans for dock work, digging canals in Maryland, working in such industries as textiles and glass, making dams to provide water-power for the giant mills in Lowell, and filling in the Back Bay of Boston for real estate speculators. But few got jobs that involved anything but back-breaking labor. In Boston, for example, two out of three domestic servants and four out of five common laborers were Irish, but only one out of thirty-six clerks was Irish.

The Irish were not only unskilled, but also newcomers to big city and industrial life. All farm people found the transition difficult. Even the Yankee farm girls who came to Lowell were regarded as "queer" by urban folk. They dressed outlandishly, wrote Harriet Robinson, and they spoke "the broken English and Scotch of their ancestors," which "when engrafted on the nasal Yankee twang" made them almost impossible to understand. They also had funny names like "Samantha,

Triphena, Plumy, Kezia, Aseneth, Elgardy, Leafy, Ruhamah, Almaretta, Sarpeta, and Florilla." And they had trouble adjusting to the dictates of the machine and the clock-work rhythms of a large cotton factory. But the Lowell girls were at least native-born Protestants. For foreign-born Catholics it was more difficult: they had to adjust to a new homeland and a hostile culture, as well as a new urban way of life.

Even worse off, however, were northern free blacks. They were always poor, and persecuted from cradle to grave. But, with the coming of the Irish, their position in northern society clearly got worse. Complained the *Colored American* in 1838: "These impoverished and destitute beings, transported from trans-atlantic shores, are crowding themselves into every place of business and of labor, and driving the poor colored American citizen out. Along the wharves, where the colored man had once done the whole business of shipping and unshipping—in stores where his services were once rendered, and in families where the chief places were filled by him, in all these situations there are substituted foreigners or white Americans." Noted Frederick Douglass ten years later: "Every hour sees us elbowed out of some employment to make room for some newly arrived immigrants, whose hunger and color are thought to give them a title to especial favor."

The loss of jobs was particularly acute in the great cities. In New York City, most servants were black in 1830; twenty years later, Irish servants outnumbered the city's entire black population by ten to one. In Philadelphia, blacks lost their places as hackney coachmen and draymen during the 1830s, were driven off the docks during the 1840s, and just barely hung on to their jobs as servants and barbers. Between 1838 and 1847, according to a recent statistical study, the per capita value of personal property among Philadelphia blacks decreased a full ten percent. The very poor thus got poorer.

The Rich. What about the other extreme? The urban rich clearly got richer. In Boston, for example, the top one percent possessed

> 16 percent of the city's assessed wealth in 1820
> 33 percent in 1833
> 37 percent in 1848

In Brooklyn, the top one percent held:

> 22 percent in 1810
> 42 percent in 1841

And in New York City, the upper one percent had:

> 29 percent in 1828
> 40 percent in 1845

Stephen Girard, the great Philadelphia merchant and banker, was worth about six million when he died in 1831. That was eighteen times as much as the combined wealth of Philadelphia's 14,000 blacks. The famous New York land speculator and merchant, John Jacob Astor, was worth three times as much as Girard when he died seventeen years later. Astor, according to one estimate, made more in an hour than the ordinary New Yorker made in a year; and more in a twenty-four hour day than the average citizen made in a lifetime. And he was only the richest of New York's 113 millionaires.

Business leaders insisted, at the time of the great merchants' funerals, that the lives of Girard and Astor proved that the "poor immigrant" who came to America as a "cabin boy" or in "common steerage" could make steady progress from "humble poverty to princely opulence" through perseverance and zeal. Hard work and good character, they claimed, was the source of great wealth. "Rubbish," replied the popular penny papers, which were read by the masses. Astor got rich, asserted the New York *Herald,* largely "at the expense of the working people of New York," and his heir William B. Astor "never did a lick of work in his life." But, due to the tireless propaganda of the mercantile press, the merchants' view prevailed and came to dominate much of American thinking.

Research has shown that the rags-to-riches experience was truly exceptional. As business historian William Miller put it, poor boys "who become business leaders have always been more conspicuous in American history books than in American history." Indeed, probably nine out of ten merchants who talked about rags-to-riches never had the experience. For every Girard or Astor, who fit the Horatio Alger stereotype, there were dozens of others who acquired their initial fortunes through marriage and inheritance.

Most merchants, in fact, started off with the aid of both a handsome inheritance and a sound marriage. The old adage that money marries money was certainly true between 1800 and 1850, and few merchants had any doubts about it. Few, to be sure, agreed with John Jacob Astor's grandson, who claimed that rich Americans only married for money. But fewer still were blind to the financial aspects of marriage. Philip Hone, for example, attended a fashionable New York wedding in 1834. When he got home, he noted in his diary that Lispenard Stewart, son of a wealthy merchant, had just "married 2 or $300,000." And Moses Yale Beech, who compiled in 1844 the first practical guidebook to credit and marriage, *The Wealthy Citizens of New York,* summed up Henry Pierpont's great wealth in just six words: "Married a daughter of John Jay." At the other extreme, when a great merchant's daughter decided "out of pure love" to marry his coachman's son, the "esteemed citizen" was so angry that he tried "to remove her from the country, and also to have her declared a lunatic."

Having a head start in the race for riches, the wealthy simply took advantage of the booming urban economies, expanded their holdings, and gained a larger slice of the economic pie. Some, of course, did better than others, and a few fell from the ranks of the mighty. But most were steady accumulators, rather than bold and daring innovators. Great fortunes, in the words of historian Edward Pessen, generally "held their own through all manner of vicissitudes." Economic cataclysms, like the Panic of 1837, might wipe out families with moderate means, but they generally strengthened rather than destroyed the very rich, who like Astor bought out hard-pressed debtors at bargain prices. Hence, gradually, financial power concentrated into the hands of a few merchants just as trade nationally came to be dominated by a few cities.

The Dimensions of Class Conflict. What did the middle and lower classes do while all this was going on? They were hardly content. Many a bitter comment appeared in the penny papers about "purse-proud aristocrats" who built colossal mansions on Broadway and Beacon Hill, formed exclusive clubs like the Century in New York and the Philadelphia Club, and dashed around town in luxurious carriages. And ordinary citizens were outraged when a few wealthy New Yorkers and Bostonians forced their servants to wear livery. That, in the eyes of a good American democrat, was like making a man "wear a halter around his neck." In response to such resentment, scores of politicians, often rich men themselves, adopted the common touch and celebrated the virtues of "hard-handed, clear-headed mechanics," while heaping nothing but scorn on "the aristocracy of the North." Indeed, in smearing the opposition, no charge was repeated with greater pertinacity than "Aristocracy! Aristocracy! Aristocracy!" And, under the political banners of Andrew Jackson and Martin Van Buren in particular, thousands of shopkeepers and workers marched to the polls in the 1830s to do battle against the "urban money power."

Yet, despite the resentment against the aggrandizement of wealth and the pretensions of the urban elite, strong words rarely led to strong action. Neither Jackson, nor Van Buren, nor the political rhetoric of the day had much effect on the urban power structure. Political parties continued to offer the very rich for high office, and the mayors of northeastern cities continued to be men of great wealth. And, even during times of rioting, mobs seldom bothered the rich and well-born.

There are two basic explanations for this paradox. One is that poverty never became so widespread that workers simply had to forget their differences and band together against the upper class. Unlike the situation in Europe, where peasants were forced off the land, the American farmer always had the choice of going West—and most did. So the American labor market was never overwhelmed with new competitors in every line of endeavor, and American wages remained "high" by European standards. Tailors and shoemakers suffered with the coming of the Irish and the Germans, but printers did not.

The other explanation is that American workers were hopelessly divided along ethnic and religious lines. Indeed, beginning in 1834, race riots and religious riots became everyday news. Time and again, the daily papers carried news of Protestants assailing nuns in Massachusetts, Protestants and Catholics battling on the streets of Philadelphia, or whites razing the Negro quarters in New York, Philadelphia, or Cincinnati. Thus, even after fifteen years of hotly contested strikes and hard times culminating in the depression of 1837 to 1843, American workers were unable to sustain class consciousness. The majority of workingmen in Boston, New York, and Philadelphia went to the polls in 1844, not to wage war against the capitalists, but to support parties whose primary targets were Roman Catholics. The minority, meanwhile, were hoping to get their hands on evangelical Protestants and "nigger lovers."

More worrisome than extreme wealth—as far as the urban elite and the upper middle class were concerned—was extreme poverty. Men and women were supposed to get rich in America—not poor. Yet it was clear, even to middle-class optimists, that the poor were becoming more plentiful.

Generally speaking, the daily grind of the poor was invisible to outsiders. But occasionally a startling event brought illumination. Of such crises, Asiatic cholera, which swept the country in 1832 and 1849, was particularly revealing since cholera was truly "a poor man's plague." In Philadelphia, the extent of the outbreak among blacks was almost twice that among whites; in New York, almost all the fatalities were buried at Potter's Field or St. Patrick's Cemetery. Everywhere, it seemed, the poor died like flies. Suddenly, men and women were overwhelmed by cramps, acute vomiting, and diarrhea; then their hands and feet turned cold and darkened, while their faces took on a bluish color; and within hours they were dead. The disease was so dreadful, and so dangerous to the city as a whole, that physicians and public officials could hardly ignore the plight of the poor. And what they found shocked them. Five New York victims, for example, were found huddled together in a tenement with twenty-two pigs; a dying black couple in Philadelphia lived in a room four-and-a-half by seven feet; a Boston patient shared his cellar-room with a tide so high that the attending physician had to build a bridge to get to the man's bed. Only on such occasions, wrote Mrs. Peter Roosevelt of New York, was the "dreadful misery and distress of the City known."

But how could such misery exist in a land of plenty? Was it the system's fault? Or the poor themselves? Many observers had doubts, but few blamed the American way. Almost all agreed that the country was truly a land of opportunity, where land was plentiful and labor scarce, and its institutions were the best on earth. The fault, therefore, must lie with the poor themselves. New York's Society for the Prevention of Pauperism concluded in 1821 that "the paupers of this city are, for the most part . . . depraved and vicious, and require support because they are so." A Philadelphia investigative committee, after visiting other eastern cities in 1827, reported that "vice" had created "here and everywhere, by far the greatest part of the poor."

Such views stimulated a demand for action. If the poor were morally debauched, as city fathers claimed, then something had to be done. They were not only dangerous to themselves but also potentially dangerous to everyone else. But what should be done? Many simply wanted to get rid of the poor. This desire, especially when coupled with white racism, led to much ugliness. Scores of politicians argued that free blacks were destined to be poor and improvident, and dozens of northern towns passed new laws, or rediscovered old ones, to keep blacks out. Others tried to drive them out. In Providence, Rhode Island, where anti-Negro feeling was particularly bitter, "respectable" whites made several attempts to expel black residents in the 1820s and 1830s. On one occasion, whites became alarmed about "Hardscrabble," a predominantly Negro slum which also harbored most of the city's drunkards, sailors, and prostitutes. The whites raised a mob which drove blacks from their homes, tore down their houses, and carried off their furniture and sold it at auction in Pawtucket.

The most serious incident of this kind occurred in Cincinnati in August 1829. For two decades the city fathers had ignored the provision of Ohio's Black Laws that compelled free Negroes entering the state to post a $500 bond as guarantee of their good behavior and providence. But between 1826 and 1829, Cincinnati's black population suddenly increased from about 4 percent to 10 percent of the total population. White citizens, claiming that the city was soon going to be overrun with "dirty black paupers," demanded that the city fathers start enforcing the Black Laws. In response, the Overseers of the Poor agreed to do so within thirty days. Almost immediately, white bands began terrorizing blacks, and soon several hundred whites invaded "Bucktown," spreading terror and destruction. By the end of 1829, half of the black population left Cincinnati, and never again in the antebellum period did the city's Negro population exceed 5 percent of the total. For many whites this fact alone justified the excesses.

The Remedy of Rehabilitation. On the other hand, many middle-class citizens thought that the poor—and especially the white poor—could be rehabilitated. As a rule, colonial Americans never had much faith in rehabilitation. But many nineteenth-century Americans accepted wholeheartedly the idea of progress and the perfectibility of man. And they were certain that "even the depraved and the vicious" could be reformed. The "depraved" were not inherently depraved, but rather the victims of poor upbringing, strong drink, bad companions, and bad habits. So dozens of well-intentioned citizens concluded that the answer to poverty was to force the "depraved" to acquire good habits.

But how could that be accomplished? It could never be done under existing circumstances, concluded most investigators, because the homes of the poor were dens of iniquity. Indeed, according to Mayor Josiah Quincy of Boston, nothing was more "destructive of industrious habits" or more "injurious to their morals" than "their own families." The first step, then, was to remove them from their homes and from the temptations of neighborhood grog shops, gambling halls, and other dives and then teach them habits of thrift, orderliness, temperance, and industry in an orderly environment.

Such thinking became the rationale for setting up dozens of institutions ranging from poorhouses to penitentiaries in the 1820s and 1830s. Boston and New York, for example, followed their investigations of poverty by erecting new poorhouses. Once inside these institutions, theoretically, able-bodied loafers would learn to live by the clock and to work hard. A bell would awaken them early in the morning; another bell would call them to breakfast; still another to work; and so on through the day. There would be no time for idle chatter or gambling, and no place or time for drinking. Discipline and hard work would be the order of the day. Armed with these virtues, which they could never learn at home, the poor would return to society, virtuous and ready to earn their keep. Unfortunately, it rarely turned out this way. The workhouses were usually poorly run, and they received not only able-bodied loafers, but also youngsters and decrepit oldsters who were unable to work long hours or profit from the regimen. So poorhouses, as a New York investigative committee put it in 1857, quickly degenerated into "the most disgraceful memorials of the public charity," where inmates were more apt to learn the latest techniques in sadism, rather than the virtues of hard work.

For the poor who turned to crime, the answer was the penitentiary. Actually, the idea of incarcerating criminals for five, ten, fifteen, or twenty years was a relatively new one. Having little or no faith in rehabilitation, colonial authorities never dreamed of burdening taxpayers by keeping a man locked up for years. Their remedies were quicker and less costly: first and second offenders were whipped, fined, sometimes branded, and publicly shamed; incorrigibles were hanged. Nineteenth-century reformers hoped to convert hardened criminals by removing them from their old haunts. Said Samuel Gridley Howe, a Massachusetts reformer, in the "Prisoner's Prayer": "In the name of justice, do not subject me to unnecessary temptation, do not expose me to further degradation . . . Remove me from my old companions, and surround me with virtuous associates."

The trick, then, was to create an institutional environment that would lead criminals away from crime. Penal reformers agreed that offenders had to be separated from corruption. The debate was generally over "how much separation was necessary." Between 1819 and 1823, New York devised what came to be known as the "Auburn System." Under it, prisoners were not allowed to communicate with one another, and they slept in solitary cells; but they worked together in large groups. Pennsylvania carried separation much further at Pittsburgh in 1826 and at Philadelphia in 1829. Under the Pennsylvania system, convicts had no contact with one another whatsoever: they were hooded when marched into their cells; once isolated, they worked, ate, and slept in their cells; they talked only to "virtuous" people such as prison officials and ministers; and they read only "morally uplifting literature"—the Bible. The two systems attracted European attention, but the Pennsylvania system failed to catch on. Some claimed that it drove prisoners crazy; others pointed to its costs. The "Auburn System" was soon modified, and penitentiaries soon degenerated into the institutions we have today.

Similarly, well-meaning reformers worked hard to get government officials to put up money for orphanages, reformatories, homes for wayward girls, and asylums for the insane. And Dorothea Dix, who campaigned far and wide in behalf of insane asylums, became a national heroine. Celebrated in both North and South, and from the Atlantic seaboard to the Far West, she soon occupied a prominent place in the nation's textbooks as "the foremost humanitarian of the day." Had she and other reformers seen the state of asylums in the 1880s or the 1970s, one suspects that they would have been disgusted. For they were kind-hearted, well-intented men and women. Nevertheless, their whole-hearted conviction in the 1820s and 1830s that institutionalization was "the" answer clearly triumphed. Indeed, it not only triumphed, but effectively eliminated the search for other solutions.

Education. Another group that effectively eliminated the search for other "answers" were educational reformers. Unlike most reformers, they never had to convince their fellow countrymen that their basic premise was sound. Nearly everyone agreed with them that there was a need for better schools and a well-educated citizenry. Romantic writers might thrill their readers with stories about untutored backwoodsmen, but most parents eagerly sought good schools for their children. Indeed, optimists claimed that education was the answer to nine tenths of the world's problems.

Still, there were vital issues at stake. Who would run the schools? Who would pay for them? And what would schools teach besides the basic "three R's"? Should schools be regarded as "levelling institutions" seeking to reduce the gulf between rich and poor? Or should they be seen primarily as "a powerful check on vice"? Should schools inculcate patriotism? Protestantism? Virtues such as thrift, hard work, respect for property?

Educators were particularly concerned about the poor. Noah Webster, for example, expressed alarm in 1819 about the prospect of the lower classes, those "miserable victims of ignorance and vice," voting in Massachusetts. Only moral and industrious men of property, he told the governor, could be trusted with the franchise. The rest had to be elevated through early instruction and discipline. That, moreover, was "the most efficacious mode of preventing crimes." Webster made his contribution to render the poor harmless through his famous "Blue-Backed Speller," which sold over 20 million copies between 1782 and 1847, and which was used in virtually every schoolroom in America. The Speller taught such virtues as industry, thrift, sobriety, honesty, and piety. And it also taught submissiveness to authority.

Sentiments like Webster's, which became commonplace by the 1820s, soon gained additional steam when boatloads of Irish Catholics began descending upon Boston, New York, Philadelphia, and other port cities. American Protestants, rich and poor alike, were certain that Rome had little respect—if not downright hostility—toward democracy and the republican form of government. And many were eager to believe the worst. Symptomatic was the fantastic reception given by the reading public to the *Awful Disclosures of the Hotel Dieu Nunnery of Montreal*, which first appeared in bookstalls in early 1836. Maria Monk, allegedly an ex-nun, had dictated this wild yarn to Theodore Dwight, the great-grandson of the eminent New England minister Jonathan Edwards, and two Protestant clergymen had edited it for a New York publishing house. The Montreal convent, so Maria said, was a hotbed of sin and debauchery and murder, where priests forced nuns to engage in weird sex acts, and where priestly offspring were strangled and dumped in a quicklime pit in the basement. Eventually pregnant herself, said Maria, she fled to save her child from certain death. *Awful Disclosures* became an immediate best-seller; and even though Maria was discredited time and again, eventually arrested for picking pockets in a New York whorehouse, and died in jail, the book continued to sell—surpassing the 300,000 mark by the Civil War.

Protestants thus watched with horror as the Catholic church, thanks largely to Irish immigration, mushroomed from five tiny dioceses in 1815 to sixteen large dioceses, with some seven hundred churches, by the 1840s. Scores of Protestants, led by the likes of the Reverend Lyman Beecher and the famous inventor Samuel F. B. Morse, quickly saw a new reason for expanding the Protestant school system. It would not only help civilize street urchins, but also overcome the heresies of the Catholic church. Indeed, where Irish settled, the "two birds—one stone" theory clearly applied. Every child, and particularly every immigrant child, must come under the sound teachings of Protestant schoolmasters, as well as the King James Bible, which was read daily at public schools.

The Catholic hierarchy, of course, wanted no part of this scheme. Moreover, they were often as belligerent and intolerant as their Protestant adversaries. Meeting at Baltimore in 1829, the first Provincial Council of Catholicity in America warned the faithful against "corrupt translations of the Bible," meaning of course the King James version, and urged parents to establish parochial schools to protect the souls of their children. And in New York, Bishop John Hughes thrived on controversy. Involved in a continuous war of words, he tore into Protestant doctrine and lashed the King James version as "the devil's work." And in a sermon at St. Patrick's Cathedral, he announced that the Church's goal was to destroy Protestantism in America:

> Everybody should know that we have for our mission to convert the world—including the inhabitants of the United States—the people of the cities, and the people of the country, the officers of the navy and the marines, commanders of the army, the Legislatures, the Senate, the Cabinet, the President, and all!

It was against this contentious background that city fathers and educators tried to find a peaceful, orderly way to elevate the masses. There were several schools of thought on how this might be done. One was the New York system. Since 1805 an unpaid, self-perpetuating board of first citizens, known first as the Free School Society and later as the Public School Society, had voluntarily run schools for the city's pauper children. They were strictly upper-class volunteers and not accountable to the people. Nevertheless, they acquired control of state funds and distributed this money to city schools. Their goal was to civilize the poor as cheaply as possible. And with this in mind, they had introduced in 1806 a system of instruction devised by an English schoolmaster named Lancaster. Under Lancaster's system, the teacher instructed older children, who in turn repeated the lesson to younger ones. Thus, said Lancaster, one teacher "from fourteen to eighteen years of age" could run "a school containing from 200 to 1,000 scholars."

The cost of Lancaster's system appealed to penny-pinching politicians everywhere, and soon Boston, Philadelphia, Baltimore, New Haven, and other cities followed the New York example. Yet, in the end, both the Lancastrian method and the paternalism of the Public School Society were rejected. Artisans denounced the Public School Society, and its counterparts elsewhere, for establishing cheap schools to which no self-respecting workingman would send his children. They wanted good, tax-supported schools to which even merchants would be willing to send their children. Simultaneously, teachers saw the Lancastrian

An anti-Catholic political party, "Native Americans," battle the militiamen in Philadelphia. In a series of Nativist-provoked riots 24 persons were killed and two famous Catholic churches were burned. *Library of Congress*

method as a threat to their calling, while democrats clamored against the Public School Society because it was not answerable to the people. Finally, Bishop Hughes raised a storm in 1840 when he challenged the upper-class and anti-Catholic bias of the Society and demanded funds for Catholic schools. That led to a bitter political fight that reverberated throughout the Northeast.

What were the alternatives to upper-class paternalism? One was the district system which prevailed in rural New York and New England. Under this system, each community ran its own school, hired its own teachers, chose its own books, determined its own curriculum, and so on. Supporters hailed it as the epitome of democracy and argued that variety would inspire competition, new ideas, and in the end produce better schools than a uniform system could ever produce. New York's Secretary of State, John C. Spencer, suggested the district system as the solution to New York City's troubles. That meant, of course, that Catholic wards could hire Catholic teachers, use Catholic books, while Protestant wards could stick with Protestant texts and teachers. It also meant that in workingmen's wards, the working class would be controlling the educational system. Upper-class reformers objected to this feature, while Protestants objected vehemently to publicly supported Catholic schools. Spencer's plan was thus rejected.

Another alternative to upper-class paternalism was a uniform system of schools run by a centralized public bureaucracy. It was the eventual winner, and the great names in the "educational revival" such as Horace Mann and Henry

Barnard supported it enthusiastically. These men, by and large, had gone to the celebrated district schools of New England. Outsiders might think these schools praiseworthy, but Mann and others knew better. The districts were usually poor, the schools run-down, and the teachers were usually the cheapest the town could find. Mann had a teacher who was an alcoholic, and his school was never open more than eight or ten weeks a year. Hating his childhood, once Mann became secretary of Massachusetts Board of Education in 1837, he fought vigorously to put down local districts, to extend the school year to six months, to modify school curriculum, to establish normal schools for training teachers, and generally to bring schools under the control of a central board.

But the desire for better schools was not the only thing that motivated the great figures in the educational revival. They, too, saw schools as weapons against urban poverty, crime, and immorality. How could the poor be elevated? How could they be taught good habits? By letting working-class parents govern their children's schools? Absolutely not, said Henry Barnard:

> No one at all familiar with the deficient household arrangements and deranged machinery of domestic life, of the extreme poor, and ignorant, to say nothing of the intemperate—of the examples of rude manners, impure and profane language, and all the vicious habits of low bred idleness, which abound in certain sections of all populous districts—can doubt, that it is better for children to be removed as early and as long as possible from such scenes and examples.

Schools, then, had to be run by the "better" sort. Since men in power agreed fully, schoolmen such as Barnard and Mann generally got their way. Attendance became compulsory, schools more or less uniform, teacher training universal and overall supervision came into the hands of superintendents of schools and boards of education. The result was the modern public school system we have today.

"Troublemakers" and "Crackpots"

Supporters of poorhouses, asylums, penitentiaries, and schools were clearly no threat to men of power. Their aim was to bring order, system, work, and production to a new social order. They wanted to create a middle-class nation, to strengthen the dominant social order, rather than to shake it up. Indeed, they were often men of power—or had the backing of men of power. And, with such clout, they scored striking victories, which in turn enhanced their reputations as "humanitarians."

But there were other reformers who paid little attention to the values of polite society, stepped on the toes of the rich as well as the poor, and often challenged or usurped the leadership role of old elites. They have often been lumped together in American histories with Horace Mann, Dorothea Dix, and other genteel reformers in one great potpourri called the "reform impulse." But they fared less well in their own lifetimes. Men of power often ridiculed them, sometimes abused them—and in the case of the abolitionists even led mobs against them. From the standpoint of the governing elites, then, there were clearly "responsible" reformers and radical ones. Let us turn now to the so-called "crackpots" and "troublemakers."

Problems of Causation. The Northeast after 1815 became a hotbed of radical reform and religious ferment. In contrast to the South, where men and women could go for weeks without hearing the cry of reform, the din of opinion and debate never ceased in parts of New England, upstate New York, and the Ohio Valley. Western New York became the scene of so many revivalists, reformers, enthusiasts, and eccentrics that some people called it the "infected district," while others insisted that "the fires of the spirit," just like a forest fire, burned over the district. Dubbed the Burned-Over District by historians, it may have had more reformers than all the slaveholding states combined. Vermont, too, was a hotbed of reform.

How come? That is an old question, and one that has never been answered to anyone's complete satisfaction. Some argue that both Yankees who moved west and Yankees who remained in New England were peculiarly touched by the reform impulse. Not every reformer, of course, was a New Englander, and most New Englanders were certainly not reformers. Indeed, many spent much of their lives fighting reformers. But with relative ease, historians can rattle off the names of scores of Yankee reformers, while they often have some difficulty coming up with an impressive list of Pennsylvania reformers, or Kentucky reformers, or Virginia reformers. Other historians note that a surprisingly large number of English immigrants were also touched by the reform impulse, and a good case can be made that some American movements were really English imports.

But why should Yankees and Englishmen be especially touched by the reform impulse? Again, there is an answer of sorts. Both people, so the leading argument goes, were stirred by the Great Revival, which began in the 1790s as vigorous counter-offensive against moral and spiritual laxity, watered down Christianity, and "French Revolutionary atheism." Really a series of religious revivals, the Great Revival swept Protestant churches on both sides of the Atlantic, kept the United States in a state of religious ferment for forty years, and fired up many men and even more women to do battle against the sins of the world.

Moreover, by the 1820s, Charles Grandison Finney of New York and other leading evangelists preached perfectionism, an idea that came to characterize much of reform thinking. Unlike the oldtime Calvinist minister, who believed strongly in man's inherent depravity, the perfectionists taught that God was much closer to the heart of man than earlier ministers believed, and that God had given man the ability to do right. If man had the ability to perfect himself, then it followed that he ought to do so, and that he ought to work zealously to perfect his society also.

Yet, even if the vast majority of abolitionists and other reformers drew heavily on the ideas and inspiration of the Great Revival, they clearly had no monopoly on evangelical Protestantism. There were thousands of Americans—probably several hundred thousands or more—who never supported a reform movement but drew spiritual and intellectual nourishment from the revivalists. Why did only a minority become reformers? No one knows for certain. But the available evidence indicates that reformers, by and large, came from the more mobile groups in northeastern society. Because their own way of life was changing drastically, perhaps they were prepared to look at their society closely, to stop taking existing social conditions for granted, to think in terms of social improvement, to demand new rules and a new social order.

Methods and goals. What kind of society were the reformers after? They have often been pictured as rampant individualists who wanted to throw off the shackles of the existing social order. But that popular explanation makes little sense. For most reformers rebelled against established institutions, not because they were too constraining, but because they were too permissive. And most reformers belonged to organizations that put a premium upon concerted action, the power of numbers, rather than individual initiative. Such organizations wanted to build up massive followings, which through pressure-group tactics would force others into line. Thus Ralph Waldo Emerson, the era's leading spokesman for individualism, insisted that reform organizations were really at odds with individualism, rather than in league with it.

For a better understanding, let us look at a few specific examples, beginning with a small, but somewhat typical reform movement that grew out of the larger concern for social depravity in the nation's cities. Among those who worried about "the depraved at home" was a small group called the Association of Gentlemen, led by Arthur and Lewis Tappan, two of the most active reformers of the age. Mainly from the Connecticut Valley, these men came to New York City in their youth, succeeded in banking and merchandizing, and joined the ranks of the newly rich. Exceptionally pious, they disliked New York's high society, especially the high life of the old Knickerbocker families, and they had little respect for the city's timid church leaders. They supported the evangelist Charles Grandison Finney, and they were involved in dozens of reforms. One was the Magdalen Society, an effort to reform the city's prostitutes, which was modeled after a similar project in London. The Magdalen Society ran a boardinghouse for whores in the heart of the city's red-light district. There, hopefully, the fallen would mend their ways after a regimen of daily Bible readings, hymn-sings, regular meals, and hope for decent employment. In charge was a young zealot, John McDowall, a recent graduate of Princeton Seminary.

McDowall raised a storm in 1831 when he issued a report on prostitution in New York. There were, according to this report, some 10,000 whores in a city of 200,000, who were not only catering to sailors and roughnecks but also to the urban elite. The city fathers were furious. A gigantic public meeting was held to denounce the Magdalen Society, and there was much talk of burning Arthur Tappan's house. In response, Tappan and others gave up the project. But a small group of women, all members of an evangelistic Presbyterian church, refused to yield. In 1834 they formed the New York Female Reform Society and hired McDowall and two other young men as missionaries to help them reform the city's whores, and to help them convert all males to moral purity, with special attention given to adulterous husbands.

So began one of the period's more militant women's movements. With incredible fanfare, McDowall and others would burst into brothels late Saturday evening or early on the Sabbath, startle the inhabitants with Bible-readings and hymns, and hold the hands of the fallen while praying for their souls. Such tactics failed to convert many lost souls, but it certainly disrupted trade and generated much publicity. The Society also published a newspaper, *The Advocate of Moral Reform*, which among other things published the names of suspected whoremongers. That, too, created a bit of a stir. With the hard work of male and female missionaries, who carried the word throughout rural New England and New York, the Society itself grew rapidly so that by 1837 the weekly *Advocate* had some 16,000 subscribers, and by 1839 the Society had 445 auxiliaries. The expanded organization was reorganized and called the American Female Reform Society. Rural members contributed the names of local lechers, and together urban and rural women petitioned state legislatures for laws to make seduction a criminal offense. After many petitions and much lobbying, the New York legislature finally passed the desired legislation in 1848.

What did such women accomplish? Probably their main contribution was to the growing conviction that in moral matters men were stunted creatures. In answer to the basic question—why did women become whores?—they essentially put the blame on lecherous men. Women, they assumed, felt little sexual desire and therefore they did not become prostitutes out of carnal desire. Instead, women joined the ranks of the fallen because some "beast" took advantage of their trusting and loving nature, "and ruined them." Yet what did society do? It ostracized fallen women, while it failed to punish their seducers. Nothing was worse than this double standard. Condemn fallen women, said the Moral Reform Society. "But let not the most guilty of the two—the deliberate destroyer of innocence—be afforded even an 'apron of fig leaves' to conceal the blackness of his crimes."

Who should lead the battle against male licentiousness? Mothers, of course! Mothers—not fathers—should have full control of the religious and moral upbringing of sons. For women had been given a moral nature that was much superior to man's. Men might dominate economic and political matters, but women should be paramount in morals and religion. They had a duty not only to keep the home clean, but also to purify the male world. Militant reformers thus joined the far-reaching trend of putting women—and especially mothers—on a pedestal.

Temperance. Women also played a key role in the largest crusade of the period—the massive campaign against Demon Rum. Beginning as a protest against drunkenness, it spread after the War of 1812 with the rising missionary zeal of Protestant churches. Lyman Beecher and scores of other Protestant ministers indicted heavy drinking not only as a barrier to triumphant Christian living, but also as a potential cause of a lower-class rebellion. Drunken workingmen, like drunken Indians, were dangerous, and thus their drinking habits had to be controlled.

Conservatives, it seems, had ample reason to be concerned. Heavy drinking was evidently on the upswing in the early nineteenth century. Estimates showed that the average citizen consumed 2.5 gallons of alcohol in 1792; 4.5 gallons in 1810; and 7.5 gallons by 1823. A small city like Albany, with only eight thousand adults in the vicinity, reported four thousand "tipplers" and five hundred "habitual drunks." In 1818 New York City boasted one liquor dealer for every one hundred inhabitants.

Yet, if conservatives hoped to use temperance to impose discipline on the masses, they quickly lost control of the movement. It was one thing to say that drunken workingmen did sloppy work, or excessive drinking led to disorder. It was quite another to say that *any* man who touched a drop was a sinner, or that an occasional after-dinner drink was ample grounds for excommunication! In 1825 many temperance advocates talked only in terms of moderation. But many more clearly wanted to go further. They asked signers of the temperance pledge to put a letter "T" next to their names if they meant to abstain completely from ardent spirits. And within the next decade, thousands of local temperance societies battled over the issue of total abstinence. The "teetotalers," who were primarily women and younger members, usually won.

But victory seldom ended the debate. Invariably a new battle would emerge over how far to carry the ban. Older advocates had no objection to beer or wine. After all, Christ Himself had turned water into wine at the wedding at Cana, and wine was clearly part of the Last Supper! Indeed, how could Christians hold communion without wine? But radicals claimed that Christ sanctioned only pure wine, which was allegedly impossible to get, while others soon accepted the teachings of Dr. Eliphalet Nott that Christ must have used unfermented grape juice. "How could this be?" asked conservatives. "Obviously the Master knew the difference between wine and grape juice!" Undaunted, the radicals plowed on, and after several stormy sessions they finally carried the national convention at Saratoga Springs in 1836 for total abstinence.

Simultaneously, the old argument that a man had to learn self-discipline—that is, when to quit—gave way to the "first fatal mistake" argument. "The moderate drinker of today is the drunkard of tomorrow." "From small drams grow great appetites."

> "'Tis but a drop," the father said,
> And gave it to his son;
> But little did he think a work
> Of death was then begun.
> The "drop" that lured him, when the babe
> Scarce lisped his father's name,
> Planted a fatal appetite,
> Deep in his infant frame.

Indeed, according to temperance propaganda, the result could be disastrous. There was the D.T.'s which tormented the drunkard's waking hours, with sensations of falling, falling, falling into some terrible abyss, with millions of spiders crawling over all his body. Then there was trouble—indeed endless trouble. Of 690 children imprisoned for crime in New York City, more that 400 came from drunken families. Of 781 maniacs in asylums, 392 were victims of strong drink. Of 647 prisoners at the Auburn State penitentiary, 467 were addicted to strong drink, and 346 were drunk at the time they committed their last crime. Statistic followed statistic. Then there were bizarre stories about drunks catching on fire. According to the *New York Times,* January 9, 1836, a student of medicine bled a common drunkard at Berwick, Maine. "A bowl containing this blood was handed to one of the spectators who lighted a match, and on bringing it into contact with the contents of the bowl, a conflagration ensued, burning with a blue flame for a space of twenty-five or thirty minutes."

The temperance crusade not only became more radical in dogma as it grew, but also more radical in methods. Older temperance advocates had always shown the utmost respect for the existing status system. They were not only mild in their criticism of excesses, but also relied mostly on pastors and community leaders to get their message across. They went through—and not around—men of power. The radicals paid little attention to such proprieties. They built massive pressure groups—over five thousand local auxiliaries by 1834—and used the power of numbers to whip the recalcitrant into line. And, along with pastors, they soon came to rely on women and children to get their message across. They horrified thousands by letting women such as Lucretia Mott, Elizabeth Cady Stanton, and Abby Kelley take the lecture platform on an equality with men. They shocked others by forming hundreds of clubs for children, especially those of the "Cold Water Army," which created a further sensation by parading through streets singing temperance songs.

Finally, the last straw for many conservatives came when the temperance movement turned to reformed drunks for its primary spokesmen. In 1840, after listening to an evangelist, six hard-drinking Baltimore artisans took the pledge and formed a society called the Washingtonians, which soon began holding "experience meetings" across the nation. Former drunks would rise, relate the horrors of dreadful debauchery, and conclude joyously on how the Pledge had pulled them out of the gutter. Generally speaking, the Washingtonians and the old church societies never felt comfortable with one another, and the Washingtonians often went their own way. But out of the new movement came a mass of orators, including John W. Hawkins and John Bartholomew Gough, two of the most popular spellbinders of the age.

The temperance crusade, then, became more radical in both dogma and methods as it grew. And both its dogma and its methods created enemies. Liquor interests of course were always hostile. And so were the millions who liked drinking—or hated "blue-noses." But even clergymen took a dislike to temperance advocates. They saw temperance lecturers as rivals—indeed as threats to their moral leadership—and they complained bitterly about the meddling of "teetotalers" in church affairs and the encroachments of women on male prerogatives. In the 1830s the Dutch Reformed Church of Breakabeen, New York, forbade church members from having anything to do with temperance, while Primitive Baptist churches in Tennessee even excommunicated members who joined temperance societies. The Episcopal Bishop of Vermont, John Henry Hopkins, never tired of denouncing the movement. Calvin Colton, an Episcopalian journalist, accused temperance leaders of being "Protestant Jesuits" who were trying to usurp for themselves the influence of Protestant churches, while destroying the liberties of the American people. At the same time, Catholics accused temperance advocates of being Protestant bigots who were merely using temperance as an excuse to attack whiskey-drinking Irish Catholics and beer-loving German Catholics. Indeed, in some communities temperance and anti-Catholicism clearly went hand in hand.

Nevertheless, women lecturers, children's parades, "experience meetings," and sensational propaganda kept interest in temperance at a fever pitch. By the late 1830s prohibitionists demanded laws restricting the sale and use of intoxicants. Hoping to duck the issue, statehouse politicians from Rhode Island to Iowa passed "local option laws" in the 1840s, thus dumping responsibility on local governments. But when Maine passed statewide prohibition in 1851, the demand for "Maine laws" swept across the North, left politicians reeling in its wake, and ended with eight states having prohibition of one sort or another by 1856.

Yet, while temperance shook up many northern communities, the crusade against Demon Rum failed to shake the nation as a whole. That honor would fall to the northern abolitionists, who, using the same methods as temperance advocates, proclaimed in the early 1830s that slavery was "SIN," the South a "brothel," and the only remedy was "IMMEDIATE ABOLITION." The crusade against slavery, as we shall see later, not only touched the nation's sorepoint, but also brought out the forces of repression in mass.

The Search for Utopia

Nothing in the turbulent North reveals the sense of social dislocation more clearly than the hundreds of utopian communities that sprang up after the War of 1812. Some were wholly secular, but most were religious. And, as a rule, the religious ones were far more durable: over half lasted over twenty-five years, and a few continued well into the twentieth century. The secular communities, by contrast, seldom lasted more than a year or two.

Nevertheless both types had much in common. Both rejected major features of the dominant social order—particularly cutthroat competition, the disparity between rich and poor, private property, orthodox religion, and marriage. Both saw themselves as harbingers of a new era—as proving grounds for alternative economic, social, and religious systems. Almost all were compact communistic villages where members worked and ate together, and owned all material things in common. Frequently, ordinary members left one community to join another which seemed, in some respects, to be an exact opposite. And utopian leaders, who on the surface seemed worlds apart, often shared a sense of comraderie, followed one another's progress, and sometimes stole one another's ideas.

A common model for many utopians, in fact, was an unusual and small group called the Shakers. It is difficult to think of a more unlikely pace-setter. Shakerism began in the heart of industrial England around 1760. Ann Lee, the founder, was a Manchester factory girl. As she grew older, she came to be deeply impressed with "the great depravity of human nature . . . and especially the impure nature of sexual coition." She had four children who died in infancy or early childhood. She joined a radical religious sect, which preached that the second coming of Christ was the only answer to the world's miseries, and which was best known for a ritualistic dance where worship was expressed by shaking the body. In time, Ann Lee claimed to be the female equivalent of Christ, the embodiment of the second coming. The answer to the world's problems was thus here in the flesh. And while men and women had to live together, declared Mother Ann, celibacy was the key to a perfect life. Despite propinquity, her followers were to lead a celibate life.

To escape persecution in industrial England, Mother Ann and eight followers came to America in 1774. Although their religious views, particularly the interdiction of marriage and sexual intercourse, alienated many people, the Shakers began attracting adherents in the 1780s, and by the 1830s they had nineteen villages and some six thousand believers. Much more important than numbers, however, was the phenomenal success of Shaker communities. Even those who despised the religious teachings of Shakerism admired the harmony, craftsmanship, and prosperity of Shaker villages. From a background of poverty and persecution, somehow the Shakers had created communities that were more peaceful and more productive than those of the outside world. Their farms were lush. Their seeds, fruits, plants, grain, cattle, and manufactured goods had a reputation for quality. Their furniture was in great demand for being sturdy and practical—and beautiful in its simplicity—and in time became collectors' items which now sell for a small fortune.

Most important, their people obviously enjoyed a higher standard of living than ordinary people like themselves did in the outside world. They ate better, lived in cleaner surroundings, and had no fear of poverty. In Shaker society, noted an English critic, there was no fear of poverty "because they have no poor, no needy, no widows, no abandoned orphans." The Shakers proved, in short, that "utopianism paid rich dividends."

Shaker villages put a premium upon efficiency, simplicity, and order. Housing, furniture, and clothing were always simple, uniform, and functional. And people lived by the clock. "Everything they do," noted one observer, "is characterized by neatness, order and perfection." The Shakers had no policemen, no judges, no lawyers, no paid priests, no soldiers, no jails. But they had plenty of discipline. Every member of the community was essentially a policeman. Shakers had a strict code of behavior—called the Millenial Laws—which was enforced by community pressure or, as they liked to put it, by "a gentle admonition." The rules covered virtually everything. It was "contrary to order," for example, "to give the cooks any directions"; "for a brother to pass a sister on the stairs"; "to have right and left shoes"; "to cut hair, pare nails, wash feet, clean shoes, or shave on the Sabbath"; "to wear hats above the height given by the Elders"; "to kneel with the left knee first"; "to put the left foot on the stairs first when ascending"; "to spit out of the window"; "to kick a beast"; "to play with dogs and cats";"to give nicknames. " The basic rule, of course, was conform or leave in peace

Secular utopians had only a casual interest in Shaker rules. What interested them was the Shakers' ability to make utopianism work. The Shakers, so it was commonly argued, proved beyond doubt that communism, "or life and work in a community where all goods are held in common," could actually work. Thus, even atheists and agnostics looked to the Shakers for inspiration. One of the first to do so was Robert Owen, an extremely successful British industrialist, who was also a benevolent despot and utopian socialist.

Unlike most tycoons of his generation, Owen did not claim that his wealth was the result of his own genius and personal worth. He knew that it was largely the result of new technology and greater productivity. And, since industrial wealth was largely a social product, he maintained that its benefits should extend to the whole community, rather than just enrich a few capitalists. He was full of schemes for the social betterment of the working class, which in his judgment was held down not only by squalid poverty but also by ignorance and by lack of character. He gained esteem worldwide as social benefactor when he bought out his partners at New Lanark Mills, Scotland. He gradually transformed the wretched factory town into a model community by shortening working hours, establishing schools, providing relief for the aged and poor, enforcing cleanliness and "good" moral standards, and even hiring fiddlers and dancing-masters so that his workers would become devotees of music and social dancing. As a social planner of some standing, once Owen learned of the Shakers in 1817, he was certain that he could do better. If such "simple" and "superstitious" people could accomplish so much, he reasoned, a "rational" man was bound to be a smashing success.

His chance came in 1825. But, unlike the Shakers, he did not start from scratch. He bought out a ready-made colony of thirty thousand acres at Harmony, Indiana, from the Rappites, a German pietist community. Renamed New Harmony, it attracted an incredible amount of fanfare. With even more publicity, Owen himself arrived in the United States. He spoke widely and to considerable acclaim, even lecturing Congress and President Monroe on the merits of utopian socialism. The trouble with the Old Order, said Owen, was mainly private property, irrational religion, and marriage. The New Order would be created gradually, by "bringing up our children" in a different environment and by instilling different habits, and by doing away with money transactions.

In the next two years, about a dozen Owenite communities sprang up only to fail quickly. Owen's New Harmony was overwhelmed by some nine hundred citizens, who hoped, in Owen's words, to shed their old garments of individualism, selfishness, and disharmony, and learn to live in a cooperative community. But, unfortunately, they fought bitterly, and Owen's great vision of a cooperative community turned out to be a spectacular failure. Heartbroken, Owen returned to England, while his followers went in several directions. Fanny Wright, a strong-minded English woman, became a notorious spokesman for women's rights, free inquiry in religion, free love, birth control, and a system which she called "National, Rational, Republican Education, Free for All at the Expense of All, Conducted under the Guardianship of the State, apart from the Contaminating Influence of Parents." On the other hand, Frederick Evans, along with other Owenites, joined the Shakers, where Evans carved out a prominent niche for himself in the long history of the society.

Still another utopian who paid close attention to Shakerism, as well as other utopian movements, was John Humphrey Noyes, a well-educated Yankee, who like the evangelist Finney gave up the law for the ministry. While studying theology at Yale, Noyes came under the influence of a "Finney Revival" and with a group of revivalists organized a free church, where he first propounded his doctrine of "perfectionism." After announcing that he had already attained sinlessness in this life, he was booted out of Yale, dismissed from the free church, and stripped of his license to preach. He then established a Bible School at Putney, Vermont, in 1836. Shortly thereafter, he shocked people with such statements as "when the will of God is done on earth as it is in heaven there will be no marriage," and my wife "is yours, she is Christ's, and in him she is the bride of all saints."

What did Noyes mean? That became a source of controversy, and soon his followers were off in half a dozen different directions. In response, Noyes and a select few decided organization and discipline were necessary. Taking the role of God's anointed one, Noyes demanded complete submission and freely criticized the failings of each of his followers. No one escaped: Noyes even criticized his mother for failing to obey and trying to run the family. In time, mutual criticism became the means of imposing discipline, and a close-knit community soon formed. In 1846, it began to experiment with a program of "complex" marriages, which was based on the idea that all members were married to all others. This practice soon led to Noyes' arrest. He jumped bail and with his followers founded a new community at Oneida, New York, in 1848.

The Oneida experiment lasted about thirty years. And, like the Shaker communities, it was a financial success. By 1870, it had some 200 members, who jointly owned 664 acres of choice land as well as manufacturing plants worth well over $200,000. It was always work oriented and well managed. At first it produced a superior animal trap which was designed by a famous trapper, who became one of the community's early converts. Later, it produced tableware and other products. And, since it became the mainstay in the local economy, it gained support among the voices that counted in its many battles against outside authorities. Eventually, like many autocrats, Noyes lost control in his old age, and the community voted to transform itself into a business corporation, which, as Oneida Silver, still prospers by selling silverware—ironically—to June brides.

Outside observers generally regarded the Oneida perfectionists and the Shakers as exact opposites, since the Shakers were best known for a sexless existence, and the Perfectionists for "free love." Oddly enough, Noyes and other close observers insisted that the two communities had much in common. They both claimed to be inspired by the Bible. They both practiced Bible communism. They both rejected marriage as practiced in established Christian churches. And they both demanded discipline, especially in sexual matters. The Oneida Perfectionists, despite their reputation for "free love," believed strongly in birth control. Noyes' own wife had borne four stillborn children, and Noyes refused to accept the common nineteenth-century notion that this was simply woman's lot in life. He insisted that the community practice "male continence," which simply meant that a man must avoid having an orgasm during sexual intercourse. Explained Noyes:

> Now we insist that this whole process, up to the very moment of emission, is *voluntary,* entirely under the control of the moral faculty, and *can be stopped at any point.* In other words, the *presence* and the *motions* can be continued or stopped at will, and it is only the final *crisis* of emission that is automatic and uncontrollable. . . . If you say that this is impossible, I answer that I *know* it is possible—nay, that it is easy.

But it obviously took self-discipline, and the Oneida community had little trouble imposing the necessary restraint. Very few children were accidentally conceived in the community's thirty year history.

Discipline and order were the hallmarks of all successful utopian communities. The common notion that people joined utopian communities for "freedom" is misleading. They may have joined to be free from the worries of the outside world. But they were sadly misled if they thought they would be able to do as they pleased. Utopian communities clearly imposed far more restraints on their members than did the outside world. We must always remember that American governments in the nineteenth century did very little governing, and the regimentation that exists in modern society simply did not exist. Moreover, forces such as migration westward, immigration, and industrialization were destroying the old New England villages which had once exercised tight social controls. The only adults who lived under many restraints were slaves, seamen, soldiers, and prisoners. The rest lived in a world where it was virtually impossible to stop men and women from spitting on the floor, getting drunk, rioting in the streets, or having too many children. Yet all these things were effectively controlled in utopian villages. And perhaps that is why many Northerners were attracted to them.

SUGGESTED READINGS

The observations of foreign travelers are particularly valuable on northern social life in the antebellum period. Most helpful are Alexis de Tocqueville, *Democracy in America** (1835–1840); Francis Grund, *Aristocracy in America* (1839); Michael Chevalier, *Society,*

*Available in a paperback edition.

Manners, and Politics in the United States (1836); Francis Trollope, *Domestic Manners of the Americans** (1832); and Harriet Martineau, *Society in America* (1837). American literature is also valuable for recreating the atmosphere of the times, especially James Fenimore Cooper's *Home as Found** (1836), Harriet Beecher Stowe's *Uncle Tom's Cabin** (1852), and Herman Melville's *Confidence Man** (1856).

Although superceded by later scholarship, Robert Spiller, et al., eds., *The Literary History of the United States* (8 vols., 1948) provides a wealth of information on the world of Emerson. For the artist, see Neil Harris, *The Artist in American Society* (1966). For the writer, see Perry Miller, *The Raven and the Whale* (1956). The business aspects of the world in which Emerson worked are ably analyzed in William Charvat, *Literary Publishing in America, 1790–1850* (1969).

The old idea that there were no rigid class lines in the North has been demolished by recent research. For an overall perspective of the class structure, see Edward Pessen, *Riches, Class, and Power Before the Civil War* (1973); Robert Gallman, "Trends in the Size and Distribution of Wealth in the Nineteenth Century," in Lee Soltow, ed., *Six Papers on the Size Distribution of Wealth and Income* (1969); and Ralph Andreano, "Trends and Variations in Economic Welfare Before the Civil War," in Andreano, ed., *New Views on American Economic Development* (1965). For the rich, see Douglas Miller, *Jacksonian Aristocracy* (1967); Robert Lamb, "The Entrepreneur and the Community," in William Miller, ed., *Men in Business* (1962); and Ronald Story, "Harvard and the Boston Brahmins," *Journal of Social History*, Vol. 8 (1975). For the have-nots, perhaps the best introduction is in Vol. 15 of *Labor History* (1974), which is entitled "Nineteenth Century Working Class Culture." Also good are the articles in Allen F. Davis and Mark H. Haller, eds., *The Peoples of Philadelphia: A History of Ethnic Groups and Lower-Class Life, 1790–1940** (1973). See also Charles E. Rosenberg, *The Cholera Years: The United States in 1832, 1849, and 1866** (1962); Norman Ware, *The Industrial Worker** (1924); and Leon F. Litwack, *North of Slavery: The Negro in the Free States, 1790–1860** (1961).

There are scores of books on antebellum reform. A good introduction is Alice Felt Tyler, *Freedom's Ferment** (1944). More analytic are Whitney Cross, *The Burned-Over District** (1950); David Ludlum, *Social Ferment in Vermont* (1939); Frank Thistlethwaite, *America and the Atlantic Community** (1959); and David Brion Davis, ed., *Ante-Bellum Reform** (1967). On the public school movement, major studies are Jonathan Messerli, *Horace Mann* (1972); Michael Katz, *The Irony of Early School Reform* (1968); and Stanley Schultz, *The Culture Factory* (1973). On penal and asylum reform, see Harold Schwartz, *Samuel Gridley Howe: Social Reformer, 1801–1876* (1956) and David Rothman, *The Discovery of the Asylum* (1971). On temperance, nothing compares with the old study by John A. Krout, *The Origins of Prohibition* (1925).

Two outstanding surveys of utopian ferment are Arthur Bestor, *Backwoods Utopias* (1950) and Mark Holloway, *Heavens on Earth* (1951). Excellent first-hand accounts are John Humphrey Noyes, *The History of American Socialisms* (1870) and Charles Nordhoff, *Communistic Societies of the United States* (1875). Good on individual communities are Maren Carden, *Oneida: Utopian Community to Modern Corporation** (1971) and Edward Deming Andrews, *The People Called Shakers** (1953).

CHAPTER SIX

JACKSONIAN DEMOCRACY

O F THE VARIOUS FORCES that arose after the War of 1812 to shape the destiny of the nation, none has commanded more attention than the advent of democracy. Historians almost universally use the expression "Jacksonian Democracy," and a few minutes' browsing in almost any library will reveal scores of books with chapters entitled "Jacksonian Democracy."

But what does it mean? For Frederick Jackson Turner and his followers, it meant the triumph of western egalitarianism over eastern conservatism. Democracy, according to Turner, was the result of the frontier's continuous impact on American society, and with the election of Jackson, the western democrat, the long process of democratization finally triumphed. Not so, argued Arthur Schlesinger, Jr., whose *Age of Jackson* won the Pulitzer prize in 1945 and set off a historical debate that waxed hot and heavy for twenty years. Democracy triumphed with the election of Jackson, but the democratic upsurge came more from the urban masses than Turner's frontier; it was linked closely with the eastern workingmen's "enduring struggle" against the privileged, class-conscious capitalist elite. Not so, said many of Schlesinger's critics. The basic struggle was not between noncapitalists and capitalists, but rather between one set of capitalists and another; "men on the make," rather than hard-fisted workingmen, rode to power on the shoulders of Old Hickory and democratic dogma. And so it goes: in one book, the typical democrats are the urban masses; in another, simple farming folk and restless pioneers; in another, expectant capitalists; and in still another, a motley assortment of all three.

The Politics of Being Democratic

To avoid hopeless confusion, the discerning student should recognize that from the beginning two distinct phenomena—the triumph of Andrew Jackson and the growth of democracy—have been linked together. Were they inseparable developments? Not necessarily! Historians have linked the two so often that it has become habit—and habit probably has kept the two phenomena together as much as anything else.

Jackson, it is true, differed from his predecessors. Savage in his hatreds, no one ever forgot his numerous duels, stabbings, and other frays:

> He's none of your old New England stock,
> Or your gentry-proud Virginians,
> But a regular Western fighting-cock
> With Tennessee opinions.

He was the first President from west of the Appalachians, and he was the first President since Washington who was not a college graduate. Born in a Carolina

Robert Cruikshank's drawing "The President's Levee, or All Creation Going to the White House."
Library of Congress

cabin and orphaned as a teenager, he became a rich Tennessee planter, acquired all the social graces of a southern gentleman, and lived in one of the finest mansions in America, the Hermitage. Yet he never completely shed his past. Like many plain citizens, he never came close to mastering spelling and on occasion could misspell the same word in two different ways in the same letter. More important, Jackson was undoubtedly the most forceful and dramatic political figure between the Battle of New Orleans and the Civil War, the period when democracy became dogma. His followers, moreover, shrewdly called themselves Democrats.

But such facts hardly provide solid ground for the common notion that the rise of Jackson and the advent of democracy went hand in hand. Actually, in his home state of Tennessee, Jackson was hardly the champion of the "common man." When the Panic of 1819 set class against class, he was clearly on the side of the well-to-do. He pushed his own debtors to the wall, sued 129 of them in one lawsuit, and protested vehemently against the state's "relief" program. In 1821, when General William Carroll ran for governor on a popular program of democratic economic reform, Old Hickory campaigned vigorously for Carroll's opponent, Colonel Edward Ward, who was generally regarded to be an "aristocrat," a rich, college-educated planter "who despised the poor." Carroll won a smashing victory, and became invincible in Tennessee politics as the people's candidate, putting through a program of tax revision, constitutional reform, educational and penal improvement. None of this had any effect at all on national politics: the democrats of Tennessee, along with the conservatives, joined the Jackson party almost to a man.

White Man's Democracy. Actually, the Jackson party as a whole developed in a political atmosphere where politicians of all stripes tried to outdo one another in proclaiming the virtue of white man's democracy. And it was strictly white man's democracy! There was no place in it for women family heads who once had the vote in New Jersey and lost it, and there was no place in it for black men who gradually lost the right to vote in many northern states, as well as in Maryland, Tennessee, and North Carolina. Yet, even with these limitations, it was radical by the world's standards, and white Americans were extremely self-conscious about being ahead—or out of step—when hordes of European travelers descended upon them to take a close look at the "the great experiment in popular government."

Advocates of white man's democracy suffered a smashing defeat in Jefferson's Virginia, ran into trouble where Federalist conservatism still lingered on, and railed constantly against the evil machinations of insidious aristocrats. But generally most politicians, rich and poor alike, sang the praises of the ordinary white man. In this atmosphere the future supporters of Jackson sometimes damned the aristocrats and celebrated the virtues of the common man with a bit more zeal than the supporters of Clay and Adams. At times, however, they lagged behind and suffered the consequences. For the democratic dogma came out of many streams and took some striking twists and turns.

The Case of New York. For a better understanding of the whole process, let us look at some of the twists and turns that enlivened New York politics. There was, first of all, a concerted drive after the War of 1812 to get rid of the state constitution of 1777. It had long been regarded as a backward and aristocratic document. Under it there were two classes of voters: the governor and state senators were elected by well-to-do townsmen and the farmers of the state, "free and independent lords of the soil," who were worth at least $250 in freehold estate; the assemblymen were chosen by freeholders who had land worth at least $50, and renters who paid $5 or more yearly. As a result, about 40 percent of the adult male population could vote for governor, and 70 percent for assemblymen. Also under this document, the governor and leading judges, sitting as the Council of Revision, had a veto power over all legislation and the judges could only be removed by impeachment. Finally, the governor and four senators, sitting as the Council of Appointment, controlled all kinds of local offices; they appointed officers of the militia, local judges, district attorneys, sheriffs, coroners, mayors, and so forth; altogether, they controlled fifteen thousand jobs. So power was concentrated in the hands of a few men who were completely beyond the control of ordinary citizens.

By 1815 the old constitution had few defenders, and the swarms of Yankees who had come into the state since the Revolution never tired of pointing out its defects. "Only drunken Dutchmen," so the Yankee saying went, "would consent to live under such tyranny." Then in 1818 Connecticut revised its constitution, and Yankee pressure for change became intense. At the same time, Martin Van Buren and his followers decided to jump on the bandwagon and use the popular demand for constitutional reform to rout Governor DeWitt Clinton and the Clintonians. They forced upon the reluctant governor and the Council of Revision legislation calling for revision of the state constitution.

When the constitutional convention met in 1821, Van Buren had little trouble with the conservatives, who were outnumbered by at least five to one. His problem was General Erastus Root and his radical followers, who were generally Yankee farmers—and not lawyers. They trusted only "the majesty of democracy." They wanted universal white manhood suffrage, "emancipation of the state from judicial thralldom," which included the elimination of some courts and legislative power to fire judges at will, plus an assortment of measures to curb the governor's power. Take away the governor's appointive power, strip him of his veto and pardoning powers, subject him to annual elections, and the people would be safe from tyranny. So said the radicals.

Van Buren preferred to think of the radicals as "Mad-caps . . . old democrats, who think nothing wise that is not violent and flatter themselves that they merit Knighthood by assailing everything that is memorable in old institutions." But the "Mad-caps" put the Van Burenites, who were known popularly as Bucktails, in the awkward position of opposing the more democratic proposals. The Bucktails went along with the majority in abolishing the old two-class system of voting, but they rejected universal suffrage as "cheapening the privilege" and pushed through a taxpaying qualification for voting. The convention voted unanimously to abolish the Council of Appointment, and a committee recommended that all but a handful of military officers should be elected by "the privates and officers of the militia," and that justices of the peace should be elected by townspeople. But the 2500 justices of the peace, along with their extensive courthouse connections, were the key to any system of political patronage. Power was at stake! So the Bucktails fought vigorously against popular election of these local magistrates, and the positions remained appointive.

"Mad-caps" and Bucktails marched shoulder to shoulder, however, on the question of race. Against the protests of conservatives, they pushed through a provision that disfranchised most of New York's thirty thousand free blacks. Previously, black men voted on equal terms with white; they too had to possess $50 worth of property or pay $5 yearly rent to vote for assemblymen. Under the new constitution, they had to possess a freehold estate worth at least $250. Van Buren, who was capable of devising an argument to support almost anything, maintained that this requirement would not close the door on Negro suffrage. It would instead encourage black men to become more provident! Another Bucktail leader, Samuel Young, was at least forthright: "Public sentiment demands it! . . . No white man will stand shoulder to shoulder with a negro in the train band [militia] or jury-room. He will not invite him to a seat at his table, nor in his pew in the church. And yet some say he must be put on a footing of equality in the right of voting. . . . Sir, he will not stand for it!"

Young's argument had wide support throughout the North. Connecticut, which served as a model for many new delegates, stripped blacks of their right to vote in 1818; New Jersey followed suit in 1820; Pennsylvania in 1838. Black men could vote in nine northern states in 1815; only five by 1840. By the latter date, 93 percent of black Northerners lived in states where they were legally barred from voting. In five states where they could vote, aversion to Negro suffrage was often so great that "the voters absolutely drive them from the polls at an election, and scorn and spit upon them." And in race baiting, no one excelled the supporters of Old Hickory. They were so vicious, noted an English visitor in 1833, that he never met a black man who was not "an anti-Jackson man."

Once New York settled on a white man's constitution in 1821, the Bucktails marketed themselves as the champions of democracy. They did this by exaggerating the influence of Chancellor James Kent and other "aristocrats" who spoke strongly in favor of the old two-class system of voting. It took strong, pragmatic, "responsible" democrats like themselves—not "Mad-caps" like Erastus Root—to overcome the "insidious influence of Federalist aristocracy." They triumphed easily over Clinton, who in 1822 decided to retire rather than face defeat. They took control of the state legislature. Then, suddenly, their image was shattered by the emergence of a new issue.

Choosing Presidential Electors. The new issue was the method of choosing presidential electors. Since the founding of the Republic, there was anything but unanimity on how electors would be chosen. But the trend was toward popular election. In 1800, electors were chosen by state legislatures in ten states, and by popular election of one kind or another in five states. By 1823, popular election was the rule in all but six of twenty-four states. New York was one of the six. The Bucktails were not only the party in control of the legislature, but they had also decided to support William Crawford, who had little chance, if any, in a popular election. The Bucktails thus had a clear stake in the old system.

Led initially by Calhoun men, supporters of other presidential contenders raised a hue and cry for popular election of presidential electors. That was the only way "democracy" would be served! A People's party soon formed to lead the charge. The Bucktails resisted, and by the time the next state election rolled around their control of the legislature was in danger. Said one stalwart, Jacob Barker: "You may rely upon it this universal Yankee notion will take out of the Republican ranks so many . . . the Federalists, Clintonians, and dissatisfied will unite and together make a majority." Barker was wrong only because many of his fellow Republicans backed down, promised to revamp the "aristocratic" electoral law, and barely hung on to their seats.

The Bucktails faced a showdown when revamping the electoral law came up for a vote in 1824. Would they support an extremely popular electoral bill? Or would they follow party strategy by defeating the bill and then delivering New York's entire electoral vote to Crawford? Van Buren urged that "Republican members of both houses act in concert and magnanimously sacrifice individual preferences for the general good." Seventeen state senators followed the dictates of their party, and thereby killed the bill. They paid dearly. People were so angry that most of the seventeen never again held elective office. And to the dismay of the Bucktail leadership, DeWitt Clinton returned to power as the candidate of the People's party. Overnight, the hated aristocrat had suddenly become a democrat, while last year's democrats had become hated "aristocrats."

Anti-Masonry. Of all the campaigns against "aristocracy," perhaps the most revealing was anti-Masonry. It highlights, as much as anything else, the temper of the times. It was, for one thing, one of the very few movements that was started by ordinary people. Most movements in behalf of the "people" or in behalf of "democracy" were clearly the work of politicians from the outset. And power, not democratic principle, was usually their primary concern. The Bucktails, as we just noticed, used democracy to get into power; the Clintonians in turn used it to drive them out. In the beginning at least, the anti-Masons were somewhat different. They were hardly tools of established politicians. Indeed, astute politicians were caught by surprise when anti-Masonry burst out, and many became its victims.

Then (as now) the Masons were a secret fraternal organization, which was not open to all members of the community. Some men were asked to join; others were blackballed; most were never even considered. Over the years, the Masons had developed the reputation of only accepting the "better sort": George Washington and Benjamin Franklin had been Masons, and so were Jackson and Clay. Masons had boasted for years that they held "almost every place of power where POWER IS OF ANY IMPORTANCE," and that their membership consisted of "men of RANK, wealth, office and talent, in power and out of power." They had bragged, too, of their ability to work in concert. After 1826, many Masons wished they had minced their words.

In the summer of 1826 bands of Masons tried to stop the printing of a manuscript revealing Freemasonry's secret, but innocuous rituals. After botching several attempts to steal the manuscript and to burn the publisher's office, they kidnapped its author, a disgruntled Mason named William Morgan, from his home in upstate New York. First, they threw Morgan in jail in a neighboring town, and then they hauled him over one hundred miles to Fort Niagara. No one knows for certain what happened to Morgan, but the kidnappers left a wide trail of evidence that indicates that they drowned him in the Niagara River. In fact, the trail was so wide that indignant citizens in four counties launched investigations to find out what happened to poor Morgan. Everywhere they were blocked by Masonic judges, Masonic sheriffs, and Masonic officeholders who sought to squelch the entire affair. Soon the investigators became convinced that they had uncovered a gigantic conspiracy to subvert the rule of law. The idea of a conspiracy, in turn, happened to coincide with a suspicion held by many churchgoers. For years they had wondered if Freemasonry, with its secret rituals and strange ceremonies, was really an organized plot to overthrow Christianity. In France, they noted, Masonic lodges had been centers of anticlerical propaganda at the time of the French Revolution, as well as bastions of the aristocracy.

Hence anti-Masonry was born. And, to the dismay of seasoned politicians, it spread like wildfire—first through New York, and then through Vermont, Connecticut, Massachusetts, Pennsylvania, Ohio, and the Michigan Territory. Suddenly, ordinary citizens began counting the number of Masons in town and state offices. There were hundreds. Indeed, in some states lists of lodge members resembled a roll call of the legislature and the bar. Were they conspiring against the people, too? All anti-Masons had to do was to take some well-known Masonic boasts, add a few embellishments of their own, and rail against "this vile conspiracy which benefited the *few* at the expense of the *many*," which preferred "corrupt 'brothers' to honest citizens in appointments to office," which "hated democracy and cherished aristocratic and regal forms of power." To this basic argument, evangelical anti-Masons added that Masonry was "an infidel society at war with true Christianity." Here and there, throughout the countryside, thousands soon flocked to the polls to do battle with "the Beast with seven heads and ten horns" and "to restore equal rights, equal laws, and equal privileges to all men."

The results were startling. In the fall election of 1827, just a year after Morgan's disappearance, anti-Masons carried fifteen assembly seats in central and western New York. "The result of the election," wrote one commentator, "astonished all—even the anti-Masons themselves—and opened the eyes of politicians to the growing power of the new political group." By 1830 anti-Masons could boast of 124 newspapers across the country; 45 percent of the gubernatorial vote in Pennsylvania; 48 percent in New York; 35 percent in Vermont; 150 assembly seats in Massachusetts. Skillful leaders like Thurlow Weed and William Seward of New York, and Thaddeus Stevens of Pennsylvania, emerged to lead the charge, and even old warhorses like John Quincy Adams joined the crusade. Half of the Masonic lodges in Pennsylvania "voluntarily" surrendered their charters; college fraternities went underground; and Phi Beta Kappa saved itself by becoming an honorary society.

Eventually, the crusade subsided in some states or became part of a major party in others. Historians usually mark its death soon after the presidential election of 1832, when its national candidate, William Wirt, captured only Vermont. Yet in many parts of the Northeast, candidates continued to run until the 1850s as "Anti-Mason and Whig" or "Anti-Mason and Democrat." For many voters, that was the badge of an honest man; for others, a sign of infamy. As late as 1868, when the Senate was about to try President Andrew Johnson for "high crimes and misdemeanors," Thaddeus Stevens asked the clerk of the House for the names of all senators who were Masons. Even after more than thirty years, he would never trust a Mason to vote right!

The crusade for democracy, then, was unpredictable. Spokesmen for the "common man" always denounced the "aristocracy" and sang the praises of "democracy." They always campaigned against "privilege" and "exclusivism." Yet they invariably ended up excluding someone from "democracy" or least tried and failed, as in the case of the anti-Masons. The demand for popular government came from so many quarters, its appeal was so broad and diverse, that no party could embrace it fully. The Bucktails, the People's party, the anti-Masons—all claimed to be instruments of the common man. They all developed political apparatuses to bring thousands of ordinary citizens out of the hills, down the streams, and to the polls. But spokesmen for the common man never rallied around the same banner. Van Buren and the Bucktails went with Old Hickory, while the anti-Masons, led by Thurlow Weed and William Seward, joined the opposition. As for "Mad-cap" Erastus Root, he continued to perplex Van Buren by switching sides.

The Fall of Adams and Clay

Nationally, the Jackson party began in earnest when the House of Representatives, thanks to Henry Clay, elected John Quincy Adams to the Presidency in 1825, and Adams promptly nominated Clay to be his Secretary of State. Convinced that Clay had cheated him out of the White House, Andrew Jackson began immediately to campaign for the next election in 1828. He voted against Clay's confirmation, resigned from the Senate, and went home to Tennessee to organize his shock troops against the "corrupt bargainers" at Washington.

By then, the old political order was in hopeless disarray. Political discipline was nil, King Caucus was dead, and Jeffersonian Republicans had even failed to keep such explosive issues as slavery and southern domination out of the political arena. Vice-President Calhoun, second in the Adams administration, was opposed to it from the beginning. Even before the inauguration, according to some accounts, he began scheming to make himself President, if not by 1829, at least by 1833. Calhoun, Jackson, Clay, and Adams—all claimed to be good Jeffersonian Republicans.

Confusion thus abounded. How long would it last? What issues would dominate the political agenda? How would presidential nominees be chosen in the future? Would a new two party system emerge? If so, would political divisions follow sectional lines, class lines, or ideological lines? No one had the answers. Nothing was certain.

The Attempt at Nationalism. At the outset, the Adams administration made a major contribution to a new political order—and to its own downfall—by offering a clear-cut program of national planning. In his first year of office, Adams laid out a program that took for its time the broadest view of constitutional powers, and made Clay's American System seem modest by comparison. None of the specific proposals were new, and by modern standards the entire program seems rather commonplace—and certainly not worth getting excited about. But we must remember that nineteenth-century governments were far less active than even the more rudimentary twentieth-century governments, and Jeffersonian Americans had always hoped that their government would lead the world in governing least. Hence Adams' proposals must be examined in a different light than they would today.

"The great object of the institution of civil government," said Adams, "is the improvement of the condition of those . . . over whom it is established." Accordingly, he called for the construction of a national system of roads and canals, a national university, exploration of western territories at federal expense, a naval academy, a uniform standard of weights and measures, a more effective patent law to encourage inventors, and an astronomical observatory to observe the heavens. In Europe, he explained, there were at least 130 "lighthouses of the skies," while in America there were none. But what about the Constitution? Did *not* the Constitution limit severely the powers of the federal government? No, said Adams. There was more than enough authority to carry out this program. Indeed, if the federal government failed to exercise its power in behalf of the public good, that would be "treachery of the most sacred trust."

Adams' proposals rallied the supporters of Clay's American System. For the first time they had a President who had no constitutional doubts about the federal government building a vast system of roads and canals. That became the great effort of his administration. The government encouraged internal improvements by buying nearly two million dollars of stock in four major canal-building companies, including a million dollars in the Chesapeake and Ohio Canal Company. Altogether, the Adams administration spent nearly as much on internal improvements in four years as had been spent in the previous twenty-four. In addition, it encouraged state projects through enticing grants of public lands. Ohio and Indiana got land for building both roads and canals, and Illinois got a sizable land grant for the canal from Lake Michigan to the Illinois River. By 1828 the federal government was the largest single entrepreneur in the country.

The idea of an energetic national government, however, alienated many. One substantial group was the Old Republicans of the South, who claimed to be purer Jeffersonians than the great Jefferson himself, and who were strong in areas where the postwar economic boom had made few inroads, such as the worn-out tidewater country of eastern Virginia and North Carolina. As a rule, they had no sympathy for Jackson. Jefferson himself regarded him as "most unfit" for the Presidency and as "a dangerous man." But they were fully committed to old principles such as states-rights and strict construction of the Constitution. They regarded with horror the establishment of the Second Bank, Clay's American System, the decisions of Chief Justice Marshall, the Thomas Proviso, and the death of King Caucus. They were stunned when they learned of Adams' program. Not one of them, Van Buren later commented, failed to see "the most ultra latitudinarian doctrines," the most flagrant violations of "the old Republican faith." Soon, Jefferson issued dire warnings about the revival of Federalism, and John Randolph warned that if the government acquired "such vast powers," it would soon be meddling with slavery. Quickly Thomas Ritchie, the leading voice of the old guard, sounded the alarm regarding Adams' message in the Richmond *Enquirer.* "Are we," he sneered, "really reading a state paper—or a school boy's thesis?"

The Adams administration also alienated another substantial group, the Bucktails of New York, whose primary concern was party discipline and party regularity. They had risen in New York politics in opposition to De Witt Clinton, who had ignored the state Republican caucus and dispensed political favors as he pleased, often rewarding personal friends, and often giving key jobs to Federalists at the expense of Republicans. In fighting Clinton, Van Buren and his Bucktails had come to make a fetish out of party regularity. They supported the caucus even when they were in the minority. They supported all "regular nominees," even those they disagreed with or hated personally, against any nominee of the opposition. And for the sake of party solidarity, they offered virtually no specific programs at all, no plans for internal improvements, no startling proposals for education or election reform—nothing, in fact, that might alienate any of the faithful. Unlike Adams, who loved to talk about the effect roads and canals would have on the "unborn millions of our posterity," the Bucktails preferred to talk about the past and to fight the old battles once again. Indeed, according to a recent scholar, the popular issues among Bucktails were those "that had been safely dead for twenty years."

So in national politics the Bucktails were natural allies of the Old Republicans. Conspicuously quiet during the Missouri crisis, the Bucktails had no desire to stir up controversies that would obviously divide the old party along sectional lines. It was widely assumed, in fact, that the Bucktails were anxious for sectional peace in 1820, and that they supported the corporal's guard of northern "dough faces" who voted with the South on the crucial Missouri bill. They had, moreover, supported King Caucus in 1824 and fought for William Crawford's election until the bitter end. And, like the Old Republicans, Van Buren and his colleagues had no liking for Jackson, but they were put off by Adams' proposals. They too were committed to the old principle of the "least government possible."

Hence Adams, while rallying the supporters of Clay's American System, drove

Old Republicans and Bucktails into opposition. But would the rapidly growing opposition coalesce around Jackson? Vice-President Calhoun soon decided that the surest path to the White House was to throw his support to Jackson, endear himself to the Old Hero, and become his successor. Yet many had trouble embracing Jackson. Ritchie "scarcely ever went to bed," Van Buren later recalled, ". . . without the apprehension that he would wake up to hear of some *coup d'etat* by the General." And Van Buren himself held out for assurances that Jackson and his men would "put the election on old party grounds, preserve the old system, avoid if not condemn the practices of the last campaign. . . ."

In time, both Bucktails and Old Republicans joined the Jackson-Calhoun coalition. Supporting Jackson, Van Buren explained to Ritchie in 1827, was "probably the only practicable mode of concentrating the entire vote of the opposition & of effecting what is still of greater importance, the substantial reorganization of the Old Republican Party." Reviving the old party, the sly New Yorker noted pointedly, would be especially beneficial for the South.

> We must always have party distinctions, and the old ones are the best. . . . If the old ones are suppressed, geographical divisions founded on local interests or, what is worse, prejudices between free and slave holding states will inevitably take their place. Party attachment in former times furnished a complete antidote for sectional prejudices by producing counteracting feelings. It was not until that defence had broken down that the clamor [against] Southern Influence and African Slavery could be made effectual in the North. . . . Formerly, attacks upon Southern Republicans were regarded by those of the north as assaults upon their political brethren & resented accordingly. This all powerful sympathy . . . can & ought to be revived.

In supporting Jackson, these political virtuosos were hardly looking for strong leadership. Leadership ability rated rather low on their list of priorities. These same men, we must remember, supported poor Crawford long after it became clear that he was unfit to care for himself, much less the country. They knew, of course, that Old Hickory was strong-willed, but they all thought they could steer him along a "proper" course. And, oddly enough, many of Jackson's leading supporters thought his days were numbered. Unlike the rotund Adams, who at fifty-seven still swam nude against the Potomac tide for over ninety minutes at a stretch and in the winter raced around the Capitol for exercise, the Old General never looked well. He was always a striking figure—tall and gaunt, with bushy gray hair, a high prominent forehead, and piercing blue eyes—but he had suffered from long bouts with malaria, tuberculosis, dysentery, as well as the bullets he bore in his body from near-fatal gunfights. Tired-looking and emaciated, he weighed no more than 140 pounds in 1827. Few would have predicted that he would live until 1845, and few would have guessed that he would become the towering figure he became in the White House. Many, in fact, were certain in 1827 that he would never run for a second term.

The new coalition, calling itself the Democratic-Republican party, harassed Adams in every way possible. Newmen jested about "lighthouses of the skies." Senator Thomas Hart Benton delivered a preposterous report on how the President misused his appointing power; in truth, Adams refused to fire appointees who were openly working for the opposition. And John Randolph, now a Senator from Virginia, likened Adams and Clay to "Blifil and Black George," the "puritan and the black-leg," and called for an unrelenting war against "stinking" corruption and bargain that permeated the Administration. That was too much for Clay, who quickly challenged the Senator to a duel, only to suffer the further humiliation of having the eccentric Virginian spare his life by firing deliberately into the air; some even claimed that Randolph laughed at Clay! Accordingly, with both sides trying to embarrass one another, and at the same time win the support of protectionist groups, Congress turned out a lopsided tariff in 1828 that pushed duties on both manufactured goods and farms products to absurdly high levels. The new law was dubbed the "Tariff of Abomination." The testy Virginian John Randolph asserted that "the bill referred to manufactures of no sort or kind, but the manufacture of a President of the United States."

Campaign of 1828. The campaign of 1828 marked the return of a two-man presidential race. Adams' position was clear, but Jackson was foxy on key issues. In the South, his partisans said he was against protection, but in Pennsylvania Samuel Ingham assured everyone that the Old Hero would "raise the tariff every time he touched it." In general, partisans favoring Jackson pictured him as the people's man while Adams' men depicted him as a seasoned statesman, and then both quickly descended into scurrility. The old story that Jackson had run off with another man's wife was revived. Although terribly unfair, it had some truth in it and could be expected. But the Cincinnati journalist who dug up this story concocted still another: "General Jackson's mother was a COMMON PROSTITUTE brought to this country by British soldiers! She afterwards married a MULATTO MAN, with whom she had several children, of which number General JACKSON IS ONE!!" The Jacksonians, of course, responded in kind: Isaac Hill of New Hampshire spread the fantastic story that John Quincy Adams had once pimped for the Tsar, and with straight faces Democrats in the West maintained that the President's fabulous success as a diplomat had finally been explained!

The two-man race returned in 1828, and so did dirty politics. But did a new two party system emerge in 1828? Did the nasty fight between the Adams men and the Jackson men mark the emergence of a new system of national politics? Unfortunately, the election of 1828 has become so much a part of national mythology that it is difficult to strip away the myth—and then keep fact separate from fiction. The two always seem to get tangled once again.

First of all, the election resulted in a smashing victory for the Hero in the only place it counted: the electoral college. Jackson received 178 electoral votes to Adams' 83. And as the totals mounted, many Democrats came to believe their own propaganda: the people had revolted against the privileged few; the poor and unwashed had turned on the rich; the democratic masses had spoken. And, when

herds of enthusiastic partisans romped through the Executive mansion on Inauguration Day, smashing the china and jumping enthusiastically to get a glimpse
of the tall President dressed in a plain black suit and black cravat, the propagan-
dist Amos Kendall reported: "It was a proud day for the *people*—General Jackson
is *their own* president." Even the opposition was amazed. "I never saw such a
crowd here before," said Daniel Webster. "Persons have come five hundred miles
to see General Jackson, and *they really seem to think that the country is rescued
from some dreadful danger!*" And thus the fiction gradually developed—even
among historians—that democracy triumphed in 1828.

Was it really fiction? Yes it was, and historians should have known better.
Even the old President spotted a basic fact in the election returns that historians
long ignored. Sour and uncharitable, Adams read the returns as a defeat for democracy and a victory for the South: behind the public issues, as he always expected, lay the hidden issue of slavery. Adams was hardly an unbiased observer, of
course, but neither were the Jacksonians. And, like the Jacksonians, he failed to
give the opposition their due. Jackson had been trounced in New England, which
was Adams' home ground, but Old Hickory had done well in other northern
states, and overall had won 50.3 percent of the northern vote.

There is no doubt, however, that the magnitude of Jackson's victory was due to

The Election of 1828

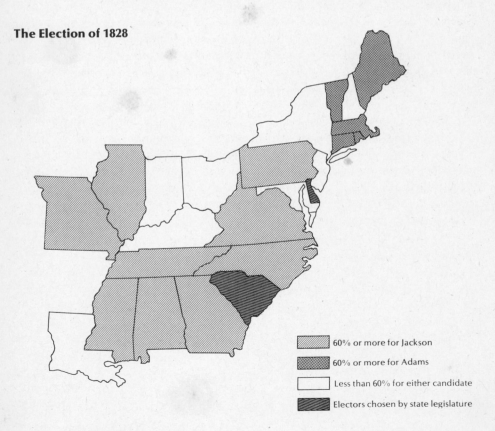

60% or more for Jackson

60% or more for Adams

Less than 60% for either candidate

Electors chosen by state legislature

the South. He carried most southern states by whopping majorities, and won 72.6 percent of the southern vote. And, thanks to the mechanics of the three-fifths clause and the electoral college, his 200,000 southern supporters provided him with far more help, man for man, than some 400,000 Northerners: 105 electoral votes as compared to 73. Hence, unless one is willing to say that the slaveholding states were much more democratic than the free states, or that Virginia was less aristocratic than states like Ohio and Vermont, then the old thesis about triumphant democracy must be laid aside.

The fact that looms largest in 1828 was the sectional appeal of the two candidates. As a result, real contests were held in no more than seven or eight of the twenty-four states; in the remainder one candidate or the other ran away with the election. The same pattern was repeated once again in 1832 when Jackson ran against Clay. The Old Hero won by a landslide in most of the South, capturing:

  75 percent of the vote in Virginia
  84 percent in North Carolina
  95 percent in Tennessee
  100 percent in Georgia and Alabama

By contrast, he lost four of the six New England states by substantial margins, and even came in third in Massachusetts and Vermont where anti-Masons made strong showings. Jackson won just

  43 percent of the vote in Rhode Island
  35 percent in Connecticut
  24 percent in Vermont
  23 percent in Massachusetts

Two-party politics, then, was largely talk in much of the nation when Jackson triumphed in 1828 and 1832. It was real enough in a handful of states, such as New York and Maryland in the East, and Ohio and Kentucky in the West, but in most states one of the major contenders simply had no chance at all on election day. In the South especially, where nearly every politician was nominally a Jacksonian, one-party politics still prevailed. In short, Jackson's candidacy came far short of nationalizing political conflict; that would come later.

Shaping the Political Agenda

Although Andrew Jackson entered the White House with only a few clear-cut positions, he almost instinctively sided with Van Buren and the Old Republicans who wanted to restore the old Jeffersonian ideal of a simple economy, and a limited and frugal government. In the 1790s, Jackson himself had got caught up in the web of easy credit and had speculated wildly; subsequent bankruptcy and the arduous struggle to pay off his debts had thoroughly chastened him. He hated debt, and he was certain that easy credit and a speculative economy only led to moral turpitude and grief. The boom-and-bust cycle of 1815 to 1819, in his judgment, was merely his own personal tragedy writ large. It proved once again the virtues of hard work and thrift. Hence, when he took office, he was determined to run a simple, frugal government so as to pay off the national debt as quickly as possible.

He offered, therefore, no striking innovations. Those who hoped for startling changes, or looked forward to a Jacksonian revolution, would wait in vain. Jackson and his chief lieutenants saw themselves as good, safe Jeffersonians, rather than as daring innovators. Indeed, in their judgment, the dangerous innovators—the men who wanted to turn the world upside down—were in the other camp. It was Adams, not Jackson, who wanted a strong central government actively and self-consciously directing the nation's economic development. It was the old President, not the new, who was dissatisfied with the old agrarian order, and who wanted drastic change. The Jacksonians would save the people from the Adamses, the Marshalls, and the Clays in American society, and destroy the dangerous centralizing tendencies in the central government. They would, in short, fight the old battles once again.

Success depended on controlling the political arena. The nation was torn by scores of conflicts, dozens of hot issues, during Jackson's eight years as President. Yeoman farmers and planters still struggled for power in Virginia. In the West settlers and claims associations fought with land speculators. On city streets, as well as in sleepy rural villages, mobs sprang up in the 1830s and lashed out against prostitutes and gamblers, abolitionists and blacks, newspaper editors, bankers, landlords, and Catholics. Five state legislatures called for the destruction of West Point before it turned the officer corps into an "aristocratic bastion of privilege." Bands of reformers launched one attack after another against "demon rum" and the "abominable SIN OF SLAVERY." Which of these issues, if any, would get into the political arena?

The number of potential battles was limited only by the popular tradition of expecting little out of Washington, and by the bias of communication. Until canals, railways, the telegraph, and a steam-powered printing press made travel and communications cheap and almost instantaneous, it was incredibly difficult to draw people with similar opinions or parallel interests into cooperative activities. Even in the East, there were still dozens of isolated communities, like the Berkshires in Massachusetts, that had absolutely nothing to do with the rest of their states. Poor and costly communications governed: it worked against national unity, but it also worked against sectionalism; it worked against all attempts—and particularly those of the poor—to build well-coordinated pressure groups. Only the voices of the wealthy and well organized could be heard. Their demands alone, however, were enough to spark plenty of controversy.

What would Congress fight over? What would parties stand for? Obviously no regime could cope with every issue that troubled the American people. If it tried, it would be blown to bits.

The Mastery of Jackson. As always, then, political leadership involved the management of conflict, suppressing some issues, and giving others plenty of fighting room. At this, Old Hickory had no master. By far the strongest of our early Presidents, nearly every issue he confronted led to an enlargement of presidential powers, and his biases, along with the settled goals of Van Buren and the Old Republicans, determined the lines of political battle. What would Congress fight over? More than anyone else, General Jackson determined what politics would be about. Indeed, he defined the platform on which Democrats would stand for decades.

His methods were simple enough. Often he simply overrode the other branches of the federal government. Arguing that the President was the only officeholder elected by the whole people, the strong-willed General insisted that his policies represented the will of the people. He was their champion, the tribune of democracy. And as such he had the right and duty to override Congress and the Supreme Court when he saw fit. He had no respect for Marshall's interpretation of the Constitution, and hence ignored decisions by the Supreme Court. He vetoed more acts of Congress than all his predecessors put together. In forty years, his predecessors had used the veto only nine times, usually on the grounds that the bills involved were unconstitutional. Jackson used the veto twelve times, against bills he thought unwise as well as those he thought unconstitutional.

Jackson not only ran the government, but he ran it with a flair. Although cautious in planning large measures, he was bold and terrifying in bringing them to fulfillment. His temper was legendary, and at times he shrewdly faked a towering rage to get what he wanted. An emotional leader, who could be gentle and kind one moment and terrifying the next, many thought his response to the assassin Richard Lawrence was characteristic.

In 1835, after a great funeral at the Capitol, Lawrence fired twice at Jackson from a distance of about eight feet. Both pistols misfired. (The chances against that happening, incidentally, were 125,000 to one.) Stunned, most of the crowd stood flatfooted. But Jackson went after the would-be assassin with a cane before the man got off the second shot, and he complained furiously when his secretary of the treasury restrained him from clubbing the man. Shortly thereafter, Van Buren found Jackson at the White House, with several children in his lap, calmly talking to General Winfield Scott about something entirely different. The authorities eventually decided Lawrence was a raving lunatic, but Jackson never believed it. He was certain that Lawrence had been hired by Senator George Poindexter of Mississippi, who "would have attempted it himself long ago, if he had had the courage."

Jackson's tendency to act with reckless abandon and brutal swiftness made most of his acts seem much bolder than they actually were. It caused many of his contemporaries—and later many historians—to jump to false conclusions. He maintained, for example, that any honest citizen could master the simple routines of government office, and thus there was no need for an office-holding elite. Why let an aristocratic, arrogant, office-holding class develop? In a democracy, offices should not be treated as "species of property" that officeholders held for life. There should be "rotation in office." Furthermore, preference should be shown for the friends of the administration that the people had just elected. Accordingly, with the Jacksonian press urging a thorough cleansing of "the Augean Stable," the new President made sixty-eight appointments in his first nine days in office.

His victims howled, and quickly the notion developed that Jackson had ruthlessly made "a clean sweep." The opposition insisted that illiterates, incompetents, and crooks were given high positions of public trust, while the Jacksonians claimed that the happy day had finally arrived when "plain, industrious men" had a say in government. Following both leads, historians later argued that Jackson had introduced the "spoils system," whereby each President would make sweeping removals and reward his own followers with the spoils of office, and that the common man rose to power with Old Hickory.

Then historians began counting. How many heads actually fell? How many common men reached the top? Such research has proven that both sides exaggerated wildly. Jackson made a few disastrous appointments like Samuel Swartwout, who was the first man to steal a million dollars from the government—and at a time when a dollar could do wondrous things. But Jackson only dismissed about one tenth of the old civil servants, and there is no evidence that he drove the "learned" out of government, or turned high offices over to the "common man." Indeed, of 127 men that Jackson appointed to high office, 109 were already officeholders, and 105 were lawyers. In a nation of farmers, where only two men out of a thousand went to college, Jackson appointed 69 college men to high office—and not one farmer! Clearly, "plain, industrious men" had little say at the top levels of government. So Jackson, as it turns out, was no bolder than Jefferson. He was just noisier, swifter, and more dramatic.

But appearances sometimes count much more than reality. And, in the eyes of his contemporaries, Old Hickory was simply incapable of halfway measures. His enemies saw him as a savage military chieftain, "King Andrew the Barbarian," whose fierce partisanship would destroy the American Republic. His friends hailed him as the father of a new democratic age, as a giant among men, as a "backwoods Napoleon" whose iron will would overcome every adversity. Said one enthusiast: "I must confess that the records of Greece and Rome—nay, the proudest days of Napoleon, cannot furnish an instance of a WILL like that of ANDREW JACKSON." A popular anecdote, which appeared in several versions after his death, held that the Old Hero's will was strong enough to set aside the judgment of God Himself:

> Has the Old General gone to heaven?
> Well, Sir, I tell you if Andrew Jackson has made up his mind to go to heaven, you may depend upon it he's there.

How did Jackson use his power? How did the man of iron will shape the political agenda? That, like everything else about Jackson, has been a subject of endless debate. On the one hand, some have argued that Jackson, with ample help from Van Buren, put the South in the saddle once again. Given Jackson's own position as a slavemaster, plus the nature of his political support, the argument has a compelling logic to it. But the standard interpretation is just the opposite. Most schol-

An opposition cartoon brands Jackson a dictator placing his will above that of the Constitution, the courts, and domestic welfare. *The Bettmann Archive, Inc.*

ars have held that Old Hickory's deepest commitments flowed not from his dependence on slavery, but from fervent patriotism. He was a nationalist, and his charisma and his actions helped create a party that had a truly national following. His most famous battles, moreover, involved pitched battles with two prominent slaveholders, Henry Clay and John C. Calhoun. To many, in fact, it seemed that Old Hickory's sole purpose was to destroy every vestige of Clay's American System. To others it seemed that the Old General had set out to ruin Calhoun's political career.

The Maysville Veto. Jackson's battle with Clay came to a head in 1830 with the Maysville Road Bill. Although the proposed road was merely sixty miles long and the bill merely called for the government to buy stock in the road-building company, the bill was widely regarded as a test measure for the whole internal improvements program. If it passed, internal improvements advocates would have a foot in the door. States-righters were vehemently opposed, and New York wanted no federally sponsored rivals competing with its Erie Canal. Advocates of a national road system, however, pushed the bill through Congress with votes to spare.

Since the proposed road was to run only within Kentucky, the home of Clay, Van Buren recommended that Jackson veto the bill on the grounds that the project was merely local in character and therefore unconstitutional. But Jackson, who took delight in slapping down one of Clay's pet projects, went far beyond Van Buren's simple objection in his veto message. On grounds of expediency and strict construction of the Constitution, he challenged the principle that the federal government had the right to build roads and canals, and expressed hostility to the entire concept of an energetic federal government. Old Republicans were delighted! Adams blamed it all on the "Sable Genius of the South," even though support for the veto crossed sectional lines. And internal improvements advocates wailed about the dismal future of public works. Their dream of a great transportation network, lacing the country together, and financed largely by the federal government, had been effectively killed.

The Bank War. Jackson's second major battle with Clay was part of a larger war against the Bank of the United States. Since Nicholas Biddle had become the Bank's president in 1823, the Bank's image had improved. It still had plenty of enemies, men who recalled bitterly that it had pushed debtors to the wall back in the grim days following the Panic of 1819, hard-money agrarians who hated all banks, new entrepreneurs who wanted easier credit, state banks which wanted to be free of its restraints, and strict constructionists who never stopped complaining about it being a gross violation of old Republican principles. Yet the Bank clearly had more friends than enemies when Jackson became President. Under Biddle the Bank ran smoothly—and the money market seemed at last to have a semblance of order. And most businessmen and politicians had become convinced that the Bank was indispensable to national growth.

Jackson shocked Biddle in his first message to Congress. He briefly questioned the constitutionality and expediency of the Bank. Biddle became even more alarmed when it became clear that Jackson would run for reelection. For if the Hero were reelected and survived another four years, he would be President when the Bank had to renew its twenty year charter, which expired in 1836. Clay, who planned to run against Jackson in 1832, urged Biddle to push for recharter before the election on the grounds that Jackson would probably not dare a veto in an election year. Other friends of the Bank argued that such a move would be folly: it would not only prove Jackson's contention that the Bank was a powerful political agency that tried to shove the government around, but it might also goad him into a veto. Biddle finally agreed with Clay to press for recharter, even though he suspected a veto. In July 1832 a recharter bill passed Congress with votes to spare. The vote indicated solid support for the Bank except in New York and in the South.

Jackson responded with a ringing veto. Despite what Chief Justice Marshall might think, the Bank was unconstitutional. Even worse, the Bank benefited the rich at the expense of the poor. The president, directors, and stockholders of the

Bank were "a favored class," "opulent citizens," who enjoyed "exclusive privileges" that gave them virtually a monopoly over foreign and domestic commerce. "It is to be regretted that the rich and powerful too often bend the acts of the government to their selfish purposes." Nothing was wrong with being rich, said the wealthy President. But when the government grants "exclusive privileges, to make the rich richer and the potent more powerful, the humble members of society—the farmers, mechanics, and laborers—who have neither the time nor the means of securing like favors to themselves, have a right to complain of the injustice of their government." Worst of all, some $8 million of the stock was held by foreigners. "If our government must sell monopolies . . . it is but justice and good policy . . . to confine our favors to our fellow citizens, and let each in turn enjoy an opportunity to profit by our bounty."

The veto message aimed at the masses—not Congress—and it soon had a life of its own. Jackson's friends rushed to embrace it, claiming that it was a second Declaration of Independence and that "the humbler members of society" at last had a President who was willing to stand for even-handed justice and against special favors for the rich. Forever after, words from the President's manifesto would be used to stir Democrats. Yet Biddle called it a "manifesto of anarchy, such as Marat or Robespierre might have issued to the mobs" during the French Revolution, and the followers of Clay lambasted it as the worst kind of demagoguery. What did the people think? No one knows for sure, but the veto probably cost Jackson votes—perhaps some 60,000 votes out of the 1,200,000 that were cast in 1832—even though he easily swamped Clay in the electoral college.

The election convinced Jackson that the Bank had to be killed quickly before it killed him. The Bank's "absolute control over the currency . . . control over property . . . control over the people" must end before its charter expired in 1836. Otherwise, said Jackson, the Bank would use the next three years to topple the verdict of 1832. Its power, moreover, was increasing since federal money was piling up in its vaults. The national debt had been paid off, and a federal surplus of millions was accumulating. To chain the "Monster," Jackson decided to remove the government's mounting deposits.

That decision disrupted the Jacksonian coalition. Many Democrats, including the Secretary of the Treasury, Louis McLane, vehemently opposed it and predicted disaster if the old General went through with such a radical proposal. Since removal could not be accomplished without the approval of the Secretary of the Treasury, McLane had to be kicked upstairs into the State Department. William Duane of Pennsylvania was brought in to do the job of removal. But, after several state banks had been chosen to receive government money, the new Secretary of the Treasury defied the President and refused to authorize the transfer. So he too had to be removed. Finally, with the compliant Roger B. Taney of Maryland as his Treasury Secretary, Jackson ordered in September 1833 that all future government deposits be placed in selective state banks, which the opposition quickly dubbed "pet banks."

Biddle was outraged. "This worthy President thinks that because he has scalped Indians and imprisoned Judges, he is to have his way with the Bank. He is mistaken." Defiantly, Biddle threw the full economic power of the Bank against the government. He ordered a general curtailment of loans by all branches of the Bank, hoping thereby to create such a severe contraction of credit that public pressure would force Congress to restore the deposits—and with any luck to continue the charter. Mounting bankruptcies, unemployment, and distress generally put enormous pressure on Congress during the winter of 1833–1834, and scores of Democrats left the fold. Along with Clay men and other dissidents, they formed a new party, which they called Whig to signify their opposition to executive tyranny. Like the Whigs of old England, they claimed to be fighting "Old World despotism." Their newspapers crowned Jackson "King Andrew I," and by March 1834 they had enough votes in the Senate to censure Jackson for the misuse of presidential power. Democratic leaders feared a full-scale revolt. But Jackson refused to budge, and his anti-Bank majority in the House held firm. At last Biddle gave way—and the Bank was forever doomed.

The Search for Alternatives. What would take its place? Jackson and many of his followers were hard-money men who wanted to drive all bank notes out of circulation, leaving only gold and silver as the circulating medium. They hoped to use the "pet banks" to reform the state banks. Hence they submitted to Congress in 1834 a bill that required the "pet banks," as a condition for receiving government deposits, to stop issuing or receiving bank notes under five dollars. Gradually, the prohibition would extend to notes under ten dollars, and then under twenty dollars. Driving small notes from circulation, said Thomas Hart Benton in a two day Senate speech, would restore a sound "farmer's" currency. It would end the boom and bust financial cycles where insiders and bankers got richer and the poor poorer, and restore those happy days when honest coin was paid to honest men for honest work. "I did not join in putting down the Bank of the United States, to put up a wilderness of local banks; I did not strike Caesar to make Antony master of Rome." Hard money was the answer!

This scheme never got off the ground. It was popular among many workingmen, who were tired of being paid in dubious currency, but it terrified segments of the Democratic Party, especially big city financiers and rising capitalists, who were certain that Jackson would never stop at the twenty dollar mark with his hard-money proposal. How could they possibly make transactions of hundreds and hundreds of dollars without adequate paper? It was a crazy scheme, they said. The scheme, moreover, was soon swamped by massive speculation. The Jacksonians had destroyed the Bank just when a boom in the cotton trade, massive imports of English capital, and complex changes in the China trade brought good times. Cotton profits soared, business boomed, and money was plentiful. Even good Jacksonians lost interest in the simple virtues of an old-fashioned agrarian economy. Many joined the feverish speculation that caused government land sales to skyrocket from 3.8 million acres in 1833 to 20 million acres in 1836, and many joined the rush on state legislatures for bank charters which were being turned out by the hundreds.

Then in 1836, when the speculative fury was at its peak, Congress decided to

Business Activity, 1812–1848

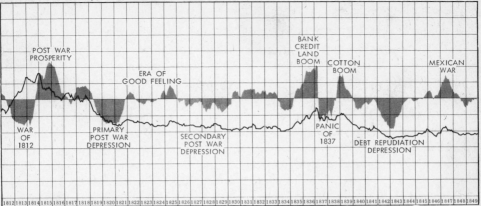

The era's economic picture, to a large degree, reflects the successes and failures of the nation's banking practices. In particular, the years (1834-1844) following the destruction of the Bank of the United States show expansion with the Bank Credit Land Boom and then depression with the Panic of 1837 and finally the refusal of the federal government to recognized the financial problems of the business community with the Debt Repudiation Depression.   *THE CLEVELAND TRUST COMPANY*

distribute the bulging federal surplus of nearly $40 million among the states. To offset the inflationary effects of this act, Jackson issued an executive order known as the Specie Circular, which said that henceforth only hard money (specie) or Virginia land scrip would be accepted in payment for public lands. Then within months, the economy turned sour: cotton prices fell, and the British cut their exportations of capital to the United States. Finally, in early 1837, only weeks after Jackson left office, a financial crisis in England set off a wave of bank failures in the United States, and once again—as in 1819—the towering pyramid of credit came crashing down.

Who was to blame? Actually, neither Jackson nor Biddle nor Clay were in any position to control the external forces that generated the boom and then the bust. But contemporaries were certain that there were home-grown villains galore. Whigs railed at Jackson and his crazy love for hard money. Killing Biddle's Bank, they said, destroyed the only restraining influence in the economy. And, without the restraining hand of the big Bank, irresponsible state banks recklessly expanded their loans and note issues, causing a runaway boom. Then Jackson, with his drastic Specie Circular, popped the land boom and precipitated a financial crisis. What was needed, said the Whigs, was another national bank to keep the economy running on an even keel. Hard-money men, on the other hand, thundered against the evils of paper currency. Once again, it had generated a disastrous boom-bust cycle. What was needed, said Benton, was the destruction of commercial, note-issuing banks.

Jackson's policies thus became a staple of American politics. For years Whigs and hard-money Democrats would fight on the state level over banking. As a result, some states continued as before; others turned banking over to a state-owned monopoly or to a mixed public-private bank; a few outlawed banks entirely.

Meanwhile, on the federal level, the Whigs tried and failed year after year to establish a third national bank. Jackson's successor Van Buren, who was left to cope with the Panic of 1837, aligned himself with the hard-money Democrats and quickly called on Congress to sever the bond between the federal government and private banks. Under his Divorce Bill banks would no longer have access to government funds, and the government would no longer be a partner with banks in the "paper" economy. Instead, the government would place its money in the "independent treasury" offices and do business only in gold and silver.

But hard-money Democrats faced an uphill struggle in overcoming the opposition of Whigs and soft-money Democrats. After three years of wrangling, they got the independent treasury bill passed in 1840 only to see it promptly repealed the next year. Then, after five more years of squabbling, they finally succeeded in reinstituting the independent treasury in 1846. It would remain the law of the land until the Civil War. So, fourteen years after Jackson's veto, the hotly contested battle over banking was finally resolved with the government, in effect, washing its hands of all responsibility for a banking system, and denying its large financial reserves to the business community and the capital of the nation.

The Nationalization of Politics

While the Bank war provided most of the fireworks and drove many Jacksonians into the opposition, Jackson's support of Van Buren over Calhoun probably did even more to split one-party states in two—and to create a truly competitive two-party system in both North and South. Both Van Buren and Calhoun were anxious to be President, and neither was willing to let the other have the first turn. In 1828 both supported Jackson in the mistaken belief that the Old General would be easy to dominate. In return, Calhoun had retained his position as Vice-President, and it seemed to most observers that Jackson's running mate would have the upper hand. But, unknown to most observers, Jackson had been repeatedly warned that Calhoun was a false friend who as Secretary of War under Monroe had wanted to censure Jackson for his invasion of Florida. Van Buren, on the other hand, was a good-natured, charming, likable little man who rarely offended anyone. His popular nicknames—"the Little Magician" and "the Red Fox of Kinderhook"—suggest something about the way he operated. Watching him maneuver to improve his standing with Jackson, Amos Kendall said he glided "along as smoothly as oil and as silently as a cat." Jackson took to him and called him "Matty."

The Eaton Affair. The announcement of Cabinet positions produced the first sign that Calhoun's position might be shaky. Instead of dominating the Cabinet as expected, the Calhoun wing of the party was given only one position, while Van Buren was made Secretary of State, and one of Calhoun's severe critics, John Eaton of Tennessee, was made Secretary of War.

Eaton's recent marriage made him highly vulnerable to attack. His new wife was the widow Peggy Timberlake. She was the daughter of a Washington tavernkeeper, with whom Eaton had boarded for many years, and she had long been suspected of sleeping with the lodgers, especially the handsome and jovial Senator Eaton of Tennessee. Her husband, a financial officer in the Navy, had just recently cut his throat while serving in the Mediterranean. There was plenty of speculation as to why, and tongues wagged even more when Eaton hastily married the pretty widow.

Accordingly, right after the appointments were announced, the wife of the Vice-President, Floride Calhoun, took the lead in snubbing Mrs. Eaton, and soon half the women in Washington refused to have anything to do with the likes of Peggy Eaton. They may have been trying to uphold moral standards as they claimed, but the timing of the whole affair makes one suspicious. They were a bit late in discovering the sinner in their midst. Many of the outraged wives, in fact, had attended the wedding, and even Mrs. Calhoun had called on Mrs. Eaton before the appointment. So, while the evidence is inconclusive, it seems that one motive for the all-out attack against Peggy Eaton was to drive her husband out of the Cabinet.

If so, it backfired. Jackson was notoriously sensitive about marriage and female virtue. He had married the wife of Lewis Robards believing that she was divorced. Two years later it became known that Robards had never gone through with the divorce proceedings. Robards then got a divorce on the grounds that Jackson's beloved Rachel was an adulteress, and Jackson and Rachel had to remarry to avoid further legal difficulties. Slanders against Rachel plagued Jackson all his married life. In 1806 he killed Charles Dickinson in a duel for dishonoring her "sacred name," and when Rachel died suddenly after the election of 1828 he blamed her death on the "vile wretches" in the Adams' camp who had just recently slandered her. "May God Almighty forgive her murderers as I know she forgave them. I never can."

So when the Eaton incident came to a head, he sided with the Eatons. He presumed that his friend John Eaton was innocent because both Eaton and Timberlake were Masons—and no Mason could ever "have criminal intercourse with another Mason's wife, without being one of the most abandoned of men." He demanded hard evidence in the case of Peggy Eaton. When that failed to come forth, he roared: "She is as chaste as a virgin!" In the end, the only one to profit from the whole unseemly mess was Calhoun's foremost rival, Van Buren. For the gallant widower was the only Cabinet member to extend every courtesy to Mrs. Eaton, and Jackson appreciated him for it.

Meanwhile, Calhoun's attempt to censure Jackson came out into the open, and Calhoun further embarrassed Jackson by printing a lengthy explanation of his side of the story, along with some details about the Eaton scandal. Jackson finally ended the scandal by reorganizing his administration. He made Van Buren minister to Great Britain, Eaton governor of Florida, and left the Calhoun men out in the cold. Calhoun got revenge when Van Buren's nomination came up for confirmation in the Senate. The Senate vote ended in a tie, and the Vice-President had the "exquisite pleasure" of casting the tie-breaking vote. Voting no, he turned to a friend: "It will kill him, Sir, kill him dead. He will never kick, Sir, never kick." Jackson was furious. "By the Eternal," shouted the President, "I'll smash them."

Nullification Crisis. A far more serious crisis between Calhoun forces and Jackson developed over the question of tariff reform. Calhoun men counted on the Jackson administration to push an all-out downward revision of the Tariff of Abominations. But that would cost Jackson thousands of votes in such crucial protariff states as Pennsylvania and Ohio, disrupt the North-South alliance that Van Buren hoped to perfect, and delay payment of the national debt. So Jackson urged his first Congress to use the "utmost caution" in handling tariff reform. And Congress responded in 1830 with revisions that barely touched the worst features of the Tariff of Abominations.

The Vice-President's South Carolina followers were outraged. They blamed the tariff for all their woes. Their economy had done well until the Panic of 1819. Their fathers and forefathers had got rich planting rice, indigo, and sea island cotton, and they had done well themselves with the addition of upland cotton. But the depression of the early 1820s had not only disrupted their economy, but it also coincided with the rise of New Orleans and the more bountiful cotton states in the Southwest. Charleston had once been the pride of the South; now it was a mere dwarf alongside New Orleans. South Carolina had once produced more cotton than the rest of the South combined; now it was being overshadowed by Georgia, Alabama, and Mississippi. Even worse, after listening to Denmark Vesey and hearing about the Missouri debate, their most trusted slaves had become rebellious.

Who was to blame for this sorry turn of events? In the early 1820s a rival states-rights faction had laid the blame on Calhoun's doorstep. It was Republican nationalism and protective tariffs, they howled, that had brought the state's decline. And soon they had raised such a storm that Calhoun men were in danger of losing control of the state. To save themselves from political extinction, the Calhounites abandoned all traces of Republican nationalism and shouted even louder than their rivals against the evils of protective tariffs and the virtues of states-rights. Indeed, they suddenly became the most radical states-righters in the entire South.

In 1828 they had responded to the Tariff of Abominations with the South Carolina Exposition and Protest. Secretly written by Calhoun, it set forth the famous doctrine of nullification. The Constitution, so the nullifiers argued, was a compact between sovereign and independent states. In creating the federal government, the states had given up none of their essential sovereignty. They had merely delegated, by common agreement, certain limited and clearly specified powers to the federal government. Since the federal government was their common agent, the states themselves were the only proper judges of whether the federal government had overstepped its powers. Should a state judge an act of Congress to be in violation of the original compact, it could declare the act unconstitutional and prevent enforcement within its border. Only an amendment to the Constitution, which would necessitate the approval of three fourths of the states, could override a state's objection.

Nullification was just a threat until it became clear that the Jackson administration had no intention of drastically cutting the tariff. After the Jacksonians failed to do so by 1830, the nullifiers called for action. But everything went wrong. First, few men could follow the fine legal points of Calhoun's argument. To most South Carolinians, as well as to most Southerners, "nullification" seemed to be just a fancy word for "treason" or "revolution." They denounced the nullifiers accordingly. Second, in the Senate, Robert Haynes of South Carolina developed a brilliant argument on how the South and West might combine against the Yankees on a platform of low land prices and low tariff rates—only to be routed in the subsequent debate by Daniel Webster, the massive New Englander, whose voice was like a "great cannon loaded to his lips." Forty thousand copies of Webster's speech were immediately printed; at least twenty editions followed, and it soon became well-known in every schoolhouse from Maine to Missouri. Finally, at the Jefferson Day dinner, Jackson made it clear where he stood. After signalling the noisy crowd to rise, he glared at Calhoun and toasted: "Our Federal Union—It must be preserved." The crowd was suddenly deathly silent, the Vice-President's hand shook, and he lamely replied: "The Union—Next to our liberties the most dear."

The nullifiers nevertheless had both determination and a solid organization. They developed, moreover, a simple-minded theory of economic affairs in 1830 that had enormous propaganda value. Before 1830, Southerners had always argued—correctly—that import duties would be passed on to consumers in higher prices, and that the tariff was unfair because southern consumers got nothing in return. It never provided them with jobs or income, for them it only meant higher prices. No one seriously argued that it affected the prices of cotton on the English market. Southerners simply got, so everyone believed, what their goods sold for overseas. Not so, argued Congressman George McDuffie of South Carolina; it was absurd to think that money was actually travelling back and forth across the Atlantic.

In reality, said McDuffie, the Atlantic trade involved little more than a simple bartering of raw cotton for manufactured goods with scores of merchants handling the paper work and obscuring what actually took place. In reality, the planter got only the proceeds from the sale of English cloth on the American market. If there was no tariff, he would get the full value of the one hundred bales of cotton he sent abroad. But with a forty percent tariff, he got the value of only sixty bales of cotton. Therefore, thundered McDuffie, the tariff robbed the planter of forty bales per hundred! The forty-bale theory was completely fallacious, but it was political dynamite. It convinced thousands of South Carolinians that Yankee manufacturers were actually stealing forty bales out of every one hundred they produced.

When Congress cautiously revised the tariff downward again in 1832, the nullifiers were better prepared for action. By this time, Calhoun had openly broken with Jackson and had openly taken the reins as head of the nullifiers. The nullifiers won the two-thirds majority in the South Carolina legislature that was necessary to call a special convention. Meeting in November 1832, the convention swiftly declared the tariff null and void, called on the state legislature to undertake all necessary military preparations, and threatened secession and war if Washington should resort to arms. In anticipation, hotheads took up arms.

Jackson also threatened force. Officially he said the nullifiers were traitors; unofficially he talked of hanging Calhoun. He sent a warship and a fleet of revenue cutters to Charleston Harbor, reinforced the federal forts in the harbor, and issued a ringing proclamation against the nullifiers in December 1832. At the same time, however, he urged South Carolina to reconsider its stand. And in January 1833, while asking Congress to enact a Force Bill that would authorize him to use the armed forces to uphold the revenue laws, he declared that the tariff was unjust and should be lowered. Shortly afterwards, the Administration stood behind the Verplanck bill, a measure that would cut tariff duties in half by 1834. In short, Jackson talked tough, but held out an enormous carrot, inviting reconciliation.

The outcome was inconclusive. Combining forces, Clay and Calhoun ganged up on the Jacksonians in Congress, snatched away the lead in tariff reform, and pushed through the Compromise Tariff of 1833. Tariff rates would be reduced over a ten year period, in gradual steps, to a uniform rate of 20 percent. Simultaneously, Congress passed a Force Bill. Ten days later, the South Carolina convention reassembled, rescinded its ordinance of nullification, and in a final gesture of defiance voted to nullify the Force Bill.

Both sides immediately claimed victory. "The Hero of New Orleans," said one Democrat after another, "had been raised up by Providence for the crisis." His iron will preserved the Constitution and saved the Union. Nullification, shouted triumphant South Carolinians, had won the day. True, rates would be cut less, and much more slowly than Carolinians had demanded, but tariff rates would go down. And, while no other southern state had endorsed nullification, and while the aged James Madison and other prominent Southerners denounced Calhoun's doctrine, the nullifiers had a sizable minority of strong sympathizers throughout the South. As Clay told Nicholas Biddle: "If South Carolina had stood alone, or if she could have been kept separated from the rest of the South in the contest which I apprehended to be impending, I should not have presented the measure which I did."

Who actually won? It is hard to say. The great French observer, Tocqueville, was absolutely certain that the federal government had been defeated. Washington, in his judgment, was just too feeble to enforce the law. So, once Congress was faced with angry citizens "with arms in their hands," it completely "abandoned the principle of the tariff" and "to conceal its defeat" passed the Force Bill. Most modern historians disagree with Tocqueville, holding instead that the nullification crisis represented a great victory for Jackson, majority rule, and democratic nationalism. Yet, modern research has also shown that the nullification crisis cost Jackson much support in the South. Nullification gave the Calhounites complete dominance over South Carolina, while in other southern states it caused many Jackson men to desert Old Hickory and join Calhoun in radical resistance to "federal tyranny." Like the Bank War, then, nullification weakened the Democratic coalition.

The Triumph of Van Buren. What of Van Buren during all of this? He was lucky. He not only benefited from Calhoun's elimination as a serious rival, but he also profited from Calhoun's attacks against him personally. When Calhoun gleefully cast the deciding vote against Van Buren's confirmation as minister to Great Britain, he expected the little New Yorker to be finished politically. He was dead wrong. As Thurlow Weed, one of Van Buren's old enemies in New York politics, had observed before the vote: "Nothing could be more gratifying to Van Buren than his rejection by the Senate. It would change the complexion of his prospects from despair to hope. His kennel presses would set up a frightful howl of 'proscription.' He would return home a 'persecuted man'—throw himself upon the sympathy of the party—be nominated for Vice-President—and huzz'ed into Office on the heels of Gen. Jackson."

That is exactly what happened. Before the rejection Van Buren was in England with little chance for the Vice-Presidency. Members of Jackson's inner circle had conspired in early 1831 to have the New Hampshire state caucus call for a national nominating convention to choose Old Hickory's running mate for the 1832 election. There was no thought of formally renominating Jackson; he was obviously the party's presidential candidate; but some way had to be found to dump Calhoun and to rally the party around one of many vice-presidential hopefuls, and a national nominating convention, which had been used recently by the anti-Masons and had a democratic aura about it, seemed like the best method. Pennsylvania and New England wanted a high tariff man, while Southerners wanted an antitariff man. A host of names were suggested—including that old favorite William Crawford. Nothing was certain. But, by December 1831, the party leaders agreed that Van Buren was too controversial to be the nominee, and Jackson reluctantly concurred.

Then in January 1832 came the Senate rejection. Jackson was furious and demanded Van Buren as his running-mate. Indignation meetings at Philadelphia, New York, and Albany cried for revenge. Selection of Van Buren, howled the Democratic press, was the only proper response to the Senate's calculated insult to the President and its persecution of "Little Van." So, by the time the convention met in May 1832, Van Buren's nomination was certain, and despite the imposition of a rule requiring a two-thirds majority he won on the first ballot.

Yet, despite Van Buren's triumph, his elevation to the Vice-Presidency was unpopular in much of the South. Many Southerners went along with his nomination only because Jackson demanded it, and they had no desire to brook his ill will. But many clearly sympathized with such dissenters as the "friends of Jackson" at Charleston, Virginia, who repudiated Van Buren and nominated Philip Barbour of Virginia in his place, or the rebellious delegates from eighteen North Carolina counties who also endorsed Barbour because of his bitter hatred of the tariff. Admirers of Calhoun were sullen about his fall from grace, while many Southerners were against putting any Northerner one step away from the White House. Indeed, it was becoming clear to all that Jackson intended to make the wily magician his successor.

The Southern Revolt. Jackson, unlike most Presidents, was such a towering figure that he had the power to choose his own successor. And once he decided upon Van Buren he made it stick. But the prospect of Van Buren in the White House drastically changed the situation for political leaders in the South and West. They never dared go against Jackson because he was so popular in their regions. But the Little Magician clearly lacked the appeal of the Old Hero. He was, in the people's view, just a clever machine politician from New York who could talk out of both sides of his mouth at the same time. He had no experience whatsoever with life on the frontier or with the management of slaves. Hence, once his candidacy became certain, restless southern politicians broke ranks and joined the opposition. Many were upset by the Bank War; others were Calhoun men or states-righters; most claimed undying loyalty to Old Hickory and his policies. They had, in short, little unity except for a common antagonism to Van Buren.

They first clashed with "regular Democrats" during the state and congressional elections of 1834 and 1835. By 1836 they were fully mobilized behind Hugh Lawson White, a former Jackson man from Tennessee, who became one of three Whig contenders for the presidency. The results were startling. In states where Jackson had encountered little more than token opposition, or no opposition at all, Van Buren was lucky to break even. In 1832 Jackson had won the major slaveholding states by a margin of nearly three to one; in the same states, four years later, Van Buren polled 173,000 votes to his opponents 174,000. Jackson had won 95 percent of the vote in Tennessee and 100 percent in Georgia; Van Buren lost both states in 1836. Suddenly, one-party politics gave way in the South, and elections became bitter and close.

How long did it last? For nearly twenty years, the South had a vigorous two-party system—an asset which it never enjoyed before—or for a century afterwards. In the election of 1836 and the succeeding presidential contests, the overall margin of difference between Whigs and Democrats was a mere 2.4 percent of the total votes.

Triumph of a New Two-Party System

At the same time Van Buren lost votes in the South, he picked up votes in New England, where Jackson had run badly. The election of 1836 thus showed all the signs of a truly national two-party system. There was still some confusion, however, because Whigs never settled on one presidential candidate.

Unlike the Democrats, the Whigs never held a national nominating convention to eliminate rival candidates. The first choice of the South was Hugh Lawson White, while the first choice of State Street in Boston and the Massachusetts legislative caucus was Daniel Webster. Some claimed that the God-like Daniel also enjoyed wide support throughout rural New England, but that was debatable. The first choice of many New England Whigs, as well as most Whig politicians in the North and the West, was clearly the Indian-fighting hero of the

Battle of Tippecanoe and the War of 1812, General William Henry Harrison of Indiana. They hoped that Webster would have the good sense to drop out. He could never compete with the popular General, they argued, even in rural New England, much less in Pennsylvania and the West.

But others thought it good strategy to run three candidates, each supposedly strong in one section of the country. "This disease," said Nicholas Biddle, "is to be treated as a local disorder—apply local remedies—if General Harrison will run better than anybody else in Pennsylvania, by all means unite upon him." Under this strategy, none of the three Whig candidates could possibly get a majority in the electoral college, but they might stop Van Buren from getting a majority. The election would then go, as in 1825, to the House of Representatives, where conceivably Whigs might rally around one of the three candidates. This strategy failed because Van Buren, in a close popular election, won a commanding majority in the electoral college.

Producing a Winner. The election proved two things to Whig strategists. First, that Harrison was by far the most popular of possible candidates. Webster took only Massachusetts; White won Tennessee and Georgia; while Harrison showed broad support by carrying Vermont, New Jersey, Delaware, Maryland, Ohio, Indiana, and Kentucky. Second, that Whigs bore the burden of being the "rich man's party," which cost them votes in such crucial states as New York and Pennsylvania. Both Webster and Clay were well-known apologists for the Bank of the United States. And Democratic newspapers had quoted Webster as saying: "Let Congress take care of the Rich, and the Rich will take care of the Poor." The party, concluded William Seward of New York, needed to shake off the Websters and Clays and to adopt the common touch.

Under the guidance of Thurlow Weed, the Whig boss of New York, hard-boiled professionals went to work to produce a winner in 1840. They joined the call for a national nominating convention to make certain that the Whigs had only one candidate in 1840. They got Henry Clay, the front-running candidate, to agree beforehand to abide by the decision of the convention. Then, in the convention at Harrisburg, Pennsylvania, they overcame the supporters of Clay, made "Old Tippecanoe" their nominee, and shrewdly avoided making any statement about party principles.

In the red-hot campaign that followed, Whig strategists abandoned the dignified approach and transformed General Harrison, who was something of a Virginia-born aristocrat, into a cider-drinking man of the people. Van Buren, on the other hand, was portrayed as an aristocrat who walked on Royal Wilton carpets, slept on a French bedstead, drank costly wines, ate off a gold plate, and traveled around in a huge, gilded coach made in England. Sober argument got lost in a mighty outpouring of songs, torchlight parades, monster rallies, and log-cabin symbolism.

"Old Tip" scored a smashing victory over "Little Van" in the electoral college, and the Whigs carried both houses of Congress for the first time. But, in the end, the Whigs were unlucky. Harrison died one month after he took office, and his

The Harrison campaign carried the promotion of a presidential candidate on hoopla alone to extremes with the excessive use of songs, torchlight parades, mammoth rallies, and log cabin–hard cider symbolism. *Franklin D. Roosevelt Library*

successor, John Tyler of Virginia, was hardly a Whig at all. He had been given second place on the Whig ticket only because his presence might win the support of Virginians, states-righters, and Democratic malcontents like himself. He twice vetoed Whig bank bills on constitutional grounds. In disgust Whigs read him out of the party.

The New Order. The strange turn of events, however, only serves to distract from the real significance of the Harrison campaign. By 1840 a new two-party system had come of age. The election brought out the largest number of votes yet seen. In 1824 no more than 27 percent of the eligible males had bothered to vote; in the Jackson campaigns of 1828 and 1832, 56 percent turned out; in 1840 a whopping 78 percent of the electorate went to the polls.

Why? What brought them out? Real contests were finally being fought in every state of the Union. Both parties had scores of strident newspapers, and dozens of spellbinding orators, trying to win supporters in virtually every town and village across the country. Both parties offered candidates for every office from sheriff to President. They were evenly matched not only on the national level, but also in every section, most states, and a majority of towns and villages. As a result, Harrison beat Van Buren by a mere 411 votes in Maine, 350 votes in Pennsylvania, while he lost Virginia by 1120 votes. For the only period in its history, the nation had a truly national two-party system.

The new two-party system had also developed a new method for choosing candidates. By 1840 both parties had settled on the convention system. The party convention has been pictured in most histories as more democratic than the old congressional caucus. But essentially they both performed the same task. Their primary function was to limit the number of political contenders, and to reduce the voters' choice to two names. There was one crucial change in the distribution of power, however. The old system gave no power whatsoever to areas where the party had little or no strength. Under the congressional caucus, if a district elected a Federalist to Congress, it had no voice at all in the Republican caucus; only Republican congressmen could vote. Under the new system, however, each district

The Election of 1840

60% or more for Harrison

60% or more for Van Buren

Less than 60% for either candidate

Electors chosen by state legislature

was equally represented.

That led to a fateful decision. In fear that weak districts might be decisive in the balloting, the Democrats in 1832 adopted a rule requiring a two-thirds majority. Aimed originally at reducing the weight of delegations from New England, where Democrats were weak, it eventually became a weapon of the South in controlling the choice of presidential candidates. And once established, it was impossible to dislodge, lasting until 1936. Thanks to the two-thirds rule, Democratic conventions were plagued by long deadlocks. It took 49 ballots to nominate Franklin Pierce in 1852; 17 for James Buchanan in 1856; 22 for Horatio Seymour in 1868; 46 for Woodrow Wilson in 1912; 44 for James Cox in 1920; and 103 for John W. Davis in 1924. On two occasions, 1844 and 1912, the two-thirds rule kept men who won a majority of the delegates from getting the nomination. Van Buren was the first victim. In 1844, southern delegates kept him from getting the necessary two thirds, and then went on to make James K. Polk of Tennessee the party's nominee. No feature of King Caucus was less democratic.

Actually, the good reputation of conventions rested on the way delegates were theoretically chosen. County conventions or public meetings chose delegates, who in turn attended district or state conventions and chose delegates to the national convention. In theory, then, political power rested with the party's rank and file, and thus political leaders had to be responsive to the whims and wishes of ordinary citizens. In fact, state and local bosses found it easy to control local conventions; they hand-picked many delegates, and sometimes one man or one committee picked an entire delegation. In 1836 Jackson managers packed the Democratic convention with federal jobholders to secure Van Buren's nomination. So irregular was this convention that when Tennessee, an anti-Van Buren state, failed to send a delegation, a traveling man from Tennessee was admitted to the floor. He cast the state's fifteen votes for Van Buren!

Facts, however, got buried in theory, and for years politicians sang the praises of conventions. They made the American government, so it was said, directly responsible to "the people." Indeed, in 1835 Jackson declared that opposition to conventions was high treason against the people. "I am always ready to bow to their will and their judgment. I consider the true policy of the friends of Republican principles to send delegates fresh from the people to a general convention, for the purpose of selecting candidates for the Presidency and Vice-Presidency, and that to impeach that selection before it is made . . . is to assail the virtue of the people, and in effect to oppose their right to govern." Historians soon agreed. It fit in nicely with a concept called "Jacksonian Democracy."

SUGGESTED READINGS

The standard accounts of politics in the Jacksonian era are George Dangerfield, *The Era of Good Feelings** (1952) and Glyndon Van Deusen, *The Jacksonian Era** (1959).

*Available in a paperback edition.

Much of the debate surrounding Jackson and Jacksonian democracy can be conveniently found in James L. Bugg, ed., *Jacksonian Democracy: Myth or Reality?** (1962). For the book that produced much of the debate, see Arthur Schlesinger, Jr., *The Age of Jackson** (1945), which is also rich in detail. Attacks on Schlesinger's hypotheses are legion, but Lee Benson, *The Concept of Jacksonian Democracy** (1958) probably carries it furthest. Two influential books, which see Jackson's appeal largely in terms of mass psychology, are Marvin Meyers, *The Jacksonian Persuasion** (1957) and John William Ward, *Andrew Jackson, Symbol for an Age** (1955).

Valuable for their examination of the new party system are Robert V. Remini, *The Election of Andrew Jackson** (1963) and Richard H. McCormick, *The Second American Party System** (1966). Two excellent studies of leading political manipulators are Robert Remini, *Martin Van Buren and the Making of the Democratic Party** (1959) and Glyndon Van Deusen, *Thurlow Weed, Wizard of the Lobby* (1947). Other good biographies of key politicians include Charles G. Sellers, Jr., *James K. Polk, Jacksonian 1795–1843* (1957); William N. Chambers, *Old Bullion Benton: Senator from the West* (1956); and Richard N. Current, *Daniel Webster and the Rise of National Conservatism** (1955). Among the many biographies of Jackson, a good short one is James C. Curtis, *Andrew Jackson and the Search for Vindication** (1976).

Much has also been written on specific elements of the new party system. Norman K. Risjord, *The Old Republicans* (1965) is good on the goals and ideology of the Old Republicans, while those of the Van Burenites are ably covered in Michael Wallace, "Changing Concepts of Party in the United States: New York 1815–1828," *American Historical Review*, Vol. 74 (1969) and Richard Hofstadter, *The Idea of a Party System** (1969). Standard on new suffrage laws is Chilton Williamson, *American Suffrage, From Property to Democracy, 1760–1860** (1960). For political conventions, see James S. Chase, *The Rise of the Presidential Nominating Convention* (1973). A modern study of anti-Masonry is desperately needed, but see Charles McCarthy, *The Antimasonic Party* (1903). Robert G. Gunderson, *The Log-Cabin Campaign* (1957), which details the 1840 election, is good on political hoopla.

Much also has been written on the specific issues of Jackson's presidency. Leonard D. White's studies, *The Jeffersonians: A Study in Administrative History, 1801–1829** (1951) and *The Jacksonians: A Study in Administrative History, 1829–1861** (1954) are good on patronage and administrative issues generally, as is Sidney Aronson, *Status and Kinship in the Higher Civil Service* (1964). William W. Freehling, *Prelude to Civil War** (1966) is excellent on South Carolina and the nullification controversy. Bray Hammond presents a pro-bank view of the bank war in *Banks and Politics in America from the Revolution to the Civil War** (1957), while Robert Remini presents a pro-Jackson view in *Andrew Jackson and the Bank War** (1967). Also useful on the bank war are W. G. Shade, *Banks or No Banks* (1972); John M. McFaul, *The Politics of Jacksonian Finance* (1972); James Roger Sharp, *The Jacksonians Versus the Banks: Politics in the States after the Panic of 1837* (1970); and Jean A. Wilburn, *Biddle's Bank: The Crucial Years* (1967). A book that challenges many sacred cows, including the widely held assumption that Jackson's policies somehow influenced the American economy, is Peter Temin's *The Jacksonian Economy** (1969).

CHAPTER SEVEN

PORTENTS
OF
TROUBLE

THERE IS NO DENYING, then, that the Jacksonians helped create a truly national two-party system. But what about the alternative interpretation? What about the contention that the Hero and his party clearly favored slaveholding interests? That argument, too, has considerable merit.

Generally speaking, the new two-party system supported slavery. Northern politicians, Whig and Democrat alike, may have felt a bit inconsistent raving about human freedom on the Fourth of July—and then supporting a slavemaster for President on Election Day. But they did it nevertheless. Some argued vociferously that the hallowed words of the Declaration of Independence that "all men are created equal" and are entitled to "Life, Liberty, and the pursuit of Happiness" applied only to whites—and not to blacks. Others knew very well that the persistence of slavery made a mockery out of the Declaration. But slavery, they argued, was clearly sanctioned by the Constitution, and they were duty-bound to uphold that sacred document.

Both parties, moreover, desperately wanted to keep slavery out of the political limelight. Knowing that slavery could easily shatter their national organizations—and perhaps the Union itself—both Whigs and Jacksonians preferred to fight over banks, tariffs, and roads. In adopting this stance, of course, they effectively supported slavery. Indeed, one could argue that this policy of keeping slavery out of the national spotlight was by far the most effective way of protecting slavery and the South's position within the Union.

Suppressing the Slavery Question

Suppressing the slavery question, while never an easy task, became increasingly difficult after 1830. For one thing, the ancient institution of slavery, which had once been quite "normal" in the Western world, had begun to give way rapidly after the turn of the nineteenth century—so rapidly, in fact, that the South soon stood out like a sore thumb. By 1804 all northern states had either freed their slaves or adopted a program of gradual emancipation. In Haiti black revolutionaries abolished slavery in 1804. Argentina and Colombia adopted gradual emancipation in 1813 and 1814; Chile abolished slavery in 1823; Central America in 1824; Mexico in 1829; Bolivia in 1831. England began using its naval power to suppress the Atlantic slave trade in 1820, and in 1833 the British antislavery movement finally succeeded in getting Parliament to abolish slavery in the British West Indies. "How can the United States boast of being the 'land of liberty' " taunted the Montreal *Herald*, "when one-fifth of its people are still in chains!"

For another thing, the wishful thinkers who said that slavery might someday disappear if blacks were shipped back to Africa ran into stiff opposition in the 1830s. Since its founding in 1817, the American Colonization Society had angered two groups. One was the planter-politicians of the Deep South, who saw coloniza-

The Alton Riot: where in disregard for freedom of the press a mob murdered newsman Elijah Lovejoy and destroyed his warehouse. Later, his brother, Owen, was elected to Congress and introduced the amendment that abolished slavery. *Brown Brothers*

tion as a front for northern "fanatics" who wanted to destroy slavery. The other was northern free blacks, who saw colonization as a plot by northern racists and southern slaveholders to drive free blacks out of the country. Lacking money and power and friends, northern free blacks faced staggering odds in battling the Colonization Society, which enjoyed the support of such prominent men as Henry Clay and James Madison. But they tried nevertheless.

It was an uphill struggle for many years. In 1827 a group of New Yorkers founded the first black newspaper, *Freedom's Journal*, which launched a full-scale attack against the colonizationists. It soon folded, however, when one of its editors, Samuel Cornish, resigned, and the other, John Russwurm, went over to the colonizationists. Then in 1829, the Boston agent for the *Journal*, an old-clothing dealer named David Walker, published a fiery pamphlet, *Walker's Appeal, in Four Articles*, which not only denounced slavery and African colonization, but also concluded that if whites refused to free their slaves voluntarily, then blacks should break the "infernal chains" by armed rebellion. Simultaneously, a group of Baltimore blacks, led by William Watkins, convinced William Lloyd Garrison, a twenty-three-year-old white newsman, that African colonization was a racist plot. Two years later in Boston, Garrison launched the *Liberator*, which came out for the "immediate abolition" of slavery, while saving its sharpest barbs for the Colonization Society— "a creature without a heart, without brains, eyeless, unnatural, hypocritical, relentless, unjust."

Yet, in an age when communications were both poor and costly, it took money to be heard. So, even after the Nat Turner insurrection in 1831, when Southerners became alarmed and demanded that Walker's *Appeal* and Garrison's *Liberator* be suppressed, most Northerners were unaware of their existence. Even in Boston few men knew the *Liberator* or its editor, and fewer still knew that Walker had been killed the year before. After hearing that an "incendiary" paper was operating in his city, the mayor of Boston made a few inquiries, but "no member of the city government, nor any person of my acquaintance, had ever heard of the publication." It took a few fat pocketbooks and a national organization to make Garrison's *Liberator* a household name across the country. That came when a few influential whites like the Tappan brothers of New York City and the land baron Gerrit Smith of upstate New York were won over to the cause.

The American Antislavery Society. Garrison, the Tappans, and other converts to the black man's cause waited until news of British emancipation reached the United States in late 1833 before launching the American Antislavery Society. Such timing, they reasoned, would give their movement momentum and the appearance of universality. Openly and self-consciously, they patterned their organization on the British model, obtained the services of the British movement's leading agitators—and thus left themselves open to the charge of being part of a British conspiracy to sow discord in the United States and to wreck the American union.

Unlike the Colonization Society, the new antislavery movement never became a "respectable" reform in northern society. Every abolitionist, from the fiery Garrison to the most pious church woman, was an extreme radical by contemporary standards. Their propaganda called for setting several million slaves free immediately. Their close ties with British abolitionists made them seem un-American—indeed, downright subversive in the eyes of many Americans. And they clearly challenged the moral authority of all leaders who were willing to compromise with the existing system. Indeed, if abolitionists had their way, at least half of the nation's institutions were clearly in danger.

Finally, there was the explosive question of race relations. By attacking the Colonization Society and by closely identifying with the free Negro, white abolitionists made it clear that they rejected the common notion that the only alternative to slavery was getting rid of the blacks. They proposed to give the free Negro citizenship—second-class citizenship to be sure—but citizenship nevertheless. They gathered free blacks into their societies, and let Frederick Douglass, a runaway slave with immense talent, become one of their leading agitators and star attractions. They opened schools in places known popularly as "Bucktown" or "Little Africa" or "Nigger Hill." And a few white abolitionists associated publicly with blacks.

What did this all mean? Northern racists and northern colonizationists had an answer. It meant "amalgamation," they thundered. White abolitionists, so the standard argument went, obviously intended to end race hatred in America by destroying the differences between the races, by marrying white to black, by "mulattoizing our posterity." Abolitionists not only denied this charge repeatedly, but went to great lengths to prove that abolishing slavery would end miscegenation in America. Look, they said, at Thomas Jefferson's half-white offspring! Look at Vice-President Richard M. Johnson's black consort and mulatto children! The life of the slaveholder, wrote Garrison, "is but one of unbridled lust, of filthy amalgamation." Abolishing slavery would put an end to "such lechery." Yet, try as they might, abolitionists never overcame the charge of being "amalgamators." No charge was repeated more tenaciously, and none was more effective in stirring up the rancor and brutality of antiabolition mobs.

All too frequently antiabolition sentiment resulted in violence. Often led by colonizationists and city fathers, scores of mobs sprang up in the 1830s to terrorize white abolitionists and blacks. In 1834 New York rioters went on a three-day rampage in which they wrecked Lewis Tappan's house, destroyed "amalgamationist" churches, and sacked the homes of free blacks. Within the next year, egg-and-rock throwing New England mobs repeatedly broke up ladies' meetings at which the English abolitionist George Thompson was speaking, and finally succeeded in driving Thompson out of the country. A Cincinnati mob, led by a wealthy mill owner, destroyed James Gillespie Birney's press and terrorized the Negro quarters in 1836. At Alton, Illinois, in 1837, a mob led by three doctors and egged on by the Attorney General of Illinois killed antislavery editor Elijah Lovejoy. A year later, well-dressed Philadelphians burned down Pennsylvania Hall, a newly built antislavery headquarters, and then razed the Negro quarters.

There was little resistance in the North to such activities. Most city officials were simply incapable of putting down riots. And usually mayors and aldermen, along with large crowds, watched and enjoyed the spectacles. Many newspapers and politicians, in fact, praised the rioters. In the United States Senate, Senator Silas Wright of New York cited the sacking of a newspaper office and the disruption of an antislavery convention in Utica, New York, as "evidences of the correct state of public opinion." And after the Alton mob killed Lovejoy, the Attorney General of Massachusetts James Trecothic Austin told a large crowd at Faneuil Hall in Boston that the mob had done its duty just like the Revolutionary heroes who dumped tea into Boston harbor.

National Impact. Violent opposition, however, did nothing to blunt the abolitionist pen or still the voice. Abolitionists invariably turned mobs to their own advantage and used them to touch the consciences of many Northerners. Trained mainly in evangelistic work and seasoned in temperance and other reform movements, the abolitionists were first-rate agitators. With few friends, thousands of enemies in the North as well as the South, and only a shoestring budget, they managed not only to be heard, but also to frighten millions out of their senses. They reworked the southern image so well, complained one Southerner, that "Christian women of the North" immediately thought of the whip and the slave trade whenever they heard the word "South." In their propaganda, the slavemaster was no patriarch, but a brute who lusted after black women, mutilated his slaves, and even sold his own mulatto children "down river."

Their success in spreading their message—and in upsetting thousands—was largely the result of taking full advantage of every advance in communications. Like Methodist circuit riders, their preachers moved from community to community, organizing scores of northern men, women, and children into antislavery societies; in 1833 there were only forty-seven such societies; by late 1836 over one thousand. They relied heavily on church women, who technically had no political voice but who industriously gathered thousands of signatures for massive petitions to Congress calling for abolition of slavery in the nation's Capitol. To present these petitions, they shrewdly chose as their primary spokesman John Quincy Adams, who after his presidency became a congressman. The ex-President not only commanded more attention than anyone else in Congress, but also gloried in keeping the House in continuous uproar.

Meanwhile Tappan and his New York associates moved quickly when the introduction of steam presses and other technological improvements suddenly halved the costs of printing. In 1835 they increased their publications by nine times and tried to flood the country with tracts, newspapers, kerchiefs, medals, emblems and even blue chocolate wrappers bearing the antislavery messages. By late July the tracts and newspapers reached southern ports. The South exploded and overnight organized antislavery became the hottest issue of the day. Almost every major city and town held antiabolitionist rallies, and mobs became everyday news. New Englanders dragged Garrison through the streets of Boston. Southern vigilance committees posted $50,000 rewards for the delivery of Arthur Tappan, dead or alive. New York City became a powder keg. The "least spark," merchant Philip Hone confided to his diary, "would create a flame in which the lives and property of Arthur Tappan and his associates would be endangered." "I have not ventured into the city," wrote abolitionist Lydia Maria Child, ". . . so great is the excitement here. . . . 'Tis like the times of the French Revolution, when no man dared trust his neighbors."

The Political Response. The "pamphlet campaign of 1835," as it was later called, created so much turmoil that politicians, North and South, had to go on record regarding antislavery agitation. And, like most politicians, Jackson came down hard against abolitionists. In his annual message in December 1835, he denounced them as "incendiaries," called for "severe penalties" to suppress their "unconstitutional and wicked" activities, and praised those Northerners who mobbed antislavery lecturers, broke up antislavery meetings, and destroyed printing presses. He recommended that postmasters publish the names of everyone who subscribed to antislavery papers "for there are few so hardened in villainy, as to withstand the frowns of all good men." He called for legislation to stop Arthur Tappan and his associates from sending "incendiary" literature through the mail into the South.

Such legislation failed to pass the Senate, but it was necessary only from a legal standpoint. The Jackson administration had already stacked the odds against a successful antislavery crusade. As soon as the controversy developed, Postmaster General Amos Kendall, with Jackson's blessing, encouraged postmasters to violate federal law by excluding antislavery materials from the mails. And, expecting such encouragement, the postmaster of New York City quickly made it his policy to stop abolitionist literature at its point of origin. That alone killed the pamphlet campaign. And, even though this policy was clearly unlawful, it remained the rule until the Civil War.

Jackson's congressional followers, in turn, took the lead in excluding antislavery from the political arena. In 1836 northern Democrats supplied the needed votes to pass the first of many "gag rules." The "gag rule" prohibited the House of Representatives from printing, discussing, or even mentioning the contents of antislavery petitions. Such petitions were to be "laid on the table" with "no further action whatever." The main purpose of the "gag," according to its sponsor, was "to arrest discussion of the subject of slavery within these walls."

That it undoubtedly did. In 1837-1838, the American Antislavery Society bombarded Congress with over 130,000 petitions (each with hundreds or even thousands of signatures) calling for the abolition of slavery in the District of Columbia, along with another 32,000 petitions for repeal of the "gag rule," 22,000 against the admission of any new slave state, 21,000 for legislation barring slavery from western territories, and 23,000 for the abolition of the interstate slave trade. The House received none of these petitions. What if it had? What if these petitions had been read and debated in the House? The tumult, fury, and shouting probably would have made the Bank War seem like a teapot tempest.

As it was, the Speaker of the House had his hands full keeping John Quincy Adams and a small band of northern Whigs from violating the "gag" and presenting the forbidden petitions. Indeed, Adams' tactics kept the House in a continuous uproar: one Alabamian got so mad he wanted to horsewhip the old man; a South Carolinian roared that the ex-President ought to be criminally indicted by the District of Columbia for inciting slaves to rebellion; and the House eventually tried the feisty old man for censure. Meanwhile, thousands of Northerners, who like Adams were temperamentally too conservative to become abolitionists, identified with the battle against the "gag rule." "The sacred right of petition," they complained, "was at stake!"

In dismay, one Virginia Whig claimed that the "gag rule" made "more abolitionists in one year, by identifying the right of petition with the question of slavery, than the abolitionists would have made for themselves in twenty-five years." Most southern politicians disagreed. To them it was worth the trouble to avoid a full-scale debate over the slavery question: the "gag" was a nuisance, but a full-scale debate would produce a debacle like the Missouri crisis.

Where did the parties stand? The Whigs divided, North versus South, while the Jacksonians supported the "gag." Over the violent objections of Adams and others, the "gag rule" was renewed at each session of the House until 1844. And on each occasion, northern Democrats supplied the crucial votes. At no time did more than forty percent of the Whigs vote for the rule, while at several sessions over eighty percent of the Democrats voted to "gag" antislavery petitions. Was such voting behavior typical? Yes, it was. After tabulating and analyzing all roll-call votes in the House from 1836 to 1860, historian Thomas B. Alexander recently found that the two parties were remarkably "consistent" and "persistent" in the way they responded to the slavery question. Beginning in 1836, says Alexander, the Whigs divided sectionally, and the party never achieved any unity on the issue of slavery. But northern Democrats stood with their southern colleagues from the beginning, and thus the party always "clung together on the essentially Southern side."

Land Hunger

In the end, it was another aspect of Jacksonianism—land hunger—that brought slavery back into the political limelight. Since several prominent Whigs, along with the Jacksonians, clamored for more land, historians have often indicated that land hunger was bipartisan. But this popular view is largely myth. Careful studies of political opinion indicate that the Jacksonians—and not the Whigs—led the expansionist impulse.

Contrary to most Whigs, who generally had little appetite for acquiring huge chunks of additional land, the Jacksonians were voracious land grabbers. While Whigs chattered constantly about the need to develop the vast country that the nation already possessed, to build a national network of roads and canals, to cultivate commerce and industry, their rivals led the chant for land, land, land. Cheap land, said the Jacksonians, would permit needy settlers to acquire a farm, and overabundance would keep the price low. "It is the exclusion of the people from the soil," said the *Democratic Review,* that "oppresses England and destroys Ireland," that keeps people poor and makes famine endemic throughout Europe. Thus making land easy to acquire should always be democracy's primary goal.

In practice, too, the Democrats sought to make land acquisition easy. Congressional Democrats, year after year, fought Whig efforts to increase the price of government lands. Senator Thomas Hart Benton, a Jacksonian stalwart from Missouri, led the fight for squatters' rights, which culminated in a permanent preemption act in 1841 that gave squatters on government lands the right to purchase up to 160 acres at the minimum price of $1.25 an acre. With less success, Benton also vigorously campaigned for severe price cuts on government lands that remained unsold year after year, which eventually led to modest reductions in 1854. Meanwhile, George H. Evans in the *Working Man's Advocate* called for free homesteads for eastern surplus labor. Simultaneously, Democrats pushed for land acquisition.

As it turned out, Jacksonian land hunger always seemed to benefit the plantation South more than the free Northwest. Was it intended that way? It was largely happenstance, but it happened enough to convince suspicious Northerners that it was not merely accident. At first, only a few radical abolitionists and inveterate Jackson haters—like Congressman John Quincy Adams—claimed that Jackson's land policy was part of a Slave Power Conspiracy. But by the 1840s, this disquieting murmur grew into a mighty roar as thousands upon thousands of Northerners became convinced that an avaricious Slave Power dictated the nation's expansionist impulse.

Historians have generally attributed the notion of a great Slave Power Conspiracy to mass paranoia. It was an age in which people saw conspirators all about them. Some thought the Pope and scheming Jesuits planned to take over the Republic; others worried about a takeover by the Masons; still others pointed to the "Monster Bank," or British abolitionists, or the Mormons. In this atmosphere, it is easy to see how the notion of the great Slave Power Conspiracy developed.

Jackson's Indian Policy. Jackson's Indian policy, for example, did far more for the South than any other part of the country. When Old Hickory took office, most northern tribes had already been stripped of their potency, while the southern tribes were not only still formidable but also in possession of some of the richest land in the South. Nearly 60,000 Cherokees, Creeks, Choctaws, and Chickasaws still possessed over 25 million acres, including pockets in western North Carolina and southern Tennessee, huge tracts in northeastern Georgia and eastern Alabama, and the northern two thirds of Mississippi. The Choctaws in Mississippi alone outnumbered all the Indians of the Northwest.

White Southerners, like Northerners in times past, dearly coveted Indian lands. Indeed, in Georgia, Alabama, and Mississippi there was no issue more central in the 1820s than getting rid of the Indians. The schemes of town promoters and speculators, the dreams of planters and farmers—all depended on getting the red man's land. But federal law and federal treaties with the Indian nations stood clearly in their way; the land belonged to the Indians, and the national gov-

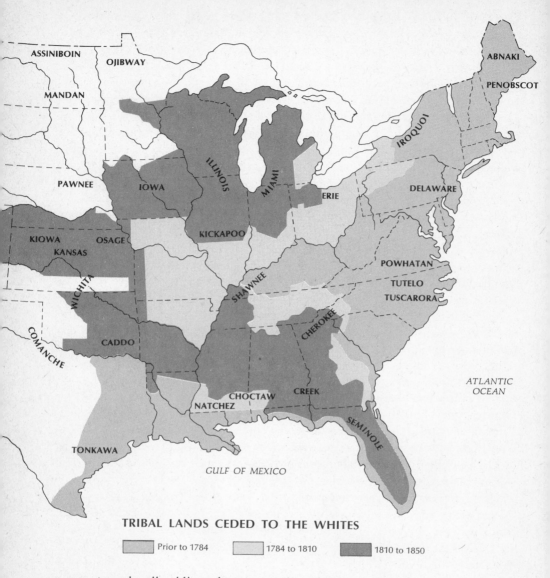

TRIBAL LANDS CEDED TO THE WHITES

Prior to 1784   1784 to 1810   1810 to 1850

ernment was legally obligated to protect them against white invasion.

Immediately upon taking office, Jackson made it clear that he would not enforce the treaties and other obligations of the United States. Georgia, Alabama, and Mississippi passed laws placing the Indian nations under state jurisdiction and outlawing tribal government. Squatters and land speculators swarmed over Indian lands. Time and again the tribes appealed to Washington for protection. Jackson and General John Eaton, his secretary of war, told them that the government was simply too feeble to enforce treaty pledges, asserted the principle of states' rights, and tried constantly to get the tribes to relinquish their lands and move beyond the Mississippi.

The Cherokees made a fight of it: Taking their case through the courts, they won a decision in the United States Supreme Court. Chief Justice Marshall declared the acts of the state of Georgia unconstitutional and in violation of sacred treaty rights. Jackson refused to execute the court's decision.

Jackson's solution was removal of the tribes beyond the Mississippi. "What good man would prefer a country covered with forests and ranged by a few thousands savages to our extensive Republic, studded with cities, towns, and prosperous farms . . . and filled with all the blessings of liberty, civilization, and religion?" His argument was an old one, and generally accepted by his countrymen: a hunting culture had to give way to farming, and savagery had to give way to civilization. But in 1830 the old argument had a hollow ring to it: the southern tribes were hardly wandering "savages." They had discarded habits of burning villages and scalping settlers, and many of them had been farmers for two or three generations. Indeed, they were known far and wide as the "civilized tribes." The Cherokees had schools and churches, many lived in fine houses, cultivated large plantations, and owned slaves like their white neighbors. They even had a constitution patterned after the federal constitution.

Given these circumstances, Jackson's policy was bound to be divisive. He could count on the avarice of planters and speculators, and the apathy of most ordinary citizens, but the opposition, spearheaded by the Methodists and the Congregationalists, was still formidable. They pointed out repeatedly that the tribes had good claims to the land, and that their claims were becoming better each day—by white man's standards—as the tribes became "more civilized." They also noted that many of these tribes had fought with Jackson during the last war. To appease the humanitarians and perhaps their own consciences as well, the Jacksonians made light of the achievements of the Cherokeees and presented removal as essentially a humanitarian gesture. Contact with white civilization, so the argument went, destroyed the red man; removal would save him from further degradation; and west of the Mississippi, away from the whiskey merchant and "Demon Rum," the noble red man could retain his nobility while shedding his savagery. Meanwhile, poor white men and yeoman farmers would take up the red man's land and gain a place in the sun. The poor of both races would thus profit.

With such arguments the Jacksonians pushed the Indian Removal Bill through Congress in 1830. The debate was exceptionally hot-tempered, and the final vote in the House was close: 103 to 97. The bill did not authorize the forced removal of any tribes. "This emigration should be voluntary," said Jackson, "for it would be as cruel as unjust to compel the aborigines to abandon the graves of their fathers and seek a home in a distant land." So the bill merely gave the President power to initiate land exchanges with various tribes.

But the President's words were merely words. In fact, Indian removal was forced removal, leading to one disgrace after another. Force, fraud, bribery, and murder—all were necessary to get the desired treaties. Shipping contractors hired the cheapest crews and rented the cheapest boats they could find, and as a result "one decrepit boat sank through mishandling and 311 Creeks drowned."

In 1832 Illinois volunteers, many of whom had joined up for "the sport of killing Indians," trapped Chief Black Hawk and his Sauk and Fox tribesmen at Bad Axe Creek, which flows into the Mississippi. Ignoring Indian attempts to surrender, the militia bayoneted and shot some 150 men, women, and children. Beginning in 1835, the army spent seven years trying to round up the Seminoles in Florida, a process that cost the lives of 1500 troops and $20 million in expenses. Even then, General T. S. Jesup had to resort to treachery to bring down Chief Osceola. When the young Seminole chief entered an American camp under a flag of truce in 1838, Jesup threw him into a military prison, where he died three months later. In the same year, General Winfield Scott was given the responsibility of herding 19,000 Cherokees from Georgia to their new homeland. Nearly one fourth of their entire nation died on the 800 mile "Trail of Tears" that led west to Oklahoma.

These atrocities shocked humanitarians, but Old Hickory's policy probably helped the Jacksonians politically. The gratitude of the avaricious seems to have run deeper than the outrage of humanitarians. As usual, the ordinary settler and the white poor failed to benefit as much as politicians had promised. For example, when the Creek lands were put on the market, three fourths of the land went to large speculators who bought 10,000 acres or more, while less than 10 percent went directly to ordinary farmers. Of course, some land was better than none at all, and among all classes Jackson's policy was popular in the South and Southwest. According to historian Edwin Miles, Mississippians were so "grateful to Old

Robert Lindneux's vision of Indian removal down the 800-mile "Trail of Tears." *Woolarac Museum*

Hickory for making these lands available . . . they were inclined to disregard differences of opinion that he might entertain on issues of less importance." In Mississippi, nearly 90 percent of the electorate gave him their vote in 1832; in Alabama and Georgia, nearly 100 percent. In 1836 Democrats offered the "man who killed Tecumseh," Richard M. Johnson, for Vice-President, while in 1840 Whigs won with another old Indian fighter, William Henry Harrison. Killing Indians apparently went a long way in American politics.

Jackson's Mexican Policy. After the Indians came the Mexicans who had the bad luck, as one Mexican official later put it, of living "too far from God and too close to the United States." Winning independence from Spain in 1821, Mexico inherited the vast northern territory of the Spanish empire which included present-day Texas, New Mexico, Colorado, Utah, Nevada, Arizona, and California. It was the new nation's most vulnerable legacy. Apart from a few missions and military outposts, the land was undeveloped and unpopulated. And the new Mexican government, torn by chaos and poverty, was clearly unable to develop or protect it. But no Mexican government dared to sell it. National pride was at stake.

The cupidity of the United States was never in doubt. Upon becoming President in 1825, John Quincy Adams instructed the State Department to buy as much of Texas as possible. And Clay tried to persuade Mexico to sell. Among other things, he told Mexican officials that if Texas was sold to the United States, then Mexico would be easier to govern, for the capital would be closer to the center of the country! When Jackson became President in 1829, he was anxious to succeed where Adams and Clay had failed. He authorized the American minister to Mexico, Joel R. Poinsett, to pay $5 million for Texas, but Mexico scorned his "generous offer." And then, since Poinsett meddled in Mexican politics in behalf of democratic forces, creating a furor in Mexico, Jackson was forced to replace him. His substitute was Anthony Butler, a fast-stepping South Carolinian who believed that bribery, extortion, and loan-sharking were the keys to successful diplomacy. Although Jackson lectured Butler on the virtues of honesty and even called him "a scamp," he allowed Butler to remain as minister to Mexico for nearly seven years—probably in the hope that one of Butler's shady deals would work.

Meanwhile Americans settled on Mexican soil. In 1821, the moribund Spanish administration granted a huge tract of land in Texas to Moses Austin, a well-traveled Connecticut Yankee who had been dealing with the Spanish since 1797, with an understanding that Austin would settle three hundred Catholic families on the land. Moses soon died, but the leaders of independent Mexico decided to let his son Stephen carry out the project. Hoping to create a buffer zone between Mexico's interior and the United States, the Mexican government set out to develop Texas by soliciting foreign colonists. Vast acreages, called empresarios, were given to big-time operators, American and Mexican alike, who agreed to settle a certain number of colonists within a given period. Unfortunately for Mexico, it was Americans from the southern and western states who came in droves. Times were hard in the United States during the 1820s, and the Land Law of 1820, requiring a minimum of $100 cash for eighty acres, came at a time when there was little cash. Across the border first-rate land could be had for about one tenth that price. In addition, there were no taxes for the first six years of settlement, and only half the normal rate for the next six years.

Good terms attracted most emigrants. But Texas also became a haven for adventurers and roughnecks—and crooks on the run. Among the more noteworthy adventurers were Davy Crockett, comic hero and fabled backwoodsman, and James Bowie, reputed inventor of the notorious Bowie knife, eighteen inches long, and known to wags throughout the Southwest as a "genuwine Arkansaw toothpick."

More important in the long run was Sam Houston, whose career was checkered to say the least. As a youth in Tennessee, he ran off from school to live with the Cherokees, who dubbed him "the Raven." After nearly four years, he rejoined white society, opened a school, fought with Jackson during the War of 1812 and suffered severe wounds at the Battle of Horseshoe Bend, and then rose in Tennessee politics to become governor in 1827. Everyone predicted a great future for the new governor; tall and captivating, and only thirty-five, he was bound to go far—certainly a Cabinet post, and maybe even the White House itself. Then in 1829 his young wife left him. Houston promptly resigned his office, and took off to live with the Cherokees, now in Arkansas, who this time dubbed him "Big Drunk." Twice Houston visited Washington, dressed in buckskins and a blanket, to speak in behalf of his tribesmen. On the second occasion, in 1832, Jackson prevailed on him to go to Texas as his representative.

By then, Mexican authorities realized that they had trouble on their hands. Texas was quickly becoming an extension of the American South. To offset the Americans, worried Mexican officials talked about settling large numbers of Germans and Swiss, Mexicans, and even convicts in Texas. Slavery was abolished throughout Mexico in 1829, and in the following year authorities enacted a new colonization law to stop American migration to Texas and to force Americans already there—including slaveholders—to abide by Mexican law and custom. But nothing worked. The Mexican government was simply too weak to enforce its authority in Texas, and the new laws were openly defied as frontiersmen and planters streamed into Texas with their slaves.

Then in 1834, General Santa Anna seized control of the Mexican government and established a dictatorship. When several Mexican states revolted in 1835, Texans joined the revolt. Seceding from Mexico, they created an army with Sam Houston as commander-in-chief. Early in 1836 Santa Anna with six thousand men stormed into Texas, devastating fields, burning villages, and shooting prisoners. Trapping 188 Texans at the Alamo in San Antonio, he massacred every last one of them, including Crockett and Bowie, after a thirteen-day siege. Shortly thereafter, he butchered more than three hundred defenders of Goliad after they had surrendered.

With ample justification, the Texans appealed to the humanitarian sentiments of the civilized world. Texas war cries—"Remember the Alamo!" "Remember Goliad!" and "Death to Santa Anna!"—soon rang through the Southwest. Angry

Americans grabbed their rifles and rushed to the aid of Texas. In the meantime, Santa Anna divided his army in three, ordering each division to seek out and destroy the fleeing Houston and his army. Shortly thereafter, while Santa Anna and 1200 men were encamped at San Jacinto, Houston stopped running, wheeled, and launched a surprise attack at siesta time. To the tune of a romantic ballad, which their band blasted out, some eight hundred Texans rushed across an open field, slaughtered half of Santa Anna's men, and eventually captured the dictator himself, who tried to escape dressed as a common soldier. In exchange for his life, the Mexican leader agreed to withdraw Mexican troops and recognize Texan independence.

Throughout this conflict, the United States government supported the rebels. In defiance of existing neutrality agreements, the Jackson administration allowed the Texans to enlist recruits and raise money and supplies in the United States. And, on the pretext of protecting the United States against Indians, Old Hickory ordered a large detachment of soldiers under General E. P. Gaines to the Texas border—and then, after Santa Anna's defeat, into Texas itself, where they remained until December 1836. Mexican authorities, who lost no time repudiating Santa Anna's agreement, concluded that United States troops were there to safeguard the results of the rebellion. They protested vigorously to Washington—only to be treated like vermin. Simultaneously, Texas appealed to the United States to recognize its independence, or to annex it.

Jackson hesitated. He wanted Texas dearly, but the price might be too high. Already in Congress, John Quincy Adams had raised a storm about Texas. At one time no one had been more enthusiastic about Texas and westward expansion than Adams. But times had changed. The Texas revolution, said Adams, was a criminal act set off by slavemasters and land speculators. Indeed, the whole affair was a wicked conspiracy plotted by Jackson and southern slavemasters, and aided by Van Buren and northern "doughfaces," to steal free soil from Mexico in order to bring in a covey of slave states so that the Slave Power would always dominate the Union. Were the Texans actually fighting for freedom? No, they were fighting to keep their slaves in chains! Did Sam Houston just happen to migrate to Texas? No, he was sent by Jackson as part of the conspiracy! Not too many Northerners, it was true, accepted such reasoning. But enough did to assure Old Hickory that Texas might touch off the whole explosive issue of slavery, at a time when he was trying to engineer the election of Van Buren, his hand-picked successor. After Van Buren was safely elected, Jackson officially recognized Texan independence, the day before he left office in 1837. But neither Jackson nor his successor dared to push for annexation.

The Road to War and Turmoil

Rebuffed by the United States, Texas looked elsewhere for help. With only seventy thousand people to Mexico's seven million, the new Lone Star Republic obviously needed all the outside aid it could get. Diplomatic agents were sent to

Europe, loans were secured from London, and by 1840 the Lone Star Republic had treaties with France, Holland, Belgium, and Great Britain. The British favored an independent Texas as a buffer against American expansion, as an independent source of cotton, and as a duty-free market for British industrial goods.

Proannexationists in the United States quickly exaggerated British interest, centering attention on English abolitionists, who hoped that Texas might be persuaded to abolish slavery in return for British gold or a guarantee of independence. For years antiabolitionists in both North and South had maintained that the American Anti-Slavery Society was a part of a gigantic British plot to destroy the American republic by sowing seeds of dissension, fomenting slave rebellions, and eventually dividing the Union itself. Now, thundered antiabolitionists, the British had a new trick up their sleeve! With the aid of Adams and other subversives, they would seize Texas and then begin a flank attack on the United States and its institutions. Annexation was thus imperative!

John Tyler. Hopes for annexation ended temporarily in 1840 when the Whig candidate, William Henry Harrison, gained the presidency. There was no chance that the Whigs would push for annexation. But, one month into his term, Harrison died and was succeeded by John Tyler of Virginia, who was more Democrat than Whig, and who was a typical Southerner of the states' rights, proslavery persuasion. Within months, all members of the Cabinet except Daniel Webster resigned, denounced Tyler publicly as a traitor to the party, and contemptuously referred to his few Whig followers as "the Corporal's Guard." And, once Webster completed negotiations with England over the boundary between Maine and Canada leading to the Webster-Ashburton Treaty of 1842, he followed suit.

Deprived of party support, Tyler pushed annexation to the fore, hoping it would enable him to run for President in 1844 as the candidate of a new pro-Texas third party, or better yet as the Democratic nominee. In both North and South, administration supporters made much of the British Conspiracy, and in the North they advanced the ingenious notion that annexation would eventually end slavery by drawing off millions of slaves to Texas, from where they would eventually disappear over the border into Mexico and Central America. Secretly, the Tyler administration began negotiating with Texas authorities for a treaty of annexation.

The secret negotiations with Texas were all but over when an explosion of a gun on the warship *Princeton* killed the Secretary of State, Abel Upshur of Virginia. Tyler turned to slavery's foremost advocate, John C. Calhoun, to complete the negotiations. That sealed the link between slavery and the annexation of Texas. Along with the treaty, which was sent to the Senate in April 1844, Calhoun sent a copy of a dispatch he had written to the British minister, Richard Pakenham, denouncing England, singing the praises of slavery, and justifying annexation as a defense measure in behalf of slavery. Calhoun's letter not only raised the cry of "Slave Power Conspiracy" to a fever pitch, but also shocked congressmen who had no sympathy at all with the antislavery movement. Two months later, Whig Senators slapped down the "renegade" President's treaty by an overwhelming majority. Of twenty-two Democrats who cast a vote, fifteen supported annexation; all but one of twenty-eight Whigs voted against it; annexation thus failed by a two to one margin.

This vote was indicative of where the two parties stood. In the wake of Calhoun's Pakenham letter, the leading contenders for the Whig and Democratic presidential nominations, Clay and Van Buren, simultaneously issued statements opposing immediate annexation. Clay had little trouble getting the Whig nomination , but Van Buren's Texas letter raised a storm of protest among Democrats, particularly in the southern and western states. Even Jackson turned on him. Since a majority of the delegates to the Democratic convention had already been instructed to vote for Van Buren, there was little chance of blocking his nomination without the two-thirds rule. Pro-Texas strategists thus insisted on a two-thirds majority for nomination—and enough delegates who were pledged to vote for Van Buren on the early ballots, but now were disillusioned with him, went along with this strategy to kill the New Yorker's chances of getting the nomination. Yet, while Van Buren could not get the necessary two thirds, neither could his arch rival, Lewis Cass of Michigan. To break the deadlock, the party finally turned to James K. Polk of Tennessee, a slaveholder whose hard-money views satisfied the Van Burenites, and whose zeal for annexation satisfied the expansionists.

Having nominated Polk, the convention then adopted a platform calling for "the reoccupation of Oregon and the reannexation of Texas, at the earliest practicable moment." The Oregon plank clearly was tacked on at the last moment. There had been no great popular demand for Oregon before the convention. The Oregon country, which stretched from the Rockies to the Pacific and from the border of Mexican California at the 42d parallel north to Russian Alaska at 54° 40′, had been occupied jointly by the United States and Great Britain since 1818. In the 1840s, several thousand Americans had made the long trek across the Rockies to the fertile meadowland of the Willamette Valley, and Democrats in the upper Mississippi Valley had begun to agitate for a more aggressive Oregon policy. But the Oregon plank was largely window-dressing to offset the charge that the Jacksonians were a prosouthern party. Likewise, the Democratic slogan of "Fifty-four Forty or Fight" was used to court northern voters and divert attention from Texas and slavery. Texas was still the crucial issue.

The election itself was extremely close. Polk received 49.6 percent of the popular vote to Clay's 48.1 percent. Despite the narrow margin, southern Democrats and outgoing President Tyler claimed that the election was a mandate "in favor of immediate annexation of Texas." Since it was obviously impossible to obtain a two-thirds majority in the Senate, which another treaty of annexation would require, Tyler recommended that Texas be annexed by a simple majority of both houses "before the British seized the prize." A joint resolution had never been used for this purpose before, and many were certain that it was illegal. Moreover, the proposed resolution would not only admit Texas as a state, but also give Texas the right to divide into two, three, or four states. Was Tyler pushing for one slave state—or four? Many thought "four." Once again, northern Whigs howled "Slave Power Conspiracy." But to their dismay, annexation passed the House, squeaked through the Senate by a 27 to 25 margin, and the lame-duck President signed the resolution on March 1, 1845.

James K. Polk. Three days later, Polk took over. A protege of Andrew Jackson, he had none of Old Hickory's charisma; indeed, he had twice failed to be re-elected governor of his state. But he was an incredibly industrious, hard-driving, aggressive President who usually got what he wanted. And he wanted a great deal.

On the Oregon question, however, he was willing to compromise. "Fifty-four Forty or Fight" and "All of Oregon or Nothing" were good campaign slogans to stir the hearts of patriots. But actually fighting Britain was another matter. As Senator Thomas Hart Benton pointed out: "Great Britain is powerful and Mexico is weak." The Oregon question thus led to a great deal of bluster and jingoism, but Polk was always ready to back off from 54° 40′, and in June 1846 he agreed to a treaty with Great Britain fixing the line between the United States and Canada at the 49th parallel, with Canada retaining all of Vancouver Island.

Against Mexico, Polk was far more aggressive. He wanted as much of northern Mexico as he could get, particularly California with its three magnificent harbors. And there is no longer much doubt that he deliberately provoked war with Mexico to get it. Mexico had never recognized Texas's independence, and thus once the United States annexed Texas, Mexico broke off diplomatic relations with Washington. Furthermore, Mexico justly claimed that the traditional southern boundary of Texas had always been the Nueces River, as all reliable maps and atlases indicated—and not the Rio Grande farther south as Texans claimed. Even Jackson, Van Buren, and Calhoun had recognized the Nueces as the true border. But Polk supported Texas's claim to the hilt, and in time ordered General Zachary Taylor and fifteen hundred men into the disputed area between the rivers. He also sent John Slidell of Louisiana to Mexico in the hope of buying California and New Mexico, and of adjusting the Texas boundary along the Rio Grande.

When the Mexicans refused to negotiate with Slidell, Polk decided to regard this rebuff as cause for war and prepared to ask Congress for a declaration of war. But just at the last minute, Polk got news that an American patrol and a Mexican force had skirmished in the disputed area, and that sixteen Americans had been killed or wounded. Hastily revising his war message, Polk told Congress that Mexico "has invaded our territory, and shed American blood upon the American soil," and thus war already "exists by the act of Mexico herself."

Polk's War. Claiming that Taylor's army desperately needed aid, or it might be destroyed, administration forces in Congress stampeded through a war bill. Debate was limited to two hours in the House, one day in the Senate. Whigs were denied time to read the documents sent with the war message. Though parts were read to them by the clerk, they were expected to rely on the President's word. Calhoun, although now back in the Democratic fold, refused to vote, proclaiming at the time that a skirmish between two patrols was hardly a war—and proclaiming later that less than ten percent of Congress would have supported Polk if they had

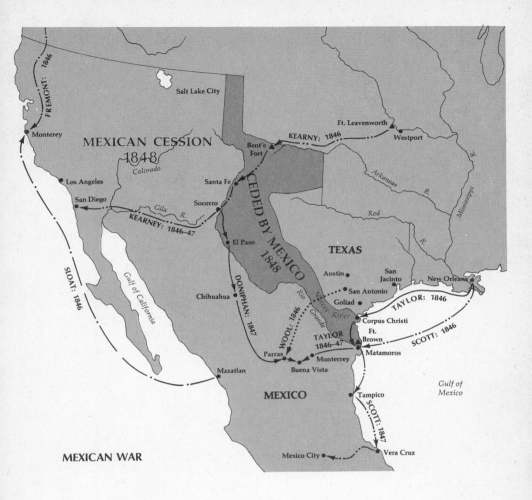

MEXICAN WAR

had the chance to examine the documents. Yet, without looking at the documents, an overwhelming majority supported Polk's war, 174 to 14 in the House, and 40 to 2 in the Senate. The naysayers were primarily Yankees, either representing districts in New England, or representing New England settlements in the West. At the head was John Quincy Adams.

War was declared on May 13, 1846. Dissent was immediate. "It is our own President who began this war," said an outspoken Whig, Garrett Davis of Kentucky, in an early discussion of war measures. Bellowed Horace Greeley of the New York *Tribune:* "People of the United States! Your rulers are precipitating you into a fathomless abyss of crime and calamity! Why sleep you thoughtless on its verge, as though this is not your business, or Murder could be hid from the sight of God by a few flimsy rags called banners? Awake and arrest the work of butchery." Whigs in the East, the West, and the South fired off similar salvos. In the

House fledgling Congressman Abraham Lincoln of Illinois called on Polk to pinpoint where blood had been first shed—was it on American or Mexican soil?

But Lincoln and other Whig congressmen were caught in a trap. Having a legally declared war on their hands, they could not abandon armies Congress had called to the field. So they supported bills for war supplies and reinforcements, lauded "our boys on the front line," and extolled the gallantry of Whig generals, who were soon covered with glory. At the same time they denounced the war and treated Polk as a war criminal—the "Father of Lies" as Greeley called him.

Meanwhile, United States' armies crushed Mexico. From the Rio Grande, Zachary Taylor led one army into northern Mexico and at Buena Vista, in February 1847, scored a smashing victory over superior Mexican forces under the command of Santa Anna. Shortly thereafter, another army under General Winfield Scott landed on the Gulf Coast at Vera Cruz and by September captured Mexico City, the enemy capital. Meanwhile, still another army under Colonel Stephen Kearney marched west from Missouri, seized Santa Fe, and then California. The fighting lasted hardly a year, cost the nation less than two thousand lives on the battlefield and some eleven thousand from disease, and made heroes by the dozens. To Polk's dismay, most of the glory fell to Whig generals, who were using

The Battle of Buena Vista claimed more American lives than any other battle of the Mexican War. The heroes of this battle were the Mississippi Rifles under the command of Colonel Jefferson Davis. *Library of Congress*

the war to gain the presidency. "Old Rough and ready" Zachary Taylor succeeded in his presidential bid, winning in 1848—while "Old Fuss and Feathers" Winfield Scott failed, losing in 1852.

The Territorial Crisis. Conquest merely sharpened the divisions within American society. How much conquered territory should the United States keep? At one extreme were antiwar Whigs who regarded any dismemberment of Mexico as stealing. But most Whigs—and particularly those who represented the commercial Northeast—were willing to forsake the golden rule when it came to California. The port of San Francisco alone, in Daniel Webster's judgment, was twenty times as valuable as all of Texas.

At the other extreme were zealous Democrats who talked incessantly about "Manifest Destiny." It was God's will, they shouted, for the United States to expand over all of North America from "the arctic to the tropic." And as American armies battered their way into the heart of Mexico, the great penny papers of New York, Philadelphia, Baltimore, and Boston whipped up support for "All Mexico." But "All Mexico" ran headlong into American racism. Could citizenship be extended to colored and mixed races? No, countered Calhoun and others, who insisted that only the sparsely populated northern parts of Mexico be considered for annexation. And even these lands were of dubious value, said Calhoun, since they were probably unsuitable for slavery and thus would probably spawn more free states.

Indeed, what was to become of the newly acquired land? Was it to become a covey of slave states—or free states? That quickly became the explosive question. As early as February 1845, more than a year before the war began, Van Buren warned northern Democrats that the Democrats must not lead the country into a war in which "the opposition shall be able to charge with plausibility, if not truth, that it is waged for the extension of slavery." And as soon as it became clear that Polk was eager to fight for a larger Texas—but not for a larger Oregon—northern Democrats knew from experience that northern Whigs were going to roast them with the proslavery, prosouthern charge. And they might make it stick! So, when Polk asked for $2 million to facilitate negotiations with Mexico in August 1846, a Pennsylvania Democrat named David Wilmot added a rider to the money bill declaring that none of the territory acquired from Mexico should ever be open to slavery. Although solid opposition from the South, plus crucial votes from northern "dough faces," killed the Wilmot Proviso, it was added to bill after bill. It was never adopted. But it infuriated southern congressmen, and it brought the slavery question into the center of the political arena long before any land was actually acquired.

Peace. Peace negotiations were the work of Nicholas P. Trist. Chief Clerk of the State Department. Sent to Mexico under the protection of Scott's army, Trist was subsequently fired by Polk and ordered home. By the time Trist got the word, Scott had captured Mexico City, and a new Mexican government was willing to negotiate. With Scott's blessing, Trist defied Polk's order and negotiated the Treaty of Guadalupe-Hidalgo in February 1848. The treaty gave the

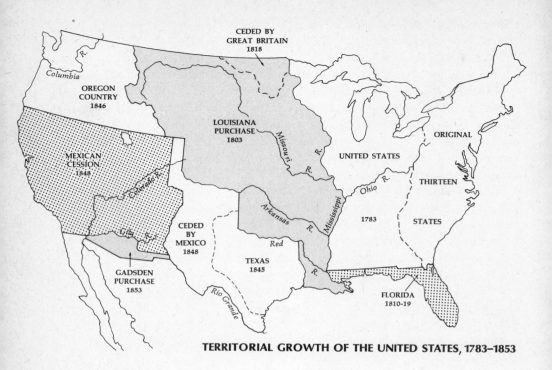

TERRITORIAL GROWTH OF THE UNITED STATES, 1783–1853

United States California and what is now the American Southwest. It took from Mexico more than one third of her territory. In return, the United States agreed to pay Mexico $15 million and settle claims of American citizens against Mexico which amounted to slightly more than $3 million.

A harsh treaty, it was still the most lenient that Trist could have negotiated under Polk's instructions. Facing growing dissension at home, Polk was in no position to reject it, and neither was the Senate. Even Horace Greeley desired ratification: "Sign anything, ratify anything, pay anything, to end the guilt, the bloodshed, the shame, the enormous waste of this horrible contest. Even with that most unfit, unstable boundary of the Rio Grande, give us Peace; and then for the reckoning!" The treaty passed easily, 38 votes to 14. Of the fourteen negative votes, seven came from Whigs protesting "the rape of Mexico"; six came from Democrats who wanted more land; and one is hard to explain.

So ended the Mexican War. Jacksonian expansionism had doubled the size of the country. But, in the process, the slavery question had become so closely tied to the land question, and so prominent in the nation's politics, that trouble lay ahead. Everyone knew it. Everyone expected it. And trouble came, time and again, tearing apart the bonds of union, shattering the national political parties, and by 1861 splitting the country itself into two warring nations.

SUGGESTED READINGS

The literature on abolitionism is vast. Detailed narratives include Louis Filler, *The Crusade Against Slavery, 1830–1860** (1960); Dwight Lowell Dumond, *Antislavery: The Crusade for Freedom in America** (1961); and Gerald Sorin, *Abolitionism: A New Perspective** (1972). Gilbert Hobbes Barnes, *The Antislavery Impulse, 1830–1844** (1933) emphasizes the western and evangelical origins of antislavery; John Thomas, *The Liberator, William Lloyd Garrison* (1963) sees the evangelical impulse coming out of New England or areas where Yankees have settled; while Frank Thistlethwaite, *America and the Atlantic Community; Anglo-American Aspects, 1790–1850** (1959) links the antislavery movement with evangelical and dissenting religious groups in both England and the United States. Benjamin Quarles, *Black Abolitionists** (1969) deals with the work of free blacks. Other general works include Martin Duberman, ed., *The Anti-Slavery Vanguard** (1965) and Aileen S. Kraditor, *Means and Ends in American Abolitionism* (1969).

Less has been written on the white majority who tried to suppress abolitionism. Leon F. Litwack, *North of Slavery: The Negro in the Free States, 1790–1860** (1961) is a good survey of northern racism, while Leonard Richards, *"Gentlemen of Property and Standing": Anti-Abolition Mobs in Jacksonian America** (1970) covers white northerners who attacked abolitionists and blacks. Russel B. Nye, *Fettered Freedom* (1963) is the handiest guide to other attempts to silence the abolitionists. Details regarding the "gag" can also be found in Samuel Flagg Bemis, *John Quincy Adams and the Union* (1956). Details on how the two parties voted are presented in Thomas B. Alexander, *Sectional Stress and Party Strength* (1967).

The literature on expansionism is also vast. Richard Van Alstyne, *The Rising American Empire** (1960) stresses the inherent expansionism of American society, while William Goetzman, *When the Eagle Screamed** (1966) emphasizes the quest for security. Frederick Merk, *Manifest Destiny and Mission** (1963) is the best analysis of the expansionist spirit among Democratic journalists. A good short analysis of how Democratic and Whig spokesmen differed on expansion can be found in Major L. Wilson, "The Concept of Time and the Political Dialogue in the United States, 1828–1848," *American Quarterly*, Vol. 19 (Winter 1967). The voting behavior of the two parties is summed up in Joel H. Silbey, *The Shrine of Party* (1967).

Grant Freeman, *Indian Removal, the Emigration of the Five Civilized Tribes* (1953) and Arthur DeRosier, *The Removal of the Choctaw Indians** (1970) describe the plight of the southern tribes. Michael Rogin, *Fathers and Children: Andrew Jackson and the Subjugation of the American Indian* (1975) attempts to psychoanalyze Jackson, focussing mainly on his relations with Indians. Bernard Sheehan, *Seeds of Extinction** (1973) discusses the major issues relating to Indian removal, while Mary Young, *Redskins, Ruffleshirts and Red Necks* (1961) examines the economic beneficiaries of Jackson's Indian policy.

The best account of the origins of the Texas issue is Eugene C. Barker, *Mexico and Texas, 1821–1835* (1928), while Norman Graebner, *Empire on the Pacific* (1955) is good

*Available in a paperback edition.

on American interest in Pacific ports. Indispensable for Polk and the Mexican War is Charles G. Sellers, Jr., *James K. Polk: Continentalist, 1843–1846* (1966). Strong on diplomatic background is David H. Pletcher, *The Diplomacy of Annexation: Texas, Oregon, and the Mexican War* (1973). Strong on the war itself is Ralph S. Henry, *The Story of the Mexican War* (1950). Bernard DeVoto, *The Year of Decision, 1846** (1942) is a classic of great literary distinction. Much of the debate regarding the Mexican War can be conveniently found in Ramón Ruiz, ed., *The Mexican War: Was It Manifest Destiny?** (1963).

INDEX